NATURAL DAM ACROSS LEES CREEK, IN CRAWFORD COUNTY, FORMED BY A BARRIER OF SANDSTONE DIPPING N. N. E. UPSTREAM

FIRST REPORT

OF A

GEOLOGICAL RECONNOISSANCE

OF THE NORTHERN COUNTIES OF

ARKANSAS,

MADE DURING THE YEARS 1857 AND 1858,

BY

DAVID DALE OWEN,

PRINCIPAL GEOLOGIST,

ASSISTED BY

WILLIAM ELDERHORST, Chemical Assistant;
EDWARD T. COX, Assistant Geologist.

LITTLE ROCK:
JOHNSON & YERKES, STATE PRINTERS.
1858.

INTRODUCTORY LETTER.

———o———

To His Excellency, E. N. Conway,
Governor of Arkansas:

Sir—In conformity to an act approved 15th January, 1857, entitled "an act to provide for a geological survey of the State of Arkansas," I had the honor of being appointed by you State Geologist of the State of Arkansas, which office I accepted with the proviso that I was to commence the geological survey of the state as early as my engagements in Kentucky permitted, say about the 1st of October, or as soon thereafter as possible, it being, however, expressly understood that my salary as Geologist of the State of Arkansas, was not to commence until I entered upon the duties of that office, as will appear from the following letter of your Excellency, addressed to me on the 20th April, 1857:

Executive Ofeice,
Little Rock, Arks.,
20th April, 1857.

Dr. D. D. Owen—

Sir: I have appointed you State Geologist of the State of Arkansas, under the act of the 15th January, 1857, as shown by the enclosed commission, which will take effect from and after the 1st day of October, 1857; and your salary is to commence upon your qualification, on or before the 15th October, 1857, that is, as soon as you shall enter upon your duties as State Geologist of Arkansas, under said law, and not before then. I hope by the first day of October, you will have completed your present engagements in the State of Kentucky, and that you will accept the commission which I send you upon the terms stated in it.

As a measure of economy, as far as this state is concerned, I was pleased to learn that the chemical work could all be done in your laboratory at New Harmony, and would be pleased to learn what annual expense this state will incur under such an arrangement, and for all instruments which I presume you have and can use in the prosecution of the work, including office-rent and fuel, whilst doing the office-work at New Harmony.

As you know best the kind of wagons and camp equipage you will require to suit you, I presume it would be better for you to procure and ship them to Jacksonport, Arkansas, than to obtain them in this state. The horses and mules which you would require, could, perhaps, be obtained in Arkansas, as well as common laborers.

We shall have to be confined to the amount of appropriation by the law, and that is so small for such an important work, we will have to use economy to accomplish much good, and I shall depend greatly on your experience and good management in the whole matter.

When you qualify before an officer of this state, you will have to take and subscribe and have authenticated and filed with the governor of Arkansas, a duplicate of the official oath which will be indorsed on your commission.

Most respectfully, your ob't serv't,

(Signed) ELIAS N. CONWAY.

In conformity with the above appointment and instructions, I commenced on the 1st October, 1857, making preparations for carrying out the provisions of said act, by procuring the necessary instruments, outfit, wagons, and means of transportation, for executing the field-work with as much dispatch as possible.

By organising *two* corps for field-duty, and continuing the work as late in the season as the weather permitted, I have, with the limited appropriation at my command, been enabled to accomplish nearly as much as I could have done with a *single* corps, during the summer and autumn months; taking into consideration that the means at my disposal would only have kept a single corps in the field during six or seven months in the year.

On account of the low stage of the Ohio river in October, 1857, the Mississippi and Ohio packets, plying along the coast of Arkansas, were not running; I therefore found it would be more expeditious to proceed by land to Arkansas, especially as by the most direct route, I would reach the north-eastern confines of that state, which your instructions designated as the portion of the state where I should commence the geological survey, so that, as soon as I reached the borders of Arkansas, the work could be immediately commenced.

The point where I first entered the State of Arkansas, and where I, therefore, commenced the field-work, was Chalk Bluffs, in Greene county.

The following report begins, for this reason, with that county.

My geological observations through the northern counties have been of a general character, with the view of gaining a knowledge of the leading geological formations, rather than of entering into minute local details; though I have made it a point, at the same time, to visit such localities as gave promise of important discoveries, even though they were, sometimes, situated a considerable distance out of the direct line of travel which would have suited the general objects I had proposed to myself.

This plan of commencing the geological survey of the state has been adopted for several reasons.

The wording of section 2, of the act providing for the survey, states: "It shall be the duty of the state geologist to make a reconnoissance of the state." This implies a general survey in the beginning; and this, in any case, I consider the proper course to pursue in conducting the survey of a new state; because, unless the geologist acquires, as soon as possible, a general knowledge of the areas and boundaries of the various formations, he cannot direct the operations of the corps to advantage.

Again, by this method, every county can receive the benefits of such a survey, in a period of time, comparatively short to that required to carry a special, detailed survey over the state—unless, indeed, very large appropriations are made, to put numerous corps in the field at the same time.

Following the instructions contained in your letter, dated the 16th September, 1857, with regard to the part of the state where you desired the survey to commence, I have devoted the first season's operations to a reconnoissance of the northern counties adjacent to the Missouri line, and those counties lying between the St. Francis and White rivers, as far south as the northern boundary of the tier of townships 10 north. I found it, however, impossible, before the close of the season, to extend the survey to the western boundary of Arkansas. The extreme limits of my western obervations of last December, only reached the confines of Carroll county.

INTRODUCTION.

---o---

The citizens of Arkansas, so far as I have had an opportunity of ascertaining by intercourse with them, are so well aware of the importance and utility of a geological survey of their state, that it is hardly necessary for me to enlarge upon the subject. But a few remarks of paramount interest suggest themselves.

It has been justly inferred, from the history of nations, that the people who have reached the highest state of civilization and intelligence, and who possess the greatest wealth and influence, are those who enjoy the most extensive facilities of commercial interchange, who possess within themselves the largest means of producing the staple articles of food, and who manufacture the substantial fabrics supplying wearing apparel, the implements of husbandry, and all kinds of useful machinery.

To accomplish these vast objects to the greatest advantage, the country itself should not only be possessed of those natural resources in soil and mineral productions, which supply the raw material for all kind of staples, but must be sufficiently populous to supply the labor necessary for carrying on those manufactures, without too great a drain upon the agricultural community. These two classes of society, under a liberal and enlightened form of government, become mutually dependent on each other, the one producing the necessaries of life, the other fashioning the implements which enable the cultivator of the soil to afford his means of subsistence at a cheap rate, and supplying, not only to the artizan but to the whole community such articles of comfort and convenience as give to life its zest, and to our home their charms.

Hence, to be in the most flourishing condition, a country should not only possess, at least, a fair average soil, but those mineral resources which contribute most essentially to the attainment of a high state of perfection in the mechanic arts.

Foremost in the list of utility, stand coal and iron ores; then platinum, gold and silver, copper, lead, tin, zinc: all producing metals for which there is a regular and constant demand in every land of active industry; ores of antimony, manganese, cobalt, nickel, cadmium, aluminum, arsenic, bismuth, sodium, yielding metals which, though in use to only a limited extent, are, many of them, very essential in the arts, and generally command high prices, on account either of their partial diffusion within the reach of the miner, or the expense of reduction.

Every commercial and civilized nation also demands a supply of a variety of saline substances and earthy minerals, found either on the surface of the earth or interstratified in its geological formations; such as common salt, alum, nitre, carbonates of soda and potash, sal-ammoniac, gypsum, potter's and other clays, ochres, and other paints; also, an abundant supply of limestone, and all the various rocks, useful as building materials and for all kinds of ornamental work, hydraulic cements, materials suitable for the manufacture of glass, fluxes for the metallurgist, are some of the most useful materials that may be enumerated as required to supply the wants of a progressive, commercial, manufacturing people: while the agriculturist, in his vocation, derives many valuable mineral manures from the strata constituting the earth's crust, such as marls, bone-earth, argillaceous and ferruginous earths, and saline deposits and efflorescences, which often form the most accessible, the cheapest and most available materials for the renovation of his land.

Such being universally recognized facts in the history of mankind from the earliest period up to the present time, is it not incumbent on every country and every state of this Union, to adopt measures calculated, first to develop their resources in the various raw materials necessary for their welfare and progress, and having done so, to direct public attention to their stores of mineral wealth; so that the capitalist, seeking profitable investments, and the skillful artizan business and employment, may take cognizance of their peculiar advantages? and, at the same time, proclaim before the immigrant farmer their agricultural resources.

What better method can a state adopt for this purpose, than to institute and support with liberality a well-conducted and *judiciously* managed geological survey of her territory and publish the results to the world in reliable, creditable and attractive geological reports, emanating from sources in which the public generally have full confidence.

This is forcibly brought home to us by a recent communication from our enlightened Minister to Prussia, writing to his friend Judge Law of Indiana, which is so pertinent to the subject that I here extract a few paragraphs bearing on the question:

"BERLIN, February 6th, 1858."

"DEAR SIR: I have often made the remark to you and to our people, that there is less known, both at home and abroad, of Indiana, her capabilities and resources, than of any state of the Union. Of the truth of this fact, I am more and more convinced. I am daily brought in contact with men of intelligence who feel a great interest in obtaining information about our country, especially how money may be invested there, so as to bring the largest return. They wish to learn, what are the most desirable portions for manufactures and trade.

Questions are often put to me about the mineral resources of Indiana. and the surprise expressed that a state, so rich in that respect, has not taken pains to let its wealth be known to the world. A few have heard of the partial survey, and the report thereon, made by Mr. Owen, some years ago, but have not seen it—and I doubt whether you can find half a dozen copies in the state, or even one in the state-library. I could distribute hundreds of those reports, imperfect as they are, with great advantage to our state.

I know the great interest you take, living as you do in the midst of the coal and iron region of the western world, in the development of the mineral resources of Indiana, and I cannot forbear urging upon you renewed exertions in this matter. Our statesmen, our literary men, our men of wealth may come to Europe and talk of the resources of the country, her mineral wealth, her capacities for improvement; but when the capitalist and intelligent mechanic desire to know, where they shall use their capital of money or mind, where they shall establish their manufactories or locate their mining operations, they wish to *see* the survey and report of the man of science, who can tell them where they may certainly find remuneration for their labor, and what it shall be.

To develop the resources of a country, the combined action of capital and labor is required. Capital and labor are annually coming to our country from Europe; but much too large a proportion passes directly through our state and finds its home and employment in Wisconsin, Illinois, Iowa and Missouri. If our state were better known, if its capacities were published abroad in a manner which could command the confidence of the capitalist and the emigrant, this would not be so.

That we have mineral wealth, *we* know. Coal, iron, lead, zinc, building stone and slate, are found in abundance, and clays useful in the arts are extensively distributed. But in how great an abundance these may be found, and how profitably the capitalist may invest his means for their development, can only be determined and made known in a manner to command the confidence of the public at home and abroad, by a careful survey under the direction of the state.

The importance of these surveys is more highly appreciated on this continent than with us. Here the necessity of developing all the resources of the country is felt, and attention is given to the subject. It is this development and the wealth which necessarily comes from it, which enables many of these countries to maintain their position and influence in the world. Money judiciously expended in these investigations yields a sure return.

In Bavaria, with less territory than the state of Indiana, millions have been expended in complete geological and topographical surveys of that country, and for a few pennies every farmer or land-owner can obtain a copy of the survey of his land, a chemical analysis of its soil, and a knowledge of the minerals which enrich it.

In Belgium, they are excavating coal at a depth of 1,500 to 1,800 feet below the surface, working veins only 18 inchs thick at an angle of 45 deg., and this coal, too, of an inferior quality, such as we would not use, and in that country, notwithstanding the amount already expended, preparations are being made for a still more thorough survey. Might not much capital thus laboriously expended be attracted towards our rich coal fields, were their existence and extent known and believed?

But it is not only in the discovery and location of the mineral resources of the state, that such a survey would be advantageous. It would call attention to the fact that all these minerals can be worked and made into manufactured articles at home, instead of being sent abroad and returned to us at an advanced price, as we know is now done, not only with our pig iron, zinc and other metals, but even with our walnut and cherry. Copper is shipped from Tennessee to England, and returned to us in the manufactured state at an advance of more than 200 per cent. I believe that zinc is not manufactured in any considerable quantities in the Mississippi valley, and yet it is well known among us, that it is found in great abundance in the north-west, equal to any in the world. How profitably to our people might the money be expended in manufacturing at home the zinc used among us for painting, for roofing, telegraphing, and in the daily employments of our mechanics. But this will not be until the attention of capital is drawn to our resources.

It may be mentioned as a striking fact, showing the extent to which we look across the water for supplies, that in South Wales and Staffordshire, England, alone, tin plates are manufactured to the amount of 900,000 boxes annually, to the value of over five millions of money, and that more than two-thirds of these are exported to the United States.

Such a survey as ought to be made, would exhibit another thing which may soon be of vital importance to the state; a thing which comes home especially to the farmers. It is well known that the supply of water is yearly becoming less abundant. Such a survey would show where artesian wells could be sunk, from which a never-failing supply of water could be obtained. This may be determined by the scientific man with as much certainty as the character of the underlying soil. A few years ago, in Paris, when water was very much needed, an artesian well was sunk under the direction of scientific men, and water was found—an everlasting fountain—though it was after eight years of labor, and at a depth of 1,900 feet.

It is said that the French in conquering Algiers, took with them men of science, and as they progressed, they established villages and sunk artesian wells, finding water even in the desert. The wandering Arabs exclaimed, 'what can we do with a people who make water rise out of the ground wherever they please?' And they conquered, perhaps, as much by the impressions made by their scientific knowledge, as by the force of their arms." * * * *

Let us look now to a few of the results of the geological survey of Kentucky, which has been in progress since 1855.

In some of the counties, where the labors of the geologist have established the existence of beds of good workable coal, the intrinsic value of the land rose, in a single season, twenty-five per cent. all over the county; while the value of the land, in many locations of the same county, offering peculiar advantages adjacent to navigable streams, rose, in the course of the same period of time, from five to ten dollars per acre, up to fifty and sixty dollars. And these prices have remained firm and permanent up to the present time, showing that the valuation was real, intrinsic and substantial.

Where the simultaneous occurrence of both coal and abundant beds of rich iron ore has been proved, the rise in the value of the property has been proportionally greater. These are, indeed, direct and tangible advantages, which all can appreciate and comprehend, and which come home to the owners of property, and to the citizens of the state.

It will be apparent, that capital and labor must speedily flow towards localities where such valuable mineral resources have been demonstrated to exist.

Further: the elaborate, comparative chemical analyses of the soils collected from various parts of the state, now numbering between two and three hundred, have developed such important, interesting and practically useful results, and thrown so much insight into the peculiar constitution of the soils, derived from particular geological formations, and the individual members of these formations, that all the well-informed and intelligent part of the farming community, whose soils yet remain unexamined for want of adequate time, is already calling loudly for an extension of the same system of chemico-agricultural investigation over their portion of the state.

Again, the iron-master, for want of a knowledge of the chemical constitution of ores easily accessible and conveniently situated to his furnace, has often been rejecting his richest and best ores, which, now that he has become aware of their composition and productiveness, through the disclosures of the geological survey, he works with greater profit and advantage than any of those ores previously employed.

Numerous instances have occurred in which deluded men, ignorant of the nature of minerals, have expended their labor and means in mining after ores, either comparatively of little value, or containing none of the metal they confidently expected to extract from them, and have only been persuaded to desist from their ruinous proceedings by the demonstrations and counsel given them by the geologist.

The capitalist, miner and business man have had their attention called to various parts of the state, and are either examining the various sections of the state in person, or sending out their agents for the purpose of making locations for future mining or manufacturing operations.

Moreover: it is incumbent on every state in the confederacy, to contribute her utmost to prevent the enormous drain made on this country, at the present time, for manufactured products imported into this country. In the article of iron, alone, and that chiefly railroad iron, recent statistics show that this country is importing upwards of 500,000 tons, at a cost of over $3,000,000 annually. Such a drain on our moneyed resources—such a serious balance of trade against us—should certainly be put an end to as speedily as possible; and this is only to be accomplished by the immediate increase in the manufacture of iron throughout the different states of the Union.

It can be shown by the most reliable calculations, that iron can be produced in the western states, where facilities exist for its manufacture, by the simultaneous occurrence of good iron ore and coal, suitable for its reduction, convenient to navigation on our larger streams, not only as cheaply as in England, but, in consequence of the duty on imported iron, and the greater cost of carriage and commission, at a cheaper rate than foreign iron can be delivered in this country, even at $15 to $20 less cost per ton; and still leave the handsome profit of twenty-five per cent. to the manufacturer, notwithstanding the advantages which Great Britain possesses in her cheap labor and in her capital. If this is true—and any one conversant with the business can satisfy himself of its correctness by investigating the subject—is it not inevitable, not only that establishments for the production of iron must rapidly spring up in the western country, where, in a year or two, four-fifths of the great demand for iron will be, and at those points that offer the greatest inducements in the required mineral resources, but it is moreover true, that the business can hardly be overdone; since the increased production, for years to come, can hardly keep even pace with the annually increased consumption in railroad iron.

So universally important is it to the interests of the United States, that this branch of business should be cherished, that it has recently called forth remarks from the executive.

The same is true, to a certain extent, in very many other branches of metallurgy, and applies, indeed, more or less, to all manufactures.

REPORT

OF A

GEOLOGICAL RECONNOISSANCE

OF PART OF

ARKANSAS.

PART FIRST.

———o———

In proceeding to record the geological observations of 1857, I shall follow nearly my line of travel through the various counties from the north-east corner of the state, towards the west, and give the results of my observations under the heads of the different counties through which the geological corps passed.

GREENE COUNTY.

The so-called Chalk Bluffs form the extreme north-east boundary of Crowley's ridge, where it abuts on the St. Francis river, a very short distance below where that stream leaves the State of Missouri and enters Arkansas, and constitute, therefore, the north-east termination of that extensive ridge of land which extends from Helena, on the Mississippi, in Phillips county, through St. Francis, Poinsett and Greene counties, dividing the waters of the St. Francis from those of White river, and giving origin to the heads of the western tributaries of the former, and the eastern tributaries of the latter streams.

This ridge, so far as it has yet been explored, i. e., to the north line of township 10 north, is composed of, comparatively, very recent deposits, mostly of incoherent or but very partially indurated materials belonging to the age of the so-called *quarternary formation*, with the exception of a few very limited areas where hard quartzose sandstones of very ancient date protrude through these beds.

The base of the quarternary deposits, forming the northern terminus of the Crowley Ridge, is a potter's clay of considerable purity, and nearly as white as chalk; hence the name of the Chalk Bluffs, where this white clay is exposed on the banks of the St. Francis river, a few feet above low water of that stream, in the north-east extremity of Greene county.

The section of the quarternary beds at the Chalk Bluffs, as far as they can be seen, is as follows:

Height above river.		*Thick-ness.*
135.	Hill on which the ferryman's house stands	
	Soil and sub-soil	
	Chert and hornstone gravel	25
110.	Lowest point to which the upper gravel bed could be traced.	
105.	Top of the first bench below the main gravel bed	
	Pink and variegated sand; locally indurated into a soft crumbling sandstone 96 feet or more in thickness	96
30.	White siliceous clay shale or marly earth, slightly indurated at the upper part	
6.	Fine white potter's clay 5 to 6 feet	6
0.	Low water of the St. Francis river.	

The materials which compose the gravel bed which underlies the sub-soil, seem to have been derived from the destruction of beds of carboniferous date, lying to the north in the State of Missouri. At this locality, it appears to be from 25 to 30 feet in thickness. It occupies the highest position of the beds of quarternary date at this locality.

No solid beds of rock have been observed in this north-east termination of Crowley's ridge. In sinking wells at levels below the gravel bed, they pass through sand, then streaks of clay and shaly materials, below which the sand continues. In this lower bed of sand the water is usually struck, which must be retained there by the lower beds of clay of the preceding section. Sometimes, in low situations, they pass through beds of clay in digging for water.

A few chert and hornstone pebbles were observed disseminated amongst the sand at 40 feet above the river, but the principal gravel deposit of this part of Crowley's ridge is in high situations above the great mass of sand.

The growth on the high ground is mostly black and white oak; in the bottoms, a mixed growth. Considerable groves of cypress timber flourish in the bottoms of St. Francis river, a short distance above Chalk Bluffs.

An erratic mass of hornstone, weighing upwards of 50 pounds, was observed on the slope of the river bluff, near the ferry; and near by are chalybeate oozings from the bank, originating, probably, from some scaly oxide of iron, sparingly disseminated in the adjacent bank.

The potter's clay at the base of the Chalk Bluffs is nearly white, or of a cream color; variegated, however, here and there, with flesh tints. Its texture is fine, and forms a plastic mass with water. Its composition is shown by the following chemical analysis:

Moisture	01.10	Silica	69.7
Insoluble siliceous earth	89.75	Alumina tinged with oxide of iron	19.0
Oxide of iron	3.86	Lime	.2
Lime	.38	Magnesia	.1
Magnesia	.33	Potash	.7
Potash	.15	Soda	.05
Carbonic acid	1.00		
Chlorine	.60		
Phosphoric acid	.075		89.75
Water of hydration (not driven off at 300 deg. F.,) trace of ammonia and loss	3.255		
	100.000		

This clay contains 4.79 per cent. less alumina than the Hickman county clay belonging to the same geological era; about 0·701 per cent. less lime, and 0·34 less alkalies. It will, therefore, make a whiter ware, be less fusible, and less liable to crack.

I have manufactured small crucibles out of this clay, and find that it produces an excellent and strong article. The moulded clay is not liable to crack in drying, without addition of silica or siliceous earth, nor during the burning; and the crucibles manufactured therefrom resist sudden changes of temperature without cracking. The burnt biscuit ware is even rather lighter colored than the original clay, which is of a very light cream color. It resists fusion at a high temperature.

Besides being valuable for the above purposes, this clay would, probably, be found of excellent quality for modelling, and various other uses; it is, therefore, well worthy the attention of the potter and the artist.

The section at Chalk Bluffs, does not extend low enough to enable the observer to see what underlies this clay; but from the position of beds of clay of, apparently, the same age, found in other western and southern states, it is probably *interstratified* amongst the orange and ferruginous sands, that are subordinate to the shell marls, which constitute the upper member of the quarternary; occupying, therefore, the same geological horizon, as the white clays at the base of the section described in the first volume of the geological report of Kentucky, on pages 20, 21 and 22 of that volume, and the corresponding clays which, I understand from Dr. E. W. Hilgard, geologist of Mississippi, are interstratified in the "orange sand," of the state of Mississippi; on this account it is probable that ferruginous, orange-colored sands occur in this part of Arkansas still beneath this clay; but concealed from view under the drainage of the country.

The quaternary beds of the northern part of Greene county afford, locally, a yellow ochre suitable both for a pigment and a dye-stuff.

One of the localities, where I had an opportunity of viewing it in place, is about one mile west of south of the "Pine," between the Gainsville and Pocahontas road, near township 21 north, range 8, east of the 5th principal meridian. It is exposed here in a steep bank, near the bottom of a hollow where a spring branch takes its rise on the north side of the ridge, 3 to 4 miles from Levi Boyd's farm. It lies a considerable distance under the main upper gravel bed which shows itself in various places near the top of this ridge and beneath underlying beds of pink, variegated, and ferruginous sands. Its original color at the bank is a yellow, but by exposure to heat, it acquires a red color, in which condition it has been used, by some of the inhabitants of this part of the county, as a dye-stuff for woolen goods.

Its chemical composition is presented in the following analysis:

Water (hygrometric)	2.99		
Insoluble silicates	81.00	Silica	68.64
		Alumina tinged with oxide of iron	10.00
		Lime	.44
		Magnesia	.18
		Potash	1.20
		Soda	trace
			80.46
Peroxide of iron	10.00		
Protoxide of iron	.78		
Oxide of manganese	.20		
Alumina	1.65		
Lime	.45		
Magnesia	.14		
Potash	.31		
Carbonic acid	.70		
Chlorine	.02		
Phosphoric acid	.14		
Sulphuric acid	trace		
Water of hydration, loss, and ammonia	1.70		
	100.00		

This ochre contains seven and a half per cent of iron: it has a good body and color; better than that of the French spruce yellow, and could be used as a pigment for brick work, and outside work, even without washing, as the texture is fine, and there is very little grit in it when carefully selected. When burnt, it acquires a light red color; this change appears to be due, more to the loss of its water of hydration, than to the peroxidation of the fraction of a per cent of protoxide of iron, which it contains. For the purposes of dying, it it used, by the country people, in its burnt condition.

At the "Pine," near by, diggings have been attempted in search of an ore, supposed to contain silver; but with no success. The gravel and sand beds, which constitute the main mass of the Crowley ridge at the " Pine," is altogether unfavorable for the discovery of ore of this description.

A qualitative chemical analysis was made of the water of the St. Francis river, in the north-east part of Greene county, which proves it to be a remarkably soft water, containing only a small quantity of carbonate of magnesia and lime, and a trace of sulphates and chlorides. It is remarkable, too, for the small proportion of lime compared with magnesia. In most river waters, the lime is in much larger proportion than the magnesia. The saline matter, altogether, is in much smaller quantity than is usually found in our western rivers; hence, the softness of the water. It is well adapted for domestic purposes. The same is true of most of the spring water in the northern part of the Crowley ridge. The spring at A. S. Stewart's was tested, qualitatively, and found to contain only a trace of lime and a very small quantity of bi-carbonate and chloride of magnesia. It is almost as soft as rain water.

Samples of soils of the northern part of the Crowley ridge, were collected from the farm of W. Raeburn, where the growth is black-oak, hickory, black and white walnut, and large poplar. Also, a sample of the genuine " black sand land," from the flat lands, at the foot of the eastern slope of the ridge, from the farm of H. W. Granada.

The ridge lands, where these soils were collected, produce from 40 to 50 bushels of corn to the acre, and 20 to 30 bushels of wheat. It would, no doubt, produce tolerably good crops of tobacco and cotton, but these have not been raised to any extent in this vicinity as yet.

The black sand soil is remarkably deep and rich, and will yield, on new land, 80 to 100 bushels of corn to the acre. It produces very fine vegetables, and appears to be especially congenial to peach trees. It is a quick warm soil, and stands both dry and wet seasons well. The growth on this land is poplar, oak, walnut, and gum, with an undergrowth of spice and papaw. This black-sand-land represents a large proportion of the flat lands, lying between Crowley's ridge and the Mississippi river, in Arkansas.

The south-western part of township 19 north, range 7 east, and the northern part of township 18 north, range 6 east, support mostly a growth of barren oak, with the upper quaternary gravel bed generally near the surface. In some of the deep hollows, 80 to 90 feet below the gravel bed, the quaternary clay is occasionally recognizable; the intervening deposition of 90 to 100 feet being mostly ferruginous orange sand, where it is exposed to view, with perhaps some subordinate interstratified beds of clay. But there are but few good sections where the quaternary sand can be satisfactorily seen. The subsoil is generally ferruginous. The surface of the country is undulating; and the growth almost universally oak.

The water of this region of Arkansas is remarkably pure, especially that which comes through the gravel beds, containing less earthy salts than I have found in any spring-waters in the western country. It lies, however, often deep, since it filters away through the porous beds of gravel and sand to the depth, sometimes, of 90 feet, except where arrested by local beds of interstratified impervious clays that lie, sometimes, at the depth of 30 to 50 feet.

In the neighborhood of Gainesville, some lead ore has been picked up, but there is very little probability that it is connected with any bodies of this species of ore, accessible to the miner, since such ores rarely, if ever, occur in the loose quaternary deposits, such as above described as prevailing through this part of Greene county. It is much more probable that they have either been brought there, and deposited, by the Indians at some of their camping grounds, or been transported along with the gravel from lead regions, lying to the north-west, either in Arkansas or Missouri. A bed of lignite of quaternary date, crops out in the bed of the Beech branch of Cache river, in Greene county, near the crossing of the Chalk Bluff road, which runs on the Cache side of the Crowley ridge. It is partly concealed under the water. It is overlaid by red and pink ferruginous sand, and underlaid by clay.

The succession and superposition, as far as they can be seen for vegetation and debris concealing the upper members of the quaternary beds, on the Beech branch at this lignite locality, are as follows:

	Feet.
Upper gravel bed 15 to 20 or 25 feet	20
Red, tenacious, ferruginous clay 7 to 10 feet in thickness	10
Second or lower gravel bed, 5 to 10 feet thick	6
Pink and variegated sand, with some disseminated gravel, passing downwards into reddish white sand, overlying the lignite bed	25?
Lignite bed partly concealed, 3 to 4 feet in thickness	3?

Some of the sand is cemented, by the infiltration of ferruginous waters, into a partially indurated rock.

This lignite is of a blackish brown color. Part of it exhibits the woody structure, and part has a more homogeneous earthy aspect, and lighter blackish brown color.

Both varieties are very similar in their character to the lignites of the same age which occur in the quaternary deposits of the western part of Ballard county, Kentucky.

The chemical analysis of this lignite, has not yet been undertaken, but will be made hereafter.*

Its appearance, however, hardly justifies the expectation that it will be found sufficiently rich in carbon and hydro-carbons, to be valuable as a fuel, even if the deposit should prove to be extensive. Lignite of a similar character occurs seven miles a little west of south form the above locality, on the Beech Fork of Cache; also, one mile north, two miles north, and four miles south.

If it be a continuous bed between all the different out-crops known at present, it would occupy an area of some seventy square miles, but this is by no means certain, since these lignite beds are often quite partial and local. Future detailed examinations in Greene county may throw farther light on its extent.

It is worthy of remark, that there occurs disseminated in this lignite a yellow pyrites, which contains a small per centage of copper, the exact amount of which will be reported on, as soon as the chemical analysis shall be completed.

Two miles from Gainesville, near Jones', the quaternary sand is indurated into a soft sandstone, which is used in the construction of chimneys. It contains impressions of leaves, one of which appears to belong to the magnolias, and others to some species of water-oak, or willows. When these have been more fully investigated, and more extensive collections made from other localities, we shall then be better able to report in specific detail.

About two-thirds of the flat Cache lands are "black sand lands," and one-third post-oak lands. The latter are too wet for cultivation, without a complete system of drainage. The highest of the former are cultivated, and are very productive. Hereafter, if the agricultural department of the survey be provided for, we hope to be able to supply comparative chemical analyses of these soils, which will give more insight into their relative productiveness, than we are able to supply in their absence.

If the flat post-oak lands of the Cache country of Arkansas, could be drained, and subsequently cultivated with profit, it would greatly increase the agricultural resources of Greene, Randolph, and Independence counties, and contribute materially to the settlement of this part of the state.

Near David Schultz's place, on the east or St. Francis side of the Crowley ridge, and about 2 miles from the St. Francis bottom, near the line between townships 18 and 19 north, range 8 east, there is a deposit of yellow ochre, similar to that previously described as occurring at the "Pine," on the other side of this ridge.*

*See Chemical Report.

Some of the geological maps, which profess to give approximate boundaries to the cretaceous formation of the United States, have indicated its northern boundary in Arkansas, as running with a north-easterly course into Greene county, passing near Lorado and Crowley. While in that vicinity, I searched for evidence of the existence of this formation above the drainage of the country, as well as in the materials penetrated in sinking wells. Since, in the western district of Tennessee, the member of this formation which reaches the surface, is a kind of chalk-marl, or soft argillaceous limestone, known popularly amongst the inhabitants as "rotten limestone," I made especial enquiry for a rock of this description in that part of Greene county. I was informed that though they knew of no "rotten limestone," some of the neighbors had obtained a different kind of water in their wells than that usually struck, all ranging in a north-east and south-west direction, which they called "rotten limestone water." I was referred particularly to J. P. Harris' well, on section 25, township 16 north, range 3 east, and accordingly made a point of examining the material removed from said well. That proved, however, to be the quaternary shell-marl; which, containing a notable quantity of lime and magnesia, imparted a harder quality to the water passing through it, than in the waters of the neighboring wells, filtering through only gravel and sand.

The quaternary marl of this part of Greene county, is of a light grey ashy appearance, and contains, disseminated, some small shells, which seem to be mostly *Helix* and *Planorbis*, but the earth was so disintegrated that no perfect specimens could be obtained.

The composition of this shell-marl, as will appear from the subjoined chemical analysis, is more siliceous and less calcareous than the Hickman county shell-marl of the same date, and is, therefore, less adapted as a mineral fertilizer of land; though it would be of some advantage to stiff clay land, improving it both physically and chemically. It could be employed, probably, to advantage in reclaiming the post-oak lands of the adjacent flats.

Chemical analysis of shell-marl, from T. P. Harris' well, Greene county, Arkansas.

Water	1.3	Silica	72.8
Insoluble silicates	84.9	Alumina tinged with iron	6.8
Carbonic acid	2.7	Lime	.8
Peroxide of iron	3.6	Magnesia	.3
Alumina	2.0	Potash	.9
Lime	2.9	Soda	3.2
Magnesia	1.2	Manganese	trace
Phosphoric acid	.45		84.8
Potash	.5		
Loss	.45		
	100.00		

For comparison, is subjoined the chemical analysis of the corresponding shell-marl of Hickman county, Kentucky:

Water	1.35	Silica	60.6
Organic matter sol. in water	.30	Alumina	7.4
Insoluble silicates	73.30	Lime	1.1
Carbonic acid	10.00	Magnesia	.4
Lime	6.8	Loss, alk, and a trace of oxide of iron not estimated	3.8
Magnesia	3.78		73.3
Alumina and peroxide of iron	2.8		
Chlorine	.12		
Loss, alkalies and phosphoric acid, not determined	1.55		
	100.00		

From the best information obtained, the materials passed through in digging this well, were:

Soil and sub-soil	3 feet.
Dark-red under-clay	14 "
Shell-marl	29 "
Gravel and white coarse sand, mixed	2 "

The water was obtained in the last member, viz: the white coarse gravel and sand.

At James Lamb's, three quarters of a mile east of Harris', the shell-marl was struck in sinking his well at 54 feet; at Henry Cook's, 48 feet; and at Daniel Martins' (where Lindley now lives), water was obtained at 18 feet in the shell-marl.

Thus I have, even to the depth of 54 feet beneath the surface, not been able to obtain the least evidence of the existence of any of the members of the cretaceous formation, as far north in the north-eastern part of Arkansas, as they have been laid down by some geological map-makers;

who, in fact, never visited the country, but plotted the boundary of that formation from what they imagined its probable bearings would be through Arkansas.

Between Gainsville and Walcott, a distance of 13 miles, the country is mostly a succession of oak and pine ridges, forming a continuation of Crowley's ridge, to the south.

On the small Colton map of Arkansas, the Walcott post-office is laid down 3 miles too far to the north, and Crowley 5 miles too far south.

The bluff below Dr. Mellon's house, Walcott post-office, is composed of the following materials:

Red ferruginous tenacious clay	10 to 15 feet.
Light-colored sand and clay, mixed	5 "
Gravel, cemented by oxide of iron into a conglomerate or pudding-stone	3 "
White, quartzose, fine-grained sand, with streaks of yellow and black sand, running irregularly through it	5 "
Indurated sandy shale, with pink and yellow streaks	14 "
" Hard pan;" indurated dark-grey shale, with impressions of leaves	1 foot.

It is probable that the post-oak soil of the Cache flats is derived from the disintegration of the indurated sandy shale, reposing on the impervious "hard-pan."

Clover does not succeed well in this part of Greene county; not even on the "black-sand lands." Herd's grass and timothy do much better, and oats and rye grow very finely — especially on the "black-sand land." This variety of soil seems, also, peculiarly well adapted to the growth of the peach-tree, which comes to perfection very rapidly. It produces both a very large and sweet peach.

Wheat succeeds best on the ridge-land; it runs too much to straw in the "black-sand land."

On section 10, township 17 north, range 4 east, near Sugar creek, in Greene county, there is a remarkable protrusion of hard quartzose sandstone through the quaternary deposits. This sandstone has all the lithological character of the Potsdam, or lowest sandstone of silurian date, as it occurs on the Minnesota and Wisconsin rivers in the north-west. It forms a hill of considerable elevation; which, however, I had no opportunity of measuring, as I examined it in the midst of that most severe thunderstorm, accompanied by heavy rain and high wind, which occurred on the 7th of November, 1857, in that part of Arkansas. I would estimate the height, by the eye, at 100 to 110 feet above the general drainage of the country.

The angle of dip of the sandstone is somewhat irregular, varying from 10 deg. to 12 deg., in the direction a little east of north, the bearing being nearly coincident with the direction of the Crowley ridge—i. e.: north-east and south-west.

These protusions of quartzose sandstone can be traced for 3 miles in a south-west direction. At W. Lane's, the quaternary deposits on the west side of the hard sandstone protrusion, are tilted at the rate of 12 feet in 20,—judging from the inclined beds passed through by him in digging his well.

These strata, passed through, were:

Red, ferruginous, tenacious clay	20 feet.
Gravel	5 "
Ledges of sandstone	5 "
Sand and clay	45 "

The water of Lane's well was tested, qualitatively, and found to be soft, containing only a trace of earthy carbonates, and slightly reddening litmus paper from the presence of free carbonic acid.

Though the protruding sandstone is, as we have said, very hard, still it can be quarried without a great deal of difficulty in certain directions. It will not stand fire, and, when heated and drenched with water, it crumbles to sand; proving its semicrystalline structure.

The color of this sandstone is mostly of a light grey or pale red tint; occasionally brown. It is of so hard and quartzose a character that it strikes fire at almost every blow of the hammer.

One or more of the violent commotions to which this part of Arkansas has been subject, evinced by the coarseness of the gravel beds, their thickness, and their wide distribution, may have been cotemporaneous with the elevation of this sandstone.

On section 9, township 15 north, range 3 east, close to William Lane's house, there is also a low range of quartzose sandstone, probably of the same date; but this sandstone lies in juxtaposition on the south-west, with a softer sandstone, containing impressions of plants, which is, no doubt, an indurated portion of the quarternary sand, through which the older, harder sandstone has protruded, and bursting it asunder, has entangled portions of this newer sandstone in the crevices and rents, so that they often appear as if of the same origin; but a close inspection of the lithological character of the rock, together with the vegetable remains, will generally serve to distinguish them.

Overlying the hard vitreous sandstone, but only partially covering it at this locality, there is also a peculiar, fine-textured, siliceous rock with vermicular or ramose-tabular perforations, either empty or partially filled with a core, and stained red with oxide of iron where these ramify the rock, while the rock itself is of a light grey. These markings have a good deal the appearance of those found in the calciferous sandstone of New York, and noted in the reports of that state under the name of Palaeophycus tubularis; but they are too indefinite to enable me to pronounce positively on their identity. They impart to the rock, however, a remarkable vermicular structure; and though they resemble, still probably differ from those impressions of plants in the *soft*, white, quaternary sandstone of the same locality.

One mile below Lane's on section 29, township 15 north, range 3 east, a similar hard standstone shows itself in a hollow.

Some lead ore has been picked up in the fields in the vicinity of Walcott; but so far as I have been able to trace the localities, invariably on the sites of Indian villages, along with other relics of the aborigenes, who, undoubtedly, brought the ore from the northwest part of the state or from Missouri.

The growth on the genuine black-sand lands of Cache and of the St. Francis river bottoms, is sweet gum, black hickory, walnut, poplar, dogwood, and occasionally box-elder and hackberry; undergrowth, papaw, spice-wood, and large grape vines. The subsoil, under the black sand, is generally clay, seldom a quicksand. About one-third of the Cache bottom is "post-oak land."

Four sets of soils were collected for chemical analysis from Abraham Tennison's farm, on Crowley's ridge, one mile from Walcott; No. 1, being the virgin or uncultivated soil; No. 2, the same soil from an old field, 35 years in cultivation, almost exclusively in corn; No. 3, subsoil, from the same old field; No. 4, the red under-clay. The growth on this land is sweet-gum, white and black-oak, with an undergrowth of dog-wood.

Should the chemical analyses of these hereafter be provided for, they will be reported.

POINSETT COUNTY.

The narrowest part of the Crowley ridge, is not far from the line between Greene and Poinsett, where it is hardly half a mile across from the St. Francis bottom to the L'Anguille bottom.

The L'Anguille bottom is mostly a bluish clay, and on the "Crab-apple barrens" a white clay. The prevalent timber in L'Anguille bottom, is red and white-oak, small scattering sweet-gum and post-oak on the "post-oak land," which, however, is not cultivated at present. The growth on the adjacent ridges is white and black-oak, poplar, and, occasionally, some pine; on the branches, poplar, gum, ash, elm, and dog-wood.

There is a stream called the St. Francis bayou, which runs from Mrs. Stott's farm, nearly parallel with the Crowley ridge, which is not laid down on the maps of Arkansas. This stream empties into the St. Francis river in the northern part of St. Francis county. The traces of earth-cracks and sandblows are numerous, almost every where in the St. Francis bottom, especially near the Morell prairie; some of the earth-cracks are eight to ten feet wide and six to eight deep. Lignite has frequently been thrown out of these rents in the earth, showing that there must be a considerable area of that mineral not far from the surface, running through the St. Francis country.

There is a peculiar soil of extraordinary fertility, occupying part of the St. Francis bottom, particularly in townships 8, 9, 10 and 11, ranges 5 and 6 east, known as the "black wax land," which was formerly overflowed by the back water of the Mississippi, but is now partly in cultivation. This soil will produce from 50 to 75 bushels of corn to the acre. The soil of the Morell prairie is sandy, but is also good corn land, yielding 40 to 50 bushels of corn to the acre, while the adjacent uplands of the Crowley ridge produce from 30 to 40 bushels.

From the Narrows of the Crowley ridge to Bolivar and Harrisburg, the new county seat, the quaternary gravel is quite conspicuous on the higher grounds, and of a very coarse character; some pieces would weigh several pounds. On Spencer creek, some little sandstone is seen underlying the gravel and resting on sandy clay.

At Hurricane creek, near Harrisburg, the Crowley ridge is about three miles wide. There are considerable cotton plantations in this part of Greene county, especially at B. Harris' and Judge Hall's, just at the edge of the L'Anguille and St. Francis bottoms.

Some specimens of amber are said to have been found on Hurricane creek. As this is sometimes an accompaniment of lignite, which occurs on the waters of this creek, it is not improbable that such a mineral may have been found, but probably only in small, isolated, disseminated lumps.

The material passed through, in sinking wells in the L'Anguille bottom, is usually 20 feet of yellow clay, underlaid by 30 to 40 feet of light-colored sand, a moderately soft water being generally obtained at 60 feet.

Immediately at the foot of the ridge, water is often obtained at 12 feet, the water gradually getting deeper for one mile into the bottom, where it is, generally, the deepest seated.

So far as I have yet been able to learn, no rotten limestone, green sand, or shell beds, referable to the cretaceous formation, have ever been reached, even in the lowest positions and excavations made in the northern part of Poinsett county.

My observations in this county have, as yet, only extended as far south as the vicinity of the northern line of township 10; but from the best information obtained from Judge Hall and others, best acquainted with this county, it seems very doubtful whether any of the members of this formation reach the surface even in the *southern* part of Poinsett.

In crossing the Crowley ridge from Benjamin Harris' to Judge Hall's, (a distance of three to three and a half miles,) gravel is found mostly in the high situations underlaid by sand and clay. At the foot of the ridge, near Judge Hall's, there is some soft sandstone, which is, no doubt, a local, partial cementation of the quaternary sand already referred to.

Samples of the cotton soil were collected for chemical analysis from Judge Hall's farm; No. 1, being the virgin soil; No. 2, twenty-four years in cultivation. The land lies just at the foot of the Crowley ridge, as it insensibly slopes down to the flats of the St. Francis bottom. This soil has a good deal of gravel mixed through it.

In passing from Judge Hall's, up the eastern edge of the Crowley ridge, the same succession of deposits prevails; the gravel occupying, as usual, the higher ground and being for the most part quite coarse.

From the west edge of the Crowley ridge, to the crossing of Cache river, by way of the Santa Fe post-office, is some eighteen miles. Of this about 8 miles is slush land, not very miry, but covered more or less with water, with only dry land enough for a few farms in the vicinity of Santa Fe post-office, and a small tract 6 miles from the crossing.

The best land of the Cache bottom for cultivation, is the sweet-gum land and red-elm, with an undergrowth of slippery-elm and dog-wood. This soil is somewhat of the nature of the black-sand land heretofore spoken of, with narrow strips of clay land running here and there through it. This soil is best adapted for corn and cotton.

JACKSON COUNTY.

There is no hill land proper in this county; the whole of the county being level land, with the farming lands bordering on White river being elevated only some 6 to 8 feet above the Cache flats.

A sample of the black sandy land was collected for analysis from land adjoining Thomas Maclerath's farm, 3 or 4 miles east of Cache river. This kind of soil forms about one-third or one-fourth of the Cache bottom. The other two-thirds are post-oak and black spice land. This latter soil is very rich when drained and reclaimed, but, in its natural state, is wet and miry. It supports a growth of large timber, viz: gum, fine ash, pen-oak, and hackberry, besides the black-spice. This land lies generally lower, if anything, than the post-oak land.

Near Driver's farm, on the Cache bottom, a specimen was collected for chemical analysis, of the higher and dryer variety of oak land which supports a growth of white-oak and gum, with only a few post-oaks.

The best farming lands in Jackson lie between Village creek and White river, occupying a low ridge rising several feet above the adjacent flats, and elevated about 10 feet above high water of White river. It supports a growth of hickory, poplar, oak, and black walnut. It is on these lands where the principal cotton crops of Jackson county are raised, and where the wealthiest portion of the population is located.*

Samples of this soil were selected for chemical analysis from two different localities; one taken from the vicinity of Jacksonport, from M. L. Robinson's farm, the other from H. J. Dowd's farm, 14 miles from Jacksonport.

The waters of White river were tested qualitatively; the sample being taken below the mouth of Black river. They were found to be soft, containing but a trace of earthy carbonates; as will be seen by consulting Dr. Elderhorst's report.

INDEPENDENCE COUNTY.

In passing from Jacksonport up the valley of White river, to examine the locality of the so-called "black marble," I traversed the "Oil-trough Bottom." This is a tract of very rich alluvial land, lying on the south-west side of White river, in the south-east part of Independence county. The fresh soil is very dark colored, even to the depth of five or six feet in some situations; the sub-soil being nearly as black as the soil, but more tenacious. This soil is particularly adapted for wheat.

On S. M. Cobb's farm, where samples of this soil were collected for future chemical analysis, an average crop of wheat is considered thirty bushels, the grain weighing 64 pounds to the bushel. It is also good corn land, yielding, on an average, 50 bushels, and would, no doubt, be excellent for tobacco.

The *palma christi*, or castor bean, grows here very large, and could, in all probability, be cultivated to great advantage, if an oil-press were established in the vicinity for the expression of the oil. The principal growth of timber on this land is pin-oak, red oak (yellow butt), water oak,

* For further particulars in regard to this tract of land, see E. T. Cox's report.

elm, pecan, black walnut, sweet-gum, hackberry, and buckeye, with an undergrowth of very large papaw, cane, grape vines, and a little spice-wood.

Rye flourishes well on this soil; but it is too rich for cotton, which grows too rank and runs too much to stalk and leaf. Timothy succeeds well; clover has not been tried. It is, however, especially adapted for small grain, for which, indeed, it is celebrated. The explanation of this will, no doubt, be found in a geological cause which will hereafter be adverted to. Since the wheat does not freeze out of this soil, and the weevil is unknown in the country, the farmers are most favorably situated for raising this grain, and the natural resources of the country would justify the erection of extensive flouring mills.

The water obtained by digging wells in the Oil-trough bottom is quite soft.

The Oil-trough bottom is about 15 miles long. At its head, the first ridge encountered is known as the Oil-trough ridge. Here I found the first ledges of solid rock which I had seen since leaving Greene county. These proved to belong to the upper members of the subcarboniferous limestone formation. At 70 feet above the Oil-trough bottom, I found one of the members of this formation which marks most decisively a most impartant geological horizon, viz: the Archimedes limestone. This rock occupies a position *below* the *lowest workable coal* throughout the western states of North America. No exception has yet been found to this geological axiom; it, therefore, serves as a sure and safe guide in pronouncing as to the existence or non-existence of coal in the vicinity, and furnishes the clue to the geologist, in connection with the dip and strike, of the formations of the country, in what direction he must search for coal.

The total height of the Oil-trough ridge was found to be 152 feet, and the following members of the upper subcarboniferous group of rocks were observed at the different elevations herewith subjoined in the approximate section of that ridge:

At 152 feet, Sandstone.
" 145 " Third bench of protruding limestone; exposed for 15 feet.
" 115 " Limestone shale.
" 92 " Second bench of protruding limestone; exposed for 15 feet.
" 75 " Productal black limestone.
" 70 " Archimedes limestone.
" 56 " First projecting ledge of limestone seen in this part of the ridge.

The Archimedes limestone, as above remarked, is the index to the discovery of coal. Where the sub-carboniferous limestone is fully developed in the west, upper and lower beds of Archimedes limestone exist, lying, sometimes, more than fifty feet apart. The upper Archimedes limestone is usually found immediately below, or within a few feet of the bottom of the conglomerate or pebbly sandstone, which lies at the base of the coal measures. This rock being of very variable thickness, from a few feet to ninety or one hundred feet or more, or even entirely absent, the space between the Archimedes limestone and lowest workable coal which usually overlies the conglomerate, may vary from 15 to 150 feet; but the first bed of workable coal never underlies this peculiar and well-marked fossiliferous limestone. This rule holds good so universally throughout the western states, viz: Indiana, Kentucky, Illinois, Tennessee, Alabama, and Missouri, that it may be applied with perfect confidence to Arkansas.

The sandstone observed capping the Oil-trough ridge, is undoubtedly the sandstone occupying the base of the coal measures, and if this ridge were 25 to 50 feet higher, we might hope to find workable coal. As it is, the south-west dip of the strata which prevails here, indicates to the geologist that he must look in that direction for coal; since the Archimedes limestone and overlying sandstone, pitching lower and lower in that course, give room for the true coal measures to come in on the hills above the drainage of the country.

We anticipate, therefore, in the farther prosecution of the survey towards Van Buren and Searcy counties, to discover coal. Whether it may be thick enough and of a good quality, are questions that can only be answered after the beds have been fairly opened and specimens obtained for chemical analysis.

The productal limestone, at 75 feet, in the preceding section of Oil-trough ridge, is of a fine black color, and is capable of receiving a polish, so that, if it can be quarried in sufficiently large slabs, free from cracks, imperfections and flaws, it may be employed for mantel-pieces and other ornamental inside work. For outside work, I fear it will be too liable to crack and split by the influence of the sun* and atmospheric agencies.

The great fertility of the soil of the Oil-trough bottom, and its adaptability, especially to small grain, is, no doubt, explained by the fact of its being bounded on the north and west by these limestone ridges, from which it has received calcareous and fertilizing washings for ages, imparting to it chemical elements found in much smaller proportions in the soil east of White river, in Jackson county.

I had again an opportunity of observing these members of the subcarboniferous limestone, in connection with some lower members, in a con-

* Some black bituminous limestones absorb heat so rapidly in the direct rays of the sun, that, from unequal expansion, they are very apt to split and crack.

spicuous hill of upwards of 500 feet, which forms a bold headland on the south side of White river, about 5 miles above Batesville, known as "Shield's Bluff," or White river mountain. It seems to be the most elevated part of a ridge which runs off to the south, forming a kind of geological culminating axis on its summit, whence the strata dip both to the south-west and north-east.

In this bluff I found the Archimedes limestone again, but in a much more elevated position than in the Oil-trough ridge, being 350 feet above the Dean farm, and some 400 feet above White river.

The total height of Shields' bluff is about 570 to 580 feet above White river. The lower 50 or 60 feet above the Dean farm is dark calcareous shale and shaly limestones; above which are some 330 to 340 feet of grey and bluish limestones with some alternations of sandstone; the summit being capped with from 80 to 100 feet of sandstone, occupying the place of the millstone grit and conglomerates that intervene between the Archimedes limestones and the coal measures.

The following are the elevations of the principal members of the sub-carboniferous group observed in Shields' bluff above the Dean farm:

At 520 feet, Top of escarpment of sandstone, capping the ridge.
" 475 " Foot of do.
" 395 " Ledge of sandstone.
" 385 " Limestone.
" 350 " Archimedes limestone.
" 345 " Encrinital limestone.
" 340 " Ledge of sandstone.
" 325 " Grey limestone.
" 315 " Sandstone (in place?)
" 300 " Top of ledges of limestone.
" 200 " Grey limestone.
" 170 " Off-set of hill-side with black limestone.
" 145 " Black limestone.
" 120 " 3d bench of limestone.
" 100 " 2d bench of limestone.
" 55 " 1st bench of limestone.
Limestone shales and shaly limestone at the foot of the hill down to the Dean farm.

Shield's bluff, where this approximate section was obtained, is a noted land-mark in Arkansas, as having been the point where the old Cherokee line commenced at White river, and ran south-west along the dividing ridge, of which it forms the terminating bluff on White river.

Eight miles south-east of Batesville, on the north-side of White river, I had a better opportunity of inspecting the shaly rocks of the subcarboniferous group, than in Shield's bluff, where they are too much concealed by debris washed from above. At this locality, I found the following succession under a ledge of sandstone:

Buff, earthy limestone	10 feet thick.	
Mudstone		6 inches thick.
Brown shale	4 "	"
Black shale	3 "	"
Limestone in pavement form	2 "	"
Brown shale	5 "	"
Black shale	1 "	"
Brown mudstone	4 "	6 inches "
Black shale	5 "	"
Calcareous septaria (hydraulic)	1 "	6 inches "
Brown shale	3 "	"

Black shale at base (thickness?) at an elevation 20 to 25 feet above the adjacent bottom.

Above these strata is apparently mostly sandstone, but much of it is out of place, having rolled down from a former higher elevation; there is evidently, however, a great thickness of millstone grit in the upper part of the adjoining ridges of 150 to 200 feet.

Four miles south-east of Batesville, a great mass of red shale crops out, which disintegrates rapidly to red clay. This underlies the above millstone grit rock.

The hills increase in height from the locality where the preceding section was taken towards Batesville; there a lower mass of intercalated sandstone rises from beneath these shales, shaly limestone, and septaria. The soil immediately over this sandstone is, as usual, thin, and supports a growth of stunted oak.

From Miller's creek up to Batesville, the hills are from 130 to 240 feet in height. Red shales, running downwards into brown and black shales, with calcareous septaria, occupy the base of the hills around Batesville; these shales are surmounted by 150 to 180 feet of sandstone.

The black shales of the above series have given rise to expectations for the discovery of coal in their vicinity; but, occupying, as they do, a geological position in the subcarboniferous group entirely below the millstone grit, and Archimedes limestone, there is no prospect of finding any thing but perhaps a few inches of coal associated with these shales, which can be of no practical value.

Between Batesville and the "Big Spring," there are high ridges elevated about 450 feet above White river, composed in their upper part of both compact and cellular chert; the latter partaking of the character of buhrstone. This chert is, in all probability, of subcarboniferous date. The surface being much encumbered with blocks and protruding masses of these siliceous rocks, the soil is necessarily thin, and supports a growth almost exclusively of small oak. Nevertheless, the soil is capable of producing much better than the forbidding nature of the rocky surface would lead one to suppose.

The descent from these chert ridges to the "Big Spring," is about 260 feet. Here, a noble volume of the clearest water silently rises from some cavernous passage at the foot of an amphitheatre of hills of cherty, siliceous limestones, sufficient in quantity to supply the wants of a small gristmill. Like all those streams having a subterranean origin, it never freezes in winter. This Big spring is quite a noted locality in Independence county. The water-power it affords, and the improvement in the soil of the country, watered by its branches, has attracted agriculturists, who have opened several good farms three miles south of the Big spring; but north-east, towards the Rocky bayou, the country is mostly rocky oak-barrens, with a broken surface, where few settlers have located.

The cavernous or barren limestone group, capped with chert, prevails to Lafferty creek, where it is underlaid in many places by a very white sandstone, some of which is sufficiently pure to make glass.

The dip is irregular; at one place the inclination was observed to be 10 deg. S. W.

I examined a salt-petre cave situated from half to three quarters of a mile north-west from Tosches' farm, and about 250 to 300 feet up in a ridge of subcarboniferous limestone. This cave is known as the "Saltpetre cave," and is owned by Col. John Miller.

It has passages from 200 to 300 yards long, and 8 to 10 feet wide. The sacks containing the earth from this cave have, unfortunately, never come to hand, so that we cannot report upon the per centage of salt-petre it contains, until a further supply is obtained.

At Peter Moser's, on Lafferty creek, the mixture of the soil, derived, in part, from the cavernous limestone, and in part from the white sandstone, produces excellent oats, and is capable of yielding 40 to 50 bushels of corn to the acre, and 800 to 1000 pounds of raw cotton in the seed, and in very favorable seasons even as high as 1500 pounds.

As the cotton loses about two-thirds in cleaning and freeing it from seed, the land may be said to yield from 250 to 350 pounds of clean ginned cotton to the acre. It is the washings from the adjacent hills of limestone that cause the land to produce so much better than its first appearance, and stunted trees of oak and pine which grow upon it, would lead one to suspect.

The cavernous limestone of Lafferty creek, is traversed by veins of different varieties of manganese ore. The most interesting locality is on the west branch of Lafferty creek, two miles above its mouth. Here, there appear to be regular veins with well-defined walls, traversing the cavernous limestone, containing the manganese ores. The course of the main vein, with probably some subordinate cross courses, runs N. N. W. and S. S. E.

I measured the space between the faces of the walls of the veins at different places where excavations had been made for the ore, and found them to vary from 14 feet 9 inches to 8½ feet. These ran down through an encrinital bed of limestone, which is elevated about 200 feet above the mouth of Lafferty creek.

The masses of manganese ore taken out of these crevices vary in weight from a few ounces to 30 or 40 pounds. From the most productive part of the vein a man could raise from 300 to 400 pounds per day.

Judging from the specimens taken out, and which lay strewed in abundant heaps on the hill-side near the crevices, there appear to be two varieties of manganese ore obtained at these mines, in the depth to which the superficial and partial mining operations have yet been carried; one a compact, close-textured ore of a dark steel-grey color, and a hardness of about 5½ to 6, having the physical aspect of that variety of compact manganese ore described in works on mineralogy under the name of "psilomelane," composed of mixtures of the oxides of manganese, with, usually, some baryta and potash; but from a partial qualitative examination made of this Lafferty creek manganese ore, it appears to contain but a trace of baryta.

The other variety is more crystalline in its structure, brighter in its lustre, and of a lighter steel-grey color; but in hardness, streak, and color of the powdered mineral (blackish brown), differs but little from the former more compact variety.*

Whether these two varieties differ only from some admixture of accidental ingredients, or have a decidedly different atomic proportion of manganese and oygen, will appear when the quantitative chemical analyses are completed and recorded in the Chemical Report; then the questions bearing on the commercial value of these ores will be decided.

So far as I can learn, the company who own these mineral lands on Lafferty creek, in Independence county, and who made an attempt to

*The analysis of these ores, recorded in the Chemical Report, proves these two varieties to be essentially of the same constitution, the first containing, however, 3 or 4 more per cent of silica.

mine and ship the ore to the eastern cities, did not find as ready a sale or as high a price for their ore as they anticipated, and seem to have suspended operations, for the present, on this account.

The explanation of this want of success in this their first enterprise on these manganese ores, is probably to be found in the fact, that the larger part, at least, of the ore which they obtained, was of this hard variety, affording rather less than one-third of its weight of oxygen; and, therefore, capable of eliminating only a proportional quantity of chlorine, for which purpose it is chiefly valuable in the arts; while they raised little or none of the soft black manganese ore; i. e. bin, or peroxide of manganese, known to mineralogists under the name of "pyrolusite," which is not only much easier to grind to powder, by reason of its greater softness, but contains about 36 per cent of oxygen, and will, therefore, evolve a larger proportion of chlorine from a given weight of the ore.

It is to be remarked, however, in this connection, that this pyrolusite or binoxide, the most valuable in commerce of the ores of manganese, is frequently associated, and even in alternating layers of different thickness, with ores of compact, grey oxide of manganese, similar to that of which there is so great an abundance on Lafferty creek and its vicinity. Hence, either a neglect to make the proper selection for the market of the ores raised, or not mining sufficiently deep to reach the best quality of ore, may be assigned as causes of the present abandonment of the mines.*

Similar ores of manganese have been found on the south-east quarter of section 25, township 15 north, range 8 west, and west of north of Batesville;† besides, at many other localities on the waters of Lafferty creek, in the north-west part of Independence county, so that if the owners of these mineral lands can obtain, by a thorough exploration of the veins, the soft black (pyrolusite) ore of manganese, there is a fair prospect of reaching well filled veins, which might return them a handsome profit.

Associated with the manganese ores of Lafferty creek, is some excellent red oxide of iron. The qualitative chemical examination, shows it to be nearly pure peroxide of iron, with but a very small per centage of foreign matter; the quantiative analysis will, therefore, no doubt, yield between 65 and 70 per cent of iron.

The lands which are most valuable for cultivation, in the north-west part of Independence county, are, first, the bottom lands supporting a growth of walnut, large Spanish-oak, ash, and overcup-oak, with an un-

* By consulting the chemical report of Dr. Elderhorst, farther information on the commercial value of these manganese ores will be obtained.

† See Ed. T. Cox's report for a description of the geological position, and external aspect of the manganese ore, which occurs three miles west of north of Batesville.

dergrowth of spice and large grape vines. These bottoms are, however, of limited extent. Secondly, the black-oak, hickory, large white-oak, and dogwood upland. Thirdly, the hazlenut and sumach thickets.

The soil of some of the hill-sides, on the slopes of the cavernous limestone, is often remarkably rich, and could be cultivated to great advantage, where not too abrupt and not too much encumbered with rock.

I examined a cave situated near the top of a ridge composed of the cavernous limestone, and reposing on the white sandstone, towards the base of the ridges. This cave is situated between Peter and Samuel Moser's farms, in the eastern part of Independence county. The entrance to this cave is very low, so that it is difficult to enter. It is only of limited extent and has but little disintegrated earth distributed through it. What little there is, is near the entrance to the cave.

A sample of this earth was collected for chemical analysis, and will be reported on when this latter is completed.

A characteristic soil of the cavernous limestone formation, was also collected for chemical analysis, from south-east half of section 25, township 15 north, range 8 west, from Peter Moser's farm, on the waters of Lafferty creek, in Independence county. The growth of timber on this land is hickory, post-oak, white-oak, persimmon, and dogwood.

This soil is said to produce 30 bushels of wheat to the acre, 20 to 25 bushels of oats, and 40 to 50 bushels of corn. The soil has some chert gravel intermixed with it; the subsoil is a dark yellowish clay.

The same geological formation prevails between Lafferty creek and Rocky bayou; white sandstone in the base of the ridges, surmounted by cavernous limestone: the ridges rising from 300 to 400 feet above the principal water courses.

For farther information in regard to the geology of this county, consult the report of the assistant geologist, Edward Cox.

IZARD COUNTY.

Five miles from Rocky bayou, the white sandstone was found to be 116 feet below the summits of the ridge, passed over in the eastern part of Izard county.

At the forks of the road leading to Mt. Olive, and the North fork, and 7 miles from the Rocky bayou, in the bed of a dry branch, about 197 feet *below* the level of the observation, on the above mentioned sandstone, is a bed of dark-grey compact limestone, charged with minute *cytherea*, which, probably, belongs to the silurian period. The adjacent ridge, bounding the valley of the branch on the north, has a sandstone near its summit, which is probably the same sandstone seen in the base of the ridges on Lafferty creek, and which is found at an elevation of 467 feet above low water of White river, at Calico Rock, and was afterwards traced through Izard county, to the high pine ridge, at the head of Sugar Loaf creek, and which is usually marked by a growth of pine, as may be observed in plate No. 1 of the Sugar Loaf mountain of Izard county, the site of that sketch being on the plateau of that pine-bearing sandstone.

No organic remains have yet been found in this sandstone, to indicate its geological position; but, taking the lithological character and order of superposition as a guide, it will probably be found to belong at the base of the subcarboniferous series of Izard and Marion counties, resting on limestones, which belong probably to the silurian period; it is, probably, the equivalent of the " Saccharoidal standstone," of the Missouri report, underlying the Cooper marble of the south-western part of that state.

This sandstone seems to increase in thickness to the north-west, towards the Lees mountain range.

Two miles from Calico, this sandstone is some 160 feet in thickness, with perhaps some intercalated layers of limestone. Most of the beds of the standstone, in this part of Izard, seem to be white or of pale yellow colors, and soft.

The dip is irregular, and often undulating, and conformable to the general contour of the country. However, the prevalent dip is to the south-west.

The limestones of this region, are of light and dark grey hues, and often singularly weathered into small furrows, radiating from a centre, and often intersected with veins of calc-spar.

The ridge of cellular buhrstone, which I passed over, before descending to the North Fork, was found, by the aneroid barometer, to be 537 feet above that river.

Before reaching Athens, the Sugar-loaf mountain of the south-eastern part of Izard county is in view, conspicuous above the intervening ridges. [See plate No. 1.]

At the mouth of the Pine bayou, the cliffs capped with sandstone are about 200 feet.

The soil of this part of Izard county, is best adapted for corn; it will yield about 30 bushels to the acre of this grain; 15 of wheat, and about the same of oats, and 800 pounds of cotton in the seed. The season for cotton is rather too short in this high, northern part of Arkansas.

The growth on the lands above cited is black-oak, hickory, and some red-oak. The sample of this soil collected for analysis may be considered an average of a large proportion of that part of Izard county, lying northeast of White river, and between that stream and Strawberry river.

Between Calico and the North Fork, the white and yellow sandstone occupies, for the first 8 miles, a position towards the summits of the ridges. Its upper layers are generally coarse-grained, and present glistening reflections. This sandstone is underlaid by the cherty limestones which form the varigated cliffs on White river, known by the name of the "Calico Rock." [See plate No. 2.]

Six miles from Calico, on the road from Calico to the North Fork, the plateau of sandstone, from which sketch No. 1 was taken, is at an elevation of 380 to 390 feet above White river.

At the widow Lafferty's farm, where a soil was collected from Izard county, for chemical analysis, the sandstone is overlaid by limestone.

In the vicinity of Friend's creek, the sandstone becomes harder and more charty; it may be designated there, a porous and cellular, cherty sandstone.

In passing over the ridges about Friend's creek, a high knob is seen off towards the south, known by the name of "Naked Joe." This hill appears to be some 150 to 200 feet higher than the main ridges of the country, and formed a conspicuous land-mark, in early times, for the guidance of hunters and explorers.

The country around Friend's creek, where there is so much cellular chert on the surface of the ground, has much the aspect of the iron region of south-western Kentucky, and though no body of iron ore has yet been discovered on the waters of this stream, the detailed survey may, perhaps, hereafter develop such.

Four miles before reaching the North Fork, the ridges at the same elevation (i.e., 380 to 390 feet) as the sandstone platform, 6 miles from Calico, are composed of cellular buhrstone chert.

The summit level, passed over about 3 miles before reaching the North Fork, and where the descent to that stream commences, is about 445 feet above Major Jacob Wolf's house, and 537 feet above the North Fork, according to observations taken with the aneroid barometer.

Beyond the North Fork, there is another high conspicuous hill, towering above the rest of the main ridges, called "Mattener's Knob," which I was told by Maj. Jacob Wolf, was reported by surveyor Smith, to be 1,100 feet high.

Maj. Jacob Wolf reports a small piece of ore, found in digging the foundation of a mill, near the North Fork, which was pronounced to be silver ore by some one, who professed to have examined it, but whose name I did not learn. I have little faith in silver occurring in the formations which prevail along the North Fork, towards its confluence with

White river, unless it be in small quantities, associated with the lead and zinc ores of this country.

The grey and red varigated limestones, which will be hereafter spoken of, under the head of Marion county, occur in the bluffs of White river, 5 or 6 miles above the mouth of the North Fork, and a mile above Big creek; but they lie under a heavy mass of superincumbent rock, which makes them difficult of access.

The cherty magnesian, and other varieties of limestones, of which the base of the hills is composed, and which form bold cliffs on the North Fork, and at Ware's mill, appear to be of silurian date, but the sandstone chert and limestones towards the tops of the ridges, must belong to the subcarboniferous group, judging from the few imperfect fossils found.

J. E. Ware showed me some ores of manganese, which he says came from the bluffs of White river, below the mouth of Big creek.

On the south side of the North Fork, the chert frequently assumes the character of hornstone and agate.

There are very fine buhr millstone rocks in the ridges of the North Fork, not far from Ware's mill, but on the opposite side of the river, according to J. E. Ware; he also found small particles of copper ore and some Terra Sienna on a prong of Morton creek, on section 17, township 18 north, range 12 west; but though he has searched a great deal for ores, adjacent to the surrounding country in Izard, he never discovered any deposit or vein of copper worth following by drifts or adit levels.

Near the line between Izard and Marion counties, at Camp spring, there is a bed of brown ochreous clay, which produces a color similar to Terra Sienna. The bed is in a ravine, about 6 or 8 feet under the spring. It is of various shades at the outcrop, mostly on account of admixtures of earths washed over it. Farther in the bank it could, probably, be obtained in greater purity, and of deeper and more uniform tints.

Lower down, on the same branch, are extensive beds of buhr millstone in "Camp creek hollow," some of which are of excellent texture and hardness for grinding corn, while other varieties are equally good for wheat. This buhrstone lies some 200 feet below the level of the ridge over which the Yellville road runs, above the Camp spring.

In consequence of the vegetation and debris of rock concealing the strata, no very satisfactory section could be obtained of the whole of the members composing the hills forming the Camp creek hollow; but the following is the succession from above, downwards, of those which can be seen:

1. Carboniferous limestone and chert.
2. Sandstone.

3. Sandstone, hard and quartzose.
4. Variegated shales, including the Terra Sienna earth and segregations of hydraulic (?) limestone, and some mudstone shale interstratified.
5. Thin-bedded, light-grey limestone.
6. Buhrstone, 6 to 8 feet thick.
7. Light-colored magnesian limestone, of silurian date?
8. Compact, flinty siliceous rocks.

J. E. Ware is of opinion, the best quality of buhrstones, of any required dimensions, can be obtained either in Camp creek hollow or the ridges opposite his flouring mill, on the North Fork, equal in quality to the French buhr.

Small particles of sulphuret of copper have been picked up by J. E. Ware, in the Camp creek hollow, disseminated sparingly in a gangue of calc-spar; but no regular vein has, as yet, been detected.

MARION COUNTY.

The prevailing rocks of this county are varieties of magnesian limestones, which crop out in terraces and low cliffs on the sides of the hills.

Some sandstone is intercalated, chiefly towards the upper and lower part of the hills. The upper sandstone is of variable thickness, from a few inches to 50 or 60 feet. It appears, in many places, as if the underlying magnesian limestone had suffered from irregular denudation; having been locally scooped out into deep hollows, into which sand was subsequently swept, and became, afterwards, indurated into a hard, solid rock.

The lower sandstone I have only had a good opportunity of examining, as yet, in the adjacent county of Carroll, on township 20 north, range 18 west, of the 5th principal meridian, where it has the hard quartzose character of the lowest sandstone of Wisconsin and Minnesota, as it occurs on the Minnesota, Baraboo, and Wisconsin rivers.

The upper sandstone is generally overlaid by limestones, capable of receiving a good polish. Some of the beds are pink, variegated with white, or light grey; others, nearly white, or light grey, and often studded with *entrochites:* that is, the disjointed stems of those singular flower-like animals, known by the name of *encrinites*, which flourished in such profusion in the ancient seas, in which the deposits and chemical precipitates were accumulating, that produced the so-called silurian, devonian, and carboniferous rocks. These contribute greatly to the beauty of the marble of which they form a part; appearing, often, of different shades of color from the matrix in which they are enclosed, and giving to the rock that variety of tint so agreeable to the eye, and so much esteemed by the worker in marble.

In the middle and north-west part of Marion county, these marble layers lie high in the hills; generally 20 to 50 feet below the tops of the ridges in which they occur.

In the high Pine ridge, which forms the water-shed between Sugar-loaf, Crooked, George's, and Jennings' creeks, there is a considerable mass of chert capping its summit, which is, probably, referable to the subcarboniferous period; judging from the few casts of crinoidea observed in it. This ridge is, at least, 200 to 250 feet higher than the subordinate ridges bounding the water courses of Sugar-loaf creek.

The summit of this high ridge is composed of chert sandstone, underlaid by limestones, dolomitic and calciferous sand-rock.

The siliceous soil, in which the pine trees flourish, is derived from the chert and sandstone, on which it is based.

The above-described marble rocks, which occur in these ridges, are, probably, the representative of the so-called "Cooper marble," of Missouri, which has been referred to the age of the Onondaga limestone of the New York system.

At present, we have not sufficient palæontological evidence to decide on its exact equivalency with rocks of other states; but in the future progress of the survey, further light will, no doubt, be thrown on the age of these beds, which intervene between the subcarboniferous and silurian rocks of northern Arkansas, and which, on account of their economical value, are of great interest.

Sufficient evidence has already been obtained to establish the age of the 300 feet of magnesian limestones and silico-calcareous rock, that underlie the marble strata, forming about 250 to 300 feet of the lower and main body of the ridges of Marion county, as of lower silurian date, and, in all probability, to that subdivision known as the calciferous sandrock of the New York system. This is the lead and zinc-bearing formation of north-western Arkansas.

Sulphuret of lead, or galena, has been found, more or less abundantly, at numerous localities, both in Marion and Carroll counties. The most noted ones, in the former county, are on the waters of Sugar-loaf, High-tower, and Jennings' creeks. No regular or systematic mining operations have yet been undertaken in Marion county, so that an opinion of the exact character and dimensions of these mineral deposits, cannot be formed; they occur, however, evidently, much in the same manner as those which were subsequently examined in the eastern part of Carroll county, at the Coka and Mitchell diggings. One partial drift, and a few prospect holes on township 20 north, range 17 east, and township 20 north, range 19 east, of the 5th principal meridian, are all that has been done in Marion county, near the head of Sugar-loaf creek, to prove this lead region.

The principal entry on township 20 north, range 17 west, on the lands of the New York company, was only carried about 8 or 10 feet into the hill-side, with a width of about 4 feet. Judge Brickey, who superintended this excavation, informs me that there were taken out of this drift from 4,500 to 5,000 pounds of lead ore; two hands obtained at the rate of about 1,000 pounds in two days. A space of about one foot deep, and three feet wide, yielded from 100 to 150 pounds. This ground was, no doubt, sufficiently productive to pay well for working; but it must be borne in mind, that this drift was entirely too limited to give a just idea of how productive the rock might prove, by regular mining operations; since it is evident from all that is at present known of this lead region, that the ore occurs irregularly disseminated in "pockets," "sheets," "joints," and crevices; the pockets being cavernous spaces of various dimensions, occurring only occasionally in the rock by local expansions of the crevice.

When ore is disseminated in this manner, it is always necessary to prove the richness of each locality, by especial trial drifts and shafts. Hence, those owning mineral lands, in this part of Arkansas, would do well, if they wish to establish the value of their mines, and induce smelters to erect furnaces, without which the mining business cannot be carried on to any advantage, to sink shafts and run drifts a sufficient depth and distance to test, satisfactorily, the productiveness of their mines.

On section 19, township 20 north, range 17 east of the 5th principal meridian, Armsted Hudson has sunk a few shallow pits on a hill, east of his house, and west 6 deg. to 8 deg. south of the New York drift. Here he discovered, likewise, more or less lead ore, and, on the opposite side of the hollow, to the west, as far as Wood's pit, where lead ore was reached at 45 feet, then two and a half miles to the south-west, near Grit's mills; while the Short mountain location of Mitchell and Walker, lies two and a half miles to the north-east.

There appear to be two sets of lead-bearing crevices, or irregular veins, traversing the magnesian limestones of Marion county; one set running nearly north-east and south-west; the other east 6 deg. to 8 deg. north; but so little has yet been done, even in the way of digging "prospect holes," that it is difficult, at present, to form a correct opinion on this subject.

Some detached pieces of lead ore have also been discovered at the junction of the magnesian limestones and underlying quartzose sandstone, on township 20 north, range 18 east of the 5th principal meridian, at what is known as McCarty's diggings; but the ore lies too close to the lower hard sandstone to give much prospect of productiveness in this rock. In the upper sections of the ridges, lying between these McCarty's diggings and the New York location, amongst the magnesian limestones, more or less ore may be expected to occur; more especially, since pieces of "float-mineral" have been found, at intervals, between the two locations.

A vein of galena of several inches traverses the limestone forming the bed of Jennings' creek, about one-and-a-half miles above the forks of that stream, at what is known as the "Molton or Sewell diggings." Here the course of the vein appears to be nearly north-west and south-east. Several shallow pits have also been sunk on the adjacent hill-side, where, I understand, small pieces of lead ore were discovered. The rock here, is a close-textured, cherty limestone, very irregular in its fracture and bedding, and is a member of the same formation in which the lead ore occurs on Sugar Loaf creek, but modified in its lithological character; since, at the latter locality, the limestone is an easily decomposing rock, weathering and splitting up like hydraulic limestone. The composition of this rock will be seen by the analysis in the Chemical Report.

There is considerable variety in the lithological character of the different strata composing the hills in the lead region of Marion county, on the waters of Sugar Loaf creek, as may be seen by the following section, taken about half way between the Hudson farm and the head of Sugar Loaf creek.

SECTION OF STRATA OF LOWER SILURIAN DATE IN THE LEAD REGION OF MARION COUNTY; WATERS OF SUGAR LOAF CREEK.

Feet.	Inches.			Feet.	Inches.
307		CH CH			
		CH			
		CH CH	Space concealed with fragments of chert, hornstone, and other varieties of flinty siliceous rocks.		
		CH			
		CH CH			
		CH			
		CH CH		37	
		L L L	White encrinital marble rock.	4	
		CH CH			
		CH			
		CH CH	Space concealed with fragments of chert and hornstone on the slope.		
		CH			
		CH CH			
		CH			
228		CH CH		38	

It will be observed by the subjoined section, in the lead region of Marion county, taken in the hills adjacent to the head of Sugar Loaf creek, that, in the space of 307 feet of the section, considerable variation is observable in the composition of the various beds of which it is made up.

The formation, as a whole, is perfectly analogous to the strata north of the Wisconsin river,

SECTION OF MARION COUNTY—Continued.

Feet.	Inches.			Feet.	Inches.
193		L / L L / L / L L	Red and variegated limestone or marble rock.	25	
194		L / L L / L / L L / L	White encrinital limestone or marble rock.	19	
194		SL SL / SL / SL SL / SL / SL SL / SL	Impure siliceous limestone.	16	
178		SS SS / SS / SS SS	Soft coarse-grained sandstone.	8	
169		ML ML / ML / ML ML	Thin-bedded magnesian limestone.	8	
161		L	White fossiliferous limestone, close-textured, brittle.	2	
159		L L / L	Birds-eye structured limestone.	5	
147		L L / L	Magnesian limestone.	5	
139		SL SL / SL / SL SL	Siliceous limestone.	10	
128		CS CS / CS / CS CS / CS	Calcareous sandstone.	11	
93		ML ML / ML / ML ML / ML / ML ML / ML	Buff, checkered magnesian limestone.	35	
71		CR CR / CR / CR CR	Light-colored limestone with chert, so-called "cotton rock."	12	
67		ML	Grey rough-weathering mag. limestone.	4	
46		L L / L / L L / L	Light-colored limestone in beds from 6 to 8 inches in thickness.	21	

in the State of Wisconsin, except that the beds of magnesian limestone are thinner-bedded and less massive, and hence, do not appear in as bold cliffs in Arkansas as on the upper Mississippi. The fossils in the limestone, at an elevation of 161 feet above Sugar Loaf creek, are, mostly, casts and imperfect imbedded impressions, so that even the genera can hardly be made out; but, so far as they are recognizable, they, as well as the lithological character of the strata, indicate the geological horizon of these rocks as cotemporaneous with the "lower magnesian limestone and interstratified sandstones" of northern Wisconsin, the "calciferous sandrock" of the New York system, and the "2nd magnesian limestone and sandstone, and 3d magnesian limestone" of the Geological Report on south-western Missouri.

SECTION OF MARION COUNTY—Continued.

Feet.	Inches.			Feet.	Inches.
42		ML ML / ML / ML ML	Bench of grey magnesian limestone.	4	
31		ML / ML ML / ML	Thin-bedded, light-colored magnesian limestone.	12	
20		ML ML / ML / ML ML	Bench of solid, grey magnesian limest.	11	
		ML / ML ML / ML / ML ML / ML / ML ML	Thin-bedded magnesian limestone, in beds of a few inches in thickness, extending down into the bed of Sugar Loaf creek.	20	
				307	

Three quarters of a mile south of the Mitchell farm, the following section was obtained in a hill known as "Mitchell's Hill:"

Height.		*Thickness.*
148 feet. / 142 "	Top of the loose pieces of chert and sandstone	6
76 "	Hard, light-grey magnesian limestone, with occasional beds of chalcedonic chert, most abundant in the lower part	76
56 "	Quartzose sandstone and chert	10
26 "	Magnesian limestone	40
25 "	Intercalated bed of siliceous magnesian limestone	1
1 "	Magnesian limestone, with red and yellow bands	15
0	Slope and bank extending down to the bed of upper Sugar-loaf creek	0

Plate 3 represents a distant view of Sugar-loaf hill, of Marion, a conspicuous land-mark, lying in the eastern part of Sugar-loaf prairie. This hill is 300 feet above the level of Sugar-loaf creek, near the Coka farm.

It is composed of thin-bedded magnesian limestones, overlaid by chert at top, and underlaid by light-colored earthy limestone, like the so-called "Cotton Rock," of Missouri.

A voluminous spring issues from the cavernous spaces in the rocks on the east side of lower Sugar-loaf creek, affording a valuable water-power, available at all seasons of the year, with but little variation as to quantity and temperature, and capable of supplying a considerable amount of machinery.

The high Pine ridge, capped with subcarboniferous chert, resting on the sandstone previously mentioned, extends for four miles between the heads of Sugar-loaf creek and those of George's creek; the pine being co-extensive with the area occupied by these higher siliceous rocks.

The white encrinital and marble rock of this region, may be very conveniently quarried in a hill just beyond this pine ridge, near Wood's mill, where it outcrops towards the top of the hill, with a gentle slope, which affords an opportunity of quarrying it with but little stripping. Also in some of the ridges, near the Hudson farm and the "New York Location," on the waters of Sugar-loaf creek.

The strata composing the lower part of the hills between Yellville and Wood's mill, are chiefly marly, earthy and hydraulic-looking calcareous rocks, very retentive of water, which flows out along the surface of the plane of dip in numerous springs. The country has a glady aspect, and the roads are soft and miry, except where they run on the bare rock.

These strata have much the character of marly, shaly limestones, described as intervening between the subcarboniferous rocks and the strata of silurian date in south-western Missouri, and may be of the same age, but, as yet, we have no positive evidence of equivalency, in the absence of the necessary palæontological evidence. The fossil nautili which have been found in chert near Mickersham's mill, about 2 miles S. W. of Yellville, indicate rocks of the subcarboniferous era, proving the south-westerly inclination of the strata, which may account for rocks of devonian (?) and subcarboniferous age being found here low in the hills, while they occupy high situations in the north and north-eastern part of Marion county.

Lee's mountain was found to be, by measurement with the aneroid barometer, 350 feet above our camp, near John Osburn's farms, on Jenning's creek.*

The ascent of this mountain from Fallen Timber creek, on the east, is very steep. Towards the summit level of the road, there are alternations of sandstone amongst the limestone, and higher up, near the summit of the ridge to the south, the marble rock is in place. The sandstone below this rock must be much thicker here than in the ridges along Sugar-loaf creek, and the rocks elevated some fifty feet higher above the drainage of the country than on Sugar-loaf creek.

The "Molton Diggings," on Jennings' creek, are a mile and a half above

*This observation was taken on the 4th of December, at noon, in the midst of a heavy shower of rain, and, therefore, may be liable to some correction hereafter.

the forks, and half a mile below John Osburn's, on both sides of the creek. The ore has been found, as yet, only in lumps and pockets, except in one place, where some blasting has been done in the limestone forming the bed of the creek. Here the ore was said to have been found in a solid vein of 4 to 6 inches wide, though this statement is not corroborated by John Osburn. Where I examined it, the work has been carried for a few yards in a N. W. and S. E. course diagonally across the bed of the Jennings' creek; but the excavations were, at the time of my exploration, completely submerged, so that little opportunity offered for seeing the vein, if such exists; but about half a pound of lead ore was found disseminated in detached pieces through the adjacent rock. Some diggings and prospect-holes have been opened along the hill-side, in a north and south course, but these are too shallow to enable any one to form an opinion as to the manner in which the ore is disseminated or concerning the true course of the ore-bearing crevice. All that can be said at present in regard to this locality, is that the formation is similar to those in the northern part of Marion, heretofore described, and the surface indications of ore probably equally as good for mining as in that part of the country from its head to the forks of the creek.

About 200 pounds of lead ore were taken out of one of the holes dug on the adjacent hill-side, three quarters of a mile above the forks of Jennings' creek. Considerable lead ore was found in lumps and small fragments by John Osburn, about a mile and a half northwest of the Molton diggings. The prevailing character of the rock on Jennings' creek, near the forks, is that of a close-textured, cherty, dark-grey limestone, very irregular in its fracture and bedding, and often fragmentary.

Below the forks of Jennings' creek, the rocks are mostly rugged ledges of magnesian and other varieties of limestone, with some alternations of marl and marly limestones, with frequent imbedded segregations of chalcedonic chert.

The principal Sewell diggings are 4 miles below the Molton diggings, township 19 north, range 16 west, of the fifth principal meridian.

Several pits and prospect-holes have been dug here in search of ore, near the tops of the ridges, and two or three tons of ore obtained. In some of the excavations crevices have been reached running in the magnesian limestone, north 30 deg. west, and lead ore is found attached to the wall-rock, and running in veins of about an inch thick.

Mr. Sewell undertook to smelt about 4 tons of this ore in a rude log furnace, but the greatest part of it oxydized and ran to slag and was lost amongst the cinders and ashes.

Small quantities of zinc ore have also been found here, associated with the lead ore at the Sewell diggings.

Some sandstones are intercalated with the magnesian limestones of this part of Jennings' creek valley.

The tops of ridges are mostly strewed over with masses of porous chert. In some of the ridges the red marble rock is in place.

The surface indications of lead ore are frequent. Mr. McCracken, whose farm adjoins the Sewell diggings, found a lump of lead ore, one foot below the surface, in digging the foundation for his chimney, and pieces weighing several pounds on the hill-sides opposite his house, on the northern side of Jennings' creek. In the tops of some of the ridges, the marble rock occurs in the vicinity of Mr. McCracken's, which appears to have generally a reddish cast.

In the valley through which the road passes up from Mr. McCracken's to the Flippen barrens, chert and buhrstone are very abundant, lying in large blocks on the surface and along the beds of the creeks, rendering the road very rough and disagreeable to travel over. There are also some glady hill-sides where marly and shaly limestones crop out, like those mentioned as occurring on the road between Yellville and Wood's mill, in this county.

The bottom lands of Jennings' creek, are of good quality, but they are narrow and limited in extent.

The high grounds at the Flippen barrens are chiefly composed of chert belonging to the subcarboniferous era, as indicated by the fossils found there, both those collected by the corps and those generously presented by Mr. William B. Flippen.

Amongst the cliffs adjacent to the west bank of White river, five or six miles from the Flippen barrens, under overhanging ledges of magnesian limestones in the "*Rock House*," known by the name of Bean's cave, peculiar nitre earths have formed in large quantities.

At this locality there are large quantities of red ferruginous dry nitre earth, above and below the red laminated layers, containing nitre salts, which, if all converted, by the usual process of manufacture, into salt-petre, would yield about 6.2 per cent. The composition of this nitre earth, is shown by the following chemical analyses, made both of the whole earth by digestion with hydrochloric acid and of the saline portion soluble in water, which extract contains the nitre salts convertible into salt-petre.

One sample of red, ferruginous, dry nitre earth gave, after being air-dried, the following result by chemical analysis:

First. By treatment with hydrochloric acid.

Hygrometric water expelled at 300 deg	3.15
Silicates insoluble in hydrochloric or nitric acid	64.68
Alumina	10.00
Peroxide of iron	7.68
Lime	3.65
Magnesia	1.50
Potash	.945
Soda	.650
Manganese	.080
Sulphuric acid	.360
Phosphoric acid	.015
Carbonic acid	.050
Chlorine	.198
Organic matter, water of hydration not expelled at 300 deg., and ammonia	2.428
Nitric acid and loss	4.614
	100.000

The saline matter extracted by water, was equal to 7 per cent of the whole, and contained the following bases and acids:

Alumina tinged with iron	0.32
Lime	0.76
Magnesia	0.40
Potash	0.282
Soda	0.068
Chlorine	0.196
Sulphuric acid	0.360
Nitric acid	3.210
Water of crystallization, loss and organic matter	1.404
	7.000

Another of the nitre earths formed in Bean's cave, is a very regularly laminated moist earth, variegated with thin bands of dark and light red of a very fine texture, and capable of being divided into thin flexible laminae, like sheets of dough.

This nitre earth, when air dried, yielded by analysis about 1.3 per cent of nitric acid, which when converted into nitrate of potash or saltpetre, by the usual process of leaching and saturation, with carbonate of potash, or the ley from ashes, would give about 2.5 per cent of saltpetre.

The artificial nitre plantations of France, afford, by a similar process, on an average, about four per cent of salt-petre. The dry nitre earths of Beans cave, which are abundant, ought, therefore, to be profitable to work.

There is a very large amount of said earths available at the cave, particularly of the laminated variety, as will be seen by reference to the Report of Mr. E. T. Cox, who was detailed to survey that locality.

It will be observed also from that Report, that this saltpetre cave is favorably situated for the transportation of its saline and other products to market, as it is located on the immediate bank of White river.

It is worthy, moreover, of note, that the red earthy residuum is of sufficiently fine texture and contains enough coloring principle, from the per centage of oxide of iron which it contains, to afford a good, durable, red ochre paint, having a good body, and being especially well adapted for painting brick walls and outdoor work generally; while the finer earths that remain long suspended in water, afford a species of polishing powder free from grit, but not rich enough in siliceous earth, to be rapid and efficient in its effects.

The magnesian limestones of lower silurian date of Marion county, afford, besides the lead ores already made mention of, some fine zinc ores.

The richest and best locality of these zinc ores, that I have yet examined in this county, is on section 13, township 19 north, range 17 west, of the 5th principal meridian, on the waters of the east branch of George's creek. The surface indications here are quite encouraging, and lead to the inference that considerable bodies of both the carbonate and sulphuret of zinc exist more deeply seated in the crevices of the rock; indeed, these ores seem to occur here in veins between well-defined walls of rock, the main vein running north 30 deg. east and south, 30 deg. west, besides some cross courses north 70 deg. to 80 deg. west. These veins or crevices are exposed in one place on George's creek, 8 feet 9 inches across from wall to wall. Several shallow openings have been made, at different points, a few hundred yards apart, on George's Creek, in all of which good specimens of these zinc ores have been exposed, associated, occasionally, with some sulphuret of lead and small quantities of sulphuret of copper.

I would particularly designate this place, as worthy of the attention and exploration of the zinc manufacturer, as the locality gives promise, as far as can be judged, from the partial openings made, of affording good rich zinc ores in sufficient quantities to supply a furnace.

There is more sulphuret of zinc at these than at the zinc mines of Lawrence county; but still there are large quantities of carbonate also, which yield from 48 to 52 per cent of zinc, as may be seen by consulting the analysis of these ores, in the Report of the Chemical Assistant. The sulphuret, it is true, contains a higher percentage of metal than the carbonate; but it is much more difficult and expensive to work, and hence a less profitable ore to mine than the carbonates, with a less per céntage of zinc in their composition.

The higher points of the hills in this part of Marion county, are capped with cherty rocks of subcarboniferous date, but the lower part of the hills belongs to the same age as the members exhibited in the geological section on Sugar-loaf creek, previously given.

The pine and other timber on the high ridge, mentioned as intervening between the head of Sugar-loaf creek and the waters of George's creek, will afford good coaling grounds for the use of zinc furnaces, which might be located some where in the vicinity of these zinc mines, as well as for the reduction of the lead ore that may be raised towards the head of Sugar-loaf creek.

CARROLL COUNTY.

As yet, only the eastern portion of this county has been examined. The lead ore of this county, occurs in the cotemporaneous formations of magnesian limestones, with occasional interstratification of sandstone and siliceous limestones, overlaid, towards the summits of the hills, by the encrinital limestones and marble rock, capped with chert. The diggings have been somewhat deeper in Carroll than in Marion county, but still quite limited, consisting of a few shallow trenches on the hill-side, and one shaft of 40 feet. These have exposed several lead-bearing crevices in the rocks, sometimes expanded into cavernous spaces forming occasional "pockets" filled with lead ore; at other times compressed in the joints of of the wall-rock, almost in contact, or only affording space enough for small "strings," and thin "sheets" of ore, irregularly distributed along its course.

In sinking the main shaft, the first layer of rock passed through, beneath the subsoil and under-clay, was:

Light grey shale	4	feet
Dark " "	8	"
Magnesian lead-bearing limestone	28	"
Total depth sunk	40	"

A hole carried a few feet further, by means of a "churn auger," passed mostly through good solid galena disseminated in the adjacent magnesian limestone.

More or less lead ore has been found at different points, over about two-thirds of township 20 north, range 19 west of the 5th principal meridian, according to the representations of Judge Brickey, who had been formerly extensively engaged in the lead business in Missouri, and has been recently employed by Coka & Mitchell, the owners of these mineral lands, to endeavor to follow the course of the veins on their property.

The ore discovered has been sometimes float or gravel ore, scattered on the surface or partially imbedded through the bare surface rock, in "strings," "sheets," thin veins, and occasional "pockets;" also in the interstices, crevices, and even horizontally between the layers of the bedded rock.

The lead-bearing Magnesian limestone, which commences, usually, about 80 to 100 feet beneath the summits of the ridges, has, in general, a capping of hard, white, quartzose sandstone, 4 to 16 inches in thickness, with intervening beds of ferruginous and argillaceous shales of, usually, only a few inches or a foot or two in thickness.

The section of the upper 90 to 100 feet of the ridges, in this lead region, may be represented approximately by the following section:

Chert	50	feet
Thin-bedded magnesian limestone	15	"
Encrinital limestone and marble rock	25 to 30	"
Sandstone, mostly hard, white and quartzose, bedded 6 to 9 or sometimes 16 inches: average say, the "cap rock" of the lead miner of Carroll county	1	"
Ferruginous and argillaceous shales 1 to	2	"
Lead-bearing magnesian limestone with some alternations of siliceous rocks extending for 200 to 250 feet down to the beds of the streams and general drainage of the country	250	"

These latter rocks are, lithologically, much of the same character as the strata represented in the 250 feet of the lower part of the section, on Sugar-loaf creek, in Marion county.

It appears that the surface of the magnesian limestone, under the sandstone, has suffered from irregular denudation, previous to the deposition of the sand, which went to form the succeeding stratum, which is, in consequence, sometimes quite irregular in its thickness, even in short distances, where the sand has been swept into the eroded cavities; such an action has taken place close to where the 40 feet shaft has been sunk in this county. There, a great mass of isolated sandstone, which has resisted the action of decomposing agencies, beyond that of the adjacent members, stands out as a bold mass, as if it might have been a wall or dike, formerly enclosed between walls of the adjacent magnesian limestone, and now forms a conspicuous feature in the landscape of that region. (See plate No. 4.)

The lead ore of this locality of Carroll county, may be expected to occur in following it, with its downward *hade*, through the different members of this formation, in irregular masses, "pockets," sheets, strings, and thin veins in the magnesian limestones; but probably sparingly, if at all, interspersed in the occasional layers of sandstone, which rock has, perhaps, not retained the openness of fissure, necessary for the reception of the infiltrated or insinuated ore.*

About 20,000 pounds of lead ore have been raised, in all, at these "diggings," the excavations being, however, for the most part, only 5 to 15 feet in depth.

About 500 to 600 pounds were raised at the 40 feet, "Brickey's" shaft, adjacent to the isolated mass of sandstone, represented on plate No. 4.

Judge Brickey, who has had long experience in the lead business, in Washington county, Missouri, is of opinion that the surface indications in township 20 north, range 19 west, of the 5th principal meridian, are fully as encouraging as in that part of Missouri, perhaps even more so, for profitable mining.

The great difficulty in pursuing lead-mining in this part of Arkansas, at present, is the want of furnaces for the reduction of ore which the miner could raise.

For want of these, the ore has either to be smelted in heaps or log furnaces at considerable loss and disadvantage, or transported at a cost which would consume the profits of the miner, to distant localities in Missouri, where smelting furnaces have been already erected.

The most common vein-stone of this region is calcareous spar; some "gozzin" is occasionally seen in the crevices; but oftener, near the surface, the materials filling the interstices of the magnesian limestones, are buff and grey argillaceous and shaly earths.

The distance from these mines to navigation on White river, at Du Buque, is from 8 to 10 miles. The growth is, mostly, small sized black and post-oak and hickory.

It will be observed, by the Chemical Report, that the lead ores, both of Carroll, Marion, and Independence counties, are, when freed from adhering gangue and rock, remarkable for their purity. The most important of them have been cupelled, to ascertain the amount of silver, but only one variety examined, up to the present time, viz: that from the Sewell

* In some few instances, in Missouri, lead ore has been found in sufficient quantity in the sandstone to pay for working.

diggings, on Jemmy's creek, promises to afford sufficient silver to pay the expense of extraction.

The rocks of the lead region of Carroll county, near the Coka and Mitchell diggings, dip to the south-west, so that the encrinital limestones descend, in that direction, at the rate of about 100 feet to the mile; and are near the level of the creeks, two miles south-west of the locality represented in plate No. 4.

FULTON COUNTY.

In the townships of land, situated in the north-western part of this county, the highest knobs are composed, like those in Marion and Izard counties, of cherty masses, referable, probably, to the subcarboniferous era, resting upon earthy, hydraulic-looking marls, limestones and shales, on which the principal tracts of arable land are based. Such is the nature of the strata in the "Rapp Barrens," between White river and the North Fork, at an elevation of about 130 or 150 feet above these streams; and corresponding in their lithological character to the strata of Marion county, formerly made mention of, occurring 4 or 5 miles north-east of Yellville, between the waters of Crooked, Jemmy's, and Fallen Timber creeks.

The following strata were observed at elevations in ascending from the North Fork to the general level of the country, in the vicinity of the Rapp barrens, in the upper 80 feet of the ridge, which overlooks the Ripple of the North Fork, near the Rapp barrens:

At 380 feet: above the North Fork, varieties of crisp and agatized chert prevail.

At 375 feet: white-weathering magnesian limestone.

At 370 feet: coarse-grained magnesian limestone and chert.

At 365 feet: porous buhrstone and chert.

At 300 feet: hard blocks of coarse-grained, glistening, siliceous rock, intermediate between chert and sandstone.

The strata of the lower part of the cliffs, along the North Fork, in the vicinity of these barrens, are mostly composed of different varieties of magnesian limestones and silico-calcareous rocks, which are remarkable for the great differences which they exhibit in their capabilities of resisting atmospheric vicissitudes; some layers being hard, compact and durable, stand out prominently in overhanging ledges; others, crumbling away, recede, even under the shelter and protection of more durable strata.* Some of the layers possess a fine oolitic structure.

* See Chemical Report for the analyses of these two different kinds of rocks.

The ridges, 150 to 160 feet above the white sandstone, which crops out near Sander's store, and elsewhere in the Barrens, are mostly strewed with agatized and chalcedonized chert. These are either destitute of timber or overgrown with thickets of low scrubby timber, while the narrow, tortuous vallies or "coves," enclosed between the ridges, are, for the most part, meadow prairie.

Though rocky and rather forbidding, at first view, the land produces well; particularly oats, wheat, wool, and honey. The crops of maize may be considered average. The country is well watered, and possesses many fine water-powers, even at the very fountain head of some of its numerous limpid calcareous streams, which frequently burst forth from amongst the ledges of rock.

One of the most remarkable of these, forms the fountain-head of the main fork of Spring river, known as the "Mammoth Spring," welling up on the south side of a low rocky ridge, from a submerged abyss beneath of sixty-four feet, and constituting, at its very source, a respectable lake of about one-sixteenth of a mile from north to south, and one-fifth to one-sixth of that distance from east to west.

It is said, by those that have sounded the bottom, that there are large cavities and crevices in the rock, and that the main body of the water issues from a large cavernous opening of some forty yards in circumference. It has been estimated that it boils up at the rate of about eight thousand barrels per minute; the correctness of this estimate, we had no means of verifying; but it may be safely estimated, that the average constant flow would be at least sufficient to propel from 12 to 15 run of stones.

The uniform temperature and composition of the water, is peculiarly congenial to the growth of a variety of cryptogamic, aquatic plants, possessing highly nutritive qualities, both for herbiverous animals and birds.

In the early settlement of the country, herds of herbiverous wild animals traveled from great distances to this fountain, of both food and water, as well as flocks of wild fowl. Now, the cattle of the neighboring farms may be seen wading in its waters, up to their middle, and browsing on the herbage, which appears peculiarly congenial to their tastes; it is, also, a general resort of ducks, geese, and other aquatic birds.

This mammoth spring is located just south of the east and west line between Missouri and Arkansas, on section 5, township 21 north, range 7 west of the 5th principal meridian, and forms the most interesting feature of this section of country, since it affords a water-power, which, if properly improved, might supply valuable mill-sites, and water-privileges, for manufacturing purposes in general. Small and rude as the present gristmill is, at this point, with its two run of 40 inch stones, it attracts the custom of farmers living 30 or 40 miles distant, who throng to its door—even though they may have to wait days and nights for their turn to come round.

The accompanying sketch [plate No. 5,] represents the present mill, looking north over the expanse of water, forming the source of this celebrated spring.

The water of this remarkable fountain, remains at a nearly uniform temperature, never freezing in winter. On the 17th of December, 1857, the temperature of the air being 17 deg. Fahrenheit, the spring showed only 57 deg. Fahrenheit. But the average temperature, when the thermometer is sunk deep in the spring, will probably be found to be 60 deg.

The extent of the range of extreme low and high water, is but 3 to 4 inches, so that the variation in the supply of water is very slight.

A large proportion of the water now runs to waste, the present mill only requiring a limited supply; but, if it were all saved, which it could very easily be, there would be enough for many grist-mills, as well as woolen factories, which would be well adapted to the resources of the country; since both the climate and herbage seem to be well suited to raising sheep. At least, the small flocks of sheep, seen in the range, appeared both healthy and vigorous.

The water is generally clear and limpid; it only becomes slightly muddy after long continued rains. From 10 to 11 feet of fall can be obtained between the fountain-head and the present site of the dam.

The principal outcrop of rock, is a white silico-calcareous rock, splitting with a slaty fracture, and presenting dendritic markings on its surface. Locally, large quantities of calcareous tufa have accumulated, and are still forming in creeks and recesses around the head of the spring; deposited from the water, partly on account of the loss of a portion of its carbonic acid, which is dissipated into the atmosphere as these calcareous waters reach the surface, and partly by gradual evaporation.

Varieties of chert, hornstone, and porous buhrstones, form the most conspicuous rocks in the ridges of the northern part of Fulton county: these repose on limestones, mostly of a siliceous character, with segregations and interpolations of chert, sandstone and calciferous sandrocks.

It is supposed that the original source of the Mammoth spring is Howel's valley, Oregon county, Missouri, since the waters of this valley, which is eight miles wide and thirty miles long, are not known to have any external outlet, losing themselves in sink-holes and subterranean caverns and passages. Uniting, as is supposed, near the southern boundary of Missouri, they again burst forth to the day through caverns and crevices in the rock, on the extreme northern confines of Arkansas, and form this immense spring, which constitutes the head of the principal branch of Spring river, watering the north-east corner of Fulton county; and then, entering Lawrence, it forms one of the main streams of that county; flowing, finally, into Black river, above Smithville.

Since the death of the former proprietor, Mr. Mills, the ownership of the spring, and the land around, has reverted to his heirs.

For the sake of the interests of the country, we hope this water-privilege, possessing so many natural advantages, will soon be improved in the manner its intrinsic value justifies, and that it may fall into the hands of enterprizing and practical manufacturers, who will give an impetus to profitable and useful branches of manufacturing industry, suited to the resources of the country, which soon attract around them an industrious, progressive, and intelligent population.

Extensive deposits of iron ore have been reported as occurring in the vicinity of the Mammoth spring. I found some superficial specimens of good ore in the north part of Fulton county, but have not seen any extensive beds; those referred to by Mr. Mills, in a notice issued of his property, before his death, are, probably, situated north of the state line, on the western fork, in Missouri. The geological formation is such as to justify the expectation that a detailed survey of Fulton county may disclose bodies of ore that might warrant the erection of furnaces.

Descending south from the head of Main Spring river, I found the country mostly constructed of low chert ridges, with prairie coves between them; the timber being, chiefly, on the ridges, of a small growth of oak and hickory.

Two miles east of the Mammoth spring, a fine, white sandstone* crops out on a slope on the Missouri side of the line.

On Jaynes' creek, the same kind of country prevails. In the valley of that stream, low benches of rugged, weathering magnesian limestone are seen projecting from the slopes of the ridges, which are mostly strewed with chert blocks, and gravel in the upper portions. The highest of these chert ridges are from 250 to 280 feet above the water courses, but the most of them are considerably lower.

* This is probably the equivalent of the sandstone represented on No. 4, which underlies the marble limestones of Carroll county.

LAWRENCE COUNTY.

Near the forks of the Jackson and Smithville road, some chert ridges, measured, were found to have an elevation of about 80 to 100 feet above the drainage of the country.

On Morton's creek, near Morgan's mill, there is some zinc, which may prove valuable, if fairly opened and exposed, as the surface indications are somewhat encouraging.

The chert of the ridges along Morton's creek is mostly dull and impure, with little or no true chalcedony.

In the cuts of the stream, grey and white varieties of magnesian limestones crop out, associated with a white rock, which has the appearance of a calciferous sandrock.

The same character of rocks prevails to the Big Lick. South of that locality, some porous buhrstones are intermixed with the dull, impure, earthy chert, and a white magnesian limestone was observed cropping out, approaching, in its character, the so-called "Cotton Rock."

On Machine creek, some zinc ore has been discovered, and a few loads hauled over to the zinc furnace, in Lawrence.

E. W. Houghton explored for lead ore on Stennett's creek, in this county, and obtained considerable lead ore, but abandoned the diggings, probably, because there was no lead furnace to smelt the ore.

The main zinc deposits of Lawrence county, on which the principal dependence is placed for supplying ore to the furnace now erected at Calamine, are the so-called Hoppe diggings, on section 19, township 16 north, range 2 west.

The ore here is very accessible, being, in some places, only one foot beneath the surface. It has been followed down 18 feet, and found occupying interstices between isolated corroded masses of limestone, and intermixed with, and imbedded in red clay. The width of the excavation was about 25 feet. The associate limestone is of a light grey color, with strings and thin veins of disseminated ore, which comprises mostly those different varieties of carbonate of zinc, described in works on mineralogy, under the name of "calamine" and "smithsonite."

The chemical analyses of these ores, made by Dr. Elderhorst, in my laboratory, gives an average yield of 51.7 per cent. of oxide, which is equal to 41.5 per cent. of metallic zinc in these carbonates.

Intermixed with the carbonates there is also some zinc blende, which will yield, when freed from adhering gangue, nearly 66 per cent. of metallic zinc; but this ore, though containing a larger proportion of zinc than the carbonates, is less valuable as an ore, since it is more expensive and difficult to roast, smelt, and reduce to the metallic state.

The chemical analyses even of the associaté dolomitic rocks and red clay, filling the interstices between the rock and ore, afford a small per centage of zinc, viz: two per cent of carbonate of zinc, in the magnesian limestone taken from the Hoppe mine, and about one-third of one per cent. in the red clay.

For the details of analysis, consult the Chemical Report of Dr. Elderhorst, where a statement will be found of the value of the Arkansas zinc ores, compared with those of the most productive zinc districts of Europe.

Since all the zinc at present consumed in this country is imported from Europe, and subject to a duty of 4 per cent. on crude zinc, and 24 per cent. on all manufactured articles, the establishment of furnaces for the smelting of these very productive ores of zinc of Arkansas, would, indeed, be a national benefit, since the quantity of crude and manufactured zinc, imported into the United States, according to the last published statements, amounts very nearly to nine hundred thousand dollars worth of this useful metal.

REPORT

OF A

GEOLOGICAL RECONNOISSANCE

OF PART OF

ARKANSAS.

PART SECOND.

———o———

In proceeding to record the observations made during the surveys of 1858, I shall commence with

WHITE COUNTY.

Mo. 6---CLIFFS OF THE "BEE ROCK," OF WHITE COUNTY, ON LITTLE RED RIVER.

The most conspicuous geological feature of this county, is the escarpment of sandstone along the bluffs of Little Red river, known as the "Bee rock." The sketch in the wood-cut at the head of this section, is taken from the summit of those rocks, looking over the valley of Little Red river, and the distant low ground to the north. The sandstone forming the cliffs in the foreground of this landscape, is part of the conglomerate and millstone grit formation that intervenes between the overlying coal measures proper, and the underlying subcarboniferous limestone.

When water-worn pebbles are disseminated through such sandstones, subordinate to the coal measures, they have received the name of conglomerates or pebbly sandstones; when pebbles are absent, and the rock constitutes merely a coarse-textured sandstone, it is called millstone grit. Both these varieties occur in White county, along the escarpments of Little Red river, which attain a thickness of 150 to 200 feet, imparting wild and romantic scenery to the country, for many miles along the bank of this stream. They constitute, also, the nucleus of the backbone ridge that runs from the Bee rock to Patterson's mill. At the latter locality, the impression of a peculiar extinct plant, characteristic of the early carboniferous era, known as the *stigmaria ficoides*, was discovered, imbedded in the sandstone, which would prove conclusively the age of this sandstone formation, if other evidence were wanting.

A particle of gold, the size of a flax-seed is said to have been pumped up with the sand from the bed of Little Red river, at Patterson's mill. Even if this is correct information, it is not probable that quantities of this metal, sufficient to pay for the extraction, could be washed out of the sands of Little Red river, since it does not flow, along any part of its course, over rocks such as have yielded profitable quantities of this precious metal in other countries.

The dip of these sandstones, on this part of Little Red river, is 1½ deg. to 2 deg. to the south, or a little west of south. The base of this formation, at this point, is schistose in its structure, i. e., thin bedded, becoming, however, more solid and massive in its upper part.

Some segregations of iron ore occur about 10 feet above the water of Little Red river, near the mill, but they are, here, too siliceous to constitute a good quality of ore for the manufacture of iron.

Three miles north-west of Searcy, at a "bald point," in the vicinity of the widow Gilbert's farm; sixty feet of shaly strata are exposed, dark or nearly black, in its lower part, and reddish yellow and ferruginous towards the top. This shale includes numerous segregations of carbonate of iron and carbonate of lime; the latter containing several fossil marine shells, amongst which the *nautilus ferratus* was discovered, a species which occurs in the ferruginous shales of Nolin, in Edmonson county, Ky.

Until levels are run, which it is contemplated doing hereafter, during the progress of the detailed surveys in the individual counties, it is difficult to pronounce positively on the relative geological position of these shales, with reference to the sandstones of the Bee rock; but, judging from the superposition as observed in Kentucky, of the cotemporaneous shales, I am, at present, disposed to consider them as immediately following these sandstones, in the order of superposition. At any rate, the cliffs of sandstone and conglomerate of Little Red river, and the Gilbert shales of White county, Arkansas, are a perfect counterpart of the high escarpment of the "Dismal rock," of which a sketch is given as the frontispiece to the first volume of the Kentucky Geological Report, and the ferruginous shales of Nolin are shown in a section at the end of the same volume.

The Gilbert shales are underlaid by heavy sandstone, passing downwards into a more schistose rock in the descent towards Panther creek.

The quantity of iron ore at this locality, both of the carbonate and limonite varieties, would go far towards supplying a furnace, and similar ores can, no doubt, be discovered in the same geological position in other parts of the county. Hereafter we shall record the constituents of this ore when the quantitative chemical analysis is completed.

In digging wells in the vicinity of Searcy, a blackish grey, indurated, argillo-siliceous shale is encountered, containing small scales of disseminated mica. This material is brittle and crumbles, by exposure, to a clay.

Similar shales are struck, usually ten feet below the surface, under the red land situated west of Searcy. The first ten feet passed through, generally consist of soil, subsoil, and gravel overlying these shales. The red-soil of these level farming lands is quite productive, yielding good crops of cotton, corn, wheat, and the finest oats in ordinary seasons, viz: 800 to 1,500 pounds of cotton in the seed to the acre, twenty to twenty-five bushels of wheat, and forty to sixty bushels of oats, when there are seasonable rains.

Samples of this soil have been collected for future chemical analysis, in case the agricultural department of the Survey should be hereafter provided for.

This description of land must have an area of some 360 square miles, extending, as it does, about thirty miles from east to west, and twelve miles from north to south, and appears to have been derived from the disintigration of the ferruginous shales, which, at one time, existed over the dark, argillo-siliceous shales, that now underlie this tract, and which still are to be seen in the slopes of the hills adjacent to these red lands.

In the southern part of the county, watered by bayou Des Arc and Caney creek, sandstones and shales of the millstone grit period prevail.

In the Royal Colony settlement, near the line between sections seven and eight, township five, range ten, a bed of coal, from ten to twelve inches in thickness, occurs sixty feet up in a ridge, known as Coal-hill, at the head of Cypress bayou.

The base of Coal-hill consists of black and ferruginous shales, surmounted by thick-bedded sandstone, capping its summit.

Ferruginous shales are strewed on the slope, under the sandstone, for seventy-five feet. Beneath this, for the depth of five feet, is a bluish shale, enclosing oval concretions.

The immediate roof of the coal is a peculiar, rusty, talcous-looking, scaly shale, unctuous to the touch, and crumbling to pieces with the least friction.

The coal varies from ten to twelve inches in thickness.

The base of the hill, for 60 feet under the coal, is composed of dark, bluish grey shale, including considerable quantities of carbonate of iron.

The same bed of coal crops out on the western declivity of Coal-hill.

This coal has been partially opened for the use of the blacksmiths in this part of White, and the adjacent portion of Conway county, but where it has been worked, it has not afforded a coal altogether free from the pyritiferous impurities required for shop use; the thickness, too, is not sufficient to warrant the expense of running drifts into it for any great distance.

Sandstone occupies the surface at Rocky point, but shale is reached about eight or nine feet under the surface. A similar sandstone crops out on the slope descending to Cypress bayou, on the confines of White and Prairie counties. All these strata are, no doubt, referrible to the millstone grit series at the base of the coal measures.

Ascending from the waters of the Cadron and Des Arc, in the western part of White county, a great mass of variegated and ferruginous shales is encountered nearly two hundred feet in thickness, including some intercalated bands of sandstone. These are surmounted by some fifty feet of heavily bedded sandstones, which are again overlapped with shales and schistose siliceous rocks, capping the mountain near the widow Norman's. Four and a half miles beyond, in the neighborhood of Theodore Goodlow's, the sandstone on the table-land is characterized by peculiar vermicular impressions,* such as were observed in Hancock county, Kentucky, in the first bench of sandstone under the main Hawesville coal, and about 50 feet above the bench of underlying conglomerate. This bench of sandstone lies, therefore, at the base of the coal measures, and though there is a thin bed of coal beneath this sandstone at Hawesville, it may be considered as underlying the productive coal measures, since no workable bed of coal has yet been found below it.

*These impressions are probably referrible to some species of fucoids or seaweeds. They bear some resemblance to drawings of *Phytogyra*, but are apparently single and more simple in their structure than that genus.

These sandstones with vermicular (fucoidal?) impressions, on the head of the Cadron, in the extreme south-western part of White county, belong, doubtless, to the geological horizon beneath the lowest workable coal.

A remarkable dislocation of the strata crosses the Cadron in the vicinity of Goodlow's. Where I examined it, on the south bank of that stream, the tilted slabs of sandstone lie at various angles from 1 deg. to 26 deg.; at one place, even at 50 deg. Yet the belt of disturbance is quite narrow, not more than six or eight feet, and some of the broken slabs of rock appear as if they had partially slipped into the yawning fissure and become entangled in the closing of the gap. The course of this disturbance runs obliquely across the bed of the Cadron, with a slightly curved bearing, south south-west, and forms a kind of artificial dam. This rupture of the strata can be traced for three quarters of a mile. In some parts of its course the fractured layers form a complete arch, dipping both ways from the central axis.

Some attempts have been made to discover ore, by sinking pits adjacent to this disturbance; but without success, at the depth to which they were carried. This axis of dislocation, may possibly be connected with those, subsequently observed on the Palerm bayou, since its course, if produced in a south-west direction, would extend to that region of country.

High cliffs of sandstone of the same geological era, appear on the south side of the Cadron, near the western confines of White county.

The Searcy sulphur water of White county, was tested qualitatively at the fountain head for its principal constituents, which proved to be as follows:

Small quantity of free sulphuretted hydrogen.
Bi-carbonate of lime.
Bi-carbonate of magnesia.
Chloride of sodium.
Chloride of magnesium.
Small quantity of sulphate of soda.
" " " " " magnesia.

This water will act as a mild alterative and laxative.

It should be remarked, that solution of acetate of lead is darkened more by the water after being boiled down, than when fresh from the spring; for this reason, I am disposed to believe, that there must be some portion of sulphur combined with some organic principle; since the free sulphuretted hydrogen would be expelled by boiling. Besides, the fresh water does not affect acetate of lead as much as the sulphur taste would indicate.

VAN BUREN COUNTY,

No. 7—SUGAR-LOAF MOUNTAIN OF VAN BUREN COUNTY.

The table-land of the south-western part of this county, on to which we ascended soon after leaving White county, supports a pine forest on the siliceous soils, derived from the disintegration of sandstones of the millstone grit series. This table land is elevated 400 feet above the general drainage of the country, and 375 above a group of dark shales, including carbonate of iron, which are well exposed at "Bald Lick," near the foot of the descent, on our route leading to Sugar-loaf springs. This shale, with its associate ore, has much the appearance of the Gilbert shales of Searcy county; but these shales of Van Buren county, occupy a position, in all probability, beneath sandstones, the equivalent of the Bee rock. From 20 to 25 feet of these shales are exposed in the ravines at the Bald Lick, having a dip to the south-west of 8 deg.; this dip is, however, local both in direction and degree, since only a mile or two to the north, the strata were observed to dip east of north at a more gentle angle.

The Sugar-loaf mountain, of which a sketch is given in the wood-cut that heads this section, is a conspicuous, isolated hill, cut off by denudation from the main ranges of this county. A measurement with the aneroid barometer, gave its height 440 feet above the Huntsucker farm. By computation, it must be about 500 feet above Little river, which sweeps around its north-eastern base.

This well known land-mark, is composed, in its upper part, of about 80 feet of schistose sandstone, forming a bold and conspicuous cliff on the heights of the mountain, which is contracted in its upper part, so that the area of the summit is only about 200 feet from north to south, by about 50 feet from east to west, with a dip of a few degrees to the south, as shown in the accompanying view. Forest and undergrowth conceal, for the most part, the strata forming the slopes below this escarpment.

The construction of the main ridges, in this part of Van Buren county, of which this may be regarded as an outlier, together with the partial exposures, here and there observed in the Sugar-loaf mountain itself, lead to the conclusion that it is composed mostly of earthy varieties of sandstone, resting on ferruginous and dark shales, similar to those observed at the Bald Lick, and which seem to exist, almost universally, under the main mass of the millstone grit of this part of the State of Arkansas.

The Sugar-loaf springs are situated about three miles from the Sugar-loaf mountain, in a course south of west. There are several fine springs of mineral water at this place.

The one known as the "Black Sulphur spring," but which might be with more propriety called the White Sulphur spring, since it deposits a white fibrous sediment in the trough, into which it first flows, though, where it subsequently dissipates itself over the ground, there is a black precipitate formed by the mutual action between the sulphur in the water and the iron contained in the soil. This has generally been regarded as the strongest mineral water on the premises.

Its principal constituents are:

Free sulphuretted hydrogen.

Bi carbonate of lime.

Bi-carbonate of magnesia.

Chloride of sodium.

Chloride of magnesium.

No appreciable quantity of sulphates could be detected in the unconcentrated water.

The "Puce spring" contains the same ingredients, though it is not so strongly impregnated with sulphuretted hydrogen, but contains more chlorides than the other spring.

The qualitative examination of the "Eye spring," so called because persons having inflamed eyes have used it most, gave the same reaction with chemical reagents as the "Puce spring."

Besides these springs there is a good chalybeate water, that issues from the bank a few paces from the "Puce spring," containing bi-carbonate of the protoxide of iron and a trace of chlorides, but no appreciable quantity of sulphates, in the unconcentrated water; also a spring of ordinary water, in which bi-carbonates of the alkaline earths are the principal constituents.

The main springs are, therefore, saline sulphuretted waters, possessing alterative, laxative, diaphoretic, and diuretic effects, well adapted for the cure of eruptive complaints, as well as of chronic diseases of the digestive organs. The properties possessed by the chalybeate, are those of a tonic, suited to cases of constitutional or temporary debility, in which preparations containing iron are indicated.

As Little Red river was too high for us to take the river road towards Clinton, we were prevented from examining any sections of the rocks that might present themselves along the route, and had again to ascend to the table-land, in which the waters of the Cadron take their rise.

The aneroid barometer indicated an elevation of 320 feet above the widow Goff's farm.

For two or three miles we again traveled through a fine pine region, with a sandy soil, derived from the underlying sandstones of the millstone grit series, but emerged soon, in township 9 north, range 12 west, on good tracts of farming lands, watered by the heads of the North Fork of the Cadron.

On section 13, township 9 north, range 12 west, sample of soils for future chemical analysis were taken from this table-land on the farm of George More.

This soil is especially adapted for the growth of oats, and will yield on an average, 20 to 25 bushels of corn, 15 bushels of wheat, and 800 pounds of cotton. It stands drought remarkably well, being based on a retentive ferruginous clayey subsoil.

In digging wells, in this part of Van Buren county, a hard reddish blue shale is penetrated under the subsoil, which overlies the beds of millstone grit. To the disintegration of these shaly rocks is no doubt to be attributed the superior fertility of these upland soils, compared with the sandy soils of the pine lands, which repose immediately on the underlying sandstones.

These table-lands are bounded on the south by a ridge, composed o sandstone and shales, rising some 70 to 100 feet above the waters of the Cadron. Two or three miles to the north-east of George More's farm, dark shaly rocks are exposed. About the same distance to the north-west, a sandstone region commences, overlaid by gravel supporting a growth of stunted oak and hickory. This kind of country extends for about six miles to the descent to the main Cadron, and the Greasy valley, which lies about 230 feet below the table-land. White, grey, banded, and mottled, schistose sandstone, are exposed in ledges. The ascent on the opposite side of the Cadron to the same description of land is only 185 feet, which indicates a dip in a westerly direction. A further ascent of 255 feet over schistose argillaceous sandstone, brought us to a table-land with a growth of black-jack, extending for three miles.

The upper beds of these sandstones, are harder and less argillaceous in their composition than the lower layers.

Oak and hickory are succeeded by oak and pine, which prevail to the descent to the valley of Little Red river.

The declivity commands an extensive view to the north-west, with high ranges of hills, both in the middle and back ground.

This elevated country is about 600 feet above Choctaw creek. The lower ledges of sandstone appear here in a kind of pavement form, dipping 40 to 50 deg. to the south-east, and checkered with segregations of oxide of iron. Beneath this is a brown massive freestone, which would make a good building stone. Still lower, near the foot of the hill, are black, rusty ferruginous shales, the base of which is some 600 feet below the summit of the ridge. About 10 feet lower, strata of flaggy sandstone form the bed of Choctaw creek, having a south-westerly dip. This is probably an intercalated band in the mass of shaly rocks which appear to extend even to the banks of Little Red river, in the vicinity of Clinton; but since there are no good exposures below the flaggy sandstone of Choctaw creek, and the aluvium of Little river, we are left to infer the character of the concealed strata from very partial out-crops, and analogy of structure with other neighboring ridges of Van Buren county.

A few miles north and north-east of Clinton, some beds of coal are reported to have been partially opened, for the use of blacksmiths; these I have not had an opportunity of examining, nor yet the coal on the waters of Sugar Camp creek, said to have been discovered by A. J. Cristopher, eight miles north-east of Clinton.

The summit level of the ridge, over which the Lebanon road runs, is 1220 feet above the town of Clinton, according to observations made with the aneroid barometer.

No limestone is visible on the east side of this ridge, as you rise from the Clinton side; the lowest rocks visible are black, grey, and ferruginous shales, surmounted by sandstone and conglomerate; the order of succession being very much the same as had been observed in the principal ridges in White county. The descent on the west side reveals, however, under these shaly rocks, Archimedes and encrinital beds of the subcarboniferous group which crop out along the bank of Lesley's ford, of Little Red river. Associated with this group, is a bed of black limestone, one to one and a half feet in thickness, which, as the fossils show white, against a black ground, will, when polished, produce a beautiful marble.

On section 12, township 13, range 15 west, the subcarboniferous limestone extends to the height of 15 to 20 feet above the bed of Lesley's creek, covered by the afore mentioned shales. This is on the immediate confines of the western boundary of Van·Buren county; the line passes through the orchard of Hatchet, who resides on the banks of Lesley's creek, at the foot of the mountain.

SEARCY COUNTY.

NO. 8---KNOB OF SEARCY COUNTY, TAKEN FROM THE DAWSON FARM, ON FORREST CREEK.

Proceeding towards Wiley's cove, in this county, from Lesley's fork of Little Red river, the Archimedes and encrinital beds of the upper subcarboniferous group gradually ascend to a higher level above the watercourses; so that there appears, beneath these, in Wiley's cove, a considerable thickness of hard, sheety, black, bituminous shale, which has all the lithological aspect of the black, bituminous shale at the foot of the falls of the Ohio. But that shale belongs to the devonian period, whereas subsequent observation showed this black shale of Searcy county to be a member of the subcarboniferous period.

Immediately overlying this black shale is a black, bituminous limestone, much of the same character as that already mentioned as occurring in the Oil-trough ridge, and occupying very nearly the same geological horizon.

The section in Wiley's cove is approximately as follows:

1. Archimedes limestones.
2. Encrinital, and Chonetes limestones, alternating with thin shaly partings.
3. Black, brittle, bituminous limestone, or marble rock.
4. Black, bituminous, hard, sheety shale.

The exact relative thickness of these beds, remains yet to be determined; the two first members are approximately 50 to 60 feet; the third member, some 15 feet; and the fourth member, from 40 to 60 feet in thickness.

The superposition in Wiley's cove, renders it highly probable that the black limestone of the Oil-trough ridge, is also underlaid by a black shale, which is concealed, however, beneath the alluvium of White river, the black soil of which is partly derived from it, and, in part, from the washings of the subcarboniferous limestones of the Oil-trough ridge. This is rendered still more probable, from the fact of dark shales and shaly limestones occurring under the same black limestones of the subcarboniferous group in Shield's bluff, as may be seen in the section given of that hill, in a previous part of this Report, under the head of "Independence county." In the centre of Wiley's cove, the grey beds of Archimedes limestone lie from 100 to 125 feet above the general level of the farms, and the top of the black shale and base of the black marble at 60 to 70 feet above the same level.

There is abundance of black chert, strewed in the water-courses of the cove, which approaches very nearly to the character and appearance of the black flints, found in the chalk formation of Europe; these appear to originate as segregations or concretions in the limestones, overlying the black shales, which, being more difficult of decomposition than their matrix, remain as gravel, while the imbedding rock, itself, has become a part of the rich, black soil of the cove. This is derived, in part, from the subcarboniferous limestone, and, in part, from the black shale.

The deep mud holes, in the road which leads up through the cove, have been washed out of and worked into the tenacious clay, derived from the disintegration of the black slate, and accumulated at the foot of the surrounding hills.

Half a mile beyond Wiley's cove, the black slate forms the bed of the Owl or Middle fork of Little Red river, with hard, heavy, dark, ferruginous, calcareous bands locally interstratified amongst the layers, exposed in the north-east bank of that stream.

At the crossing of a branch, five miles south-east of Burrowsville, the subcarboniferous limestones alternate with sandstone and grey fossiliferous shale, underlaid by some 50 feet of flaggy sandstone, resting on the dark shales which crop out about half a mile down the branch, to the left of the road. The gray fossiliferous shale, to the right of the road, lies about 85 feet above the base of the flaggy sandstones; above this are alternations of sandstone and grey limestones, while on the slope of the adjacent hillsides, gravel of black flinty chert is everywhere strewed.

Four, to four and a half miles south-east of Burrowsville, the sandstone overlying the black shale, has a disposition to split into rectangular, prismatic blocks.

At Burrowsville, the present county-seat of Searcy county, there is a buff, flaggy sandstone, which is quite fossiliferous; some of the layers are charged with casts of *Producta*. The rock has been quarried to a limited extent, in the immediate vicinity of Burrowsville, and has been used for foundations and underpinning to buildings, and in the construction of chimneys.

North-west of Burrowsville, the black shale was not seen; the descent from the productal flags, leads immediately on to chert and light-grey subcarboniferous limestone; unless, therefore, the black shale is entirely concealed from view, the productal flags of Burrowsville must underlie the black shale, so frequently exposed in Wiley's cove, and between that and Burrowsville. A black slate is said to be exposed in a ridge west of Lebanon, where there is an extensive lick; this locality, I have not yet had an opportunity of examining.

In the vicinity of Lebanon, on the north bank of Bear creek, are perpendicular cliffs of cherty, subcarboniferous limestone; one bed of which is nearly white, and of a texture passing from granular into subcrystalline, with large *Spirifers*, allied to, but probably distinct from, *Spirifer striatus*, which occurs in the same position on the Rapids of the Mississippi, above the mouth of the Des Moines, under the Archimedes beds, and above the Keokuck cherty limestone containing *Orthis crenistria*, which is superimposed on the encrinital beds of Burlington. 210 feet of these cherty members of the subcarboniferous limestone is exposed on Bear creek; above the principal escarpment there is a slope of 100 feet more, where only loose pieces of chert are visible amongst the vegetation.

At the next crossing of Bear creek, vertical walls of cherty limestone are again seen, where they dip 4 deg. to 5 deg. south-west. Here the white Spirifer bed was found in place 90 feet below the top of the ridge dividing the waters of Bear creek from those of the Buffalo fork of White river; which is 360 feet above that stream.

In this ridge, 30 feet of sandstone was found overlying cherty limestones, of the same character, and, no doubt, a continuation of the limestones forming the Bear creek cliffs.

Greyish-pink beds of this limestone extend down to the water's edge, on the north-east side of the Buffalo fork, just above the ford on the road to Carrollton.

At Spencer Adams' a *Spirifer*, allied to the *cuspidatus*, occurs in the sandstone at an elevation of about 360 feet above the bed of the Buffalo fork.

No black shale was observed, in any of the sections exposed on the streams, in this part of Searcy county.

A few hundred yards, on the north-west side of Mill creek, an abrupt dislocation has fractured the strata and thrust up the beds of limestone; which may be traced, ascending the hillside, on the north side of the road, with abrupt mural faces, resembling a dyke of basalt.

Some lead ore has been obtained in the crevices of the subcarboniferous limestone along this axis of disturbance, and some shallow excavations have been made; but these did not yield ore sufficient to encourage further search.

The occurrence of this ore, adjacent to the axis of disturbance, above mentioned, is, however, a favorable indication for the discovery of a regular lode, and more thorough and deeper explorations might lead to better discoveries.

Where the Carrollton road ascends the hill, about a mile further, the following section is exposed:

Slope, with carboniferous chert gravel.

White limestone, about 20 feet.

Encrinital limestone, 30 feet.

Red and pink limestones, or marble rock, 15 feet.

Vein of ore containing iron and manganese?

Coarse textured limestone.

Variegated white and pink beds, some of the lower layers of which, for 40 to 50 feet, have a structure similar to that of lithographic limestone.

The strata exposed below the chert slope, amount in all to about 120 feet. The summit of the ridge passed over is 470 feet above Mill creek, but in the 300 feet above the base of the chert slope, little else can be seen but gravel of this material.

Specimens of soils were collected from this county, on the farm of Albert Dugger, near the mouth of the Dry fork of Clear creek. The growth is black-jack and hickory, with an undergrowth of sumach and hazel. This soil will average about 40 bushels of corn, and 25 bushels of oats to the acre.

On the divide between the Buffalo fork and the waters of the Dry fork of Clear creek, the surface is strewed with a sharp chert gravel, overlying a pinkish limestone, occupying probably the place of the marble rock of Marion and Carroll counties. Limestones of a similar character re-appear in the descent of the ridge, towards the waters of the Dry fork, associated with a semi-oolitic variety of calciferous sand rock, perhaps of silurian date.

I have, as yet, found no conclusive evidence to enable me to form a decided opinion as to the age of the marble limestones of north-west Arkansas; but if they should, by subsequent observations, prove to be the representative of the Onondaga limestone of the New York system, then it is doubtful whether there are any rocks belonging to the *upper* silurian division in the western part of Searcy county, as the marble formation seems to rest immediately on rocks of the *lower* silurian period.

Some sandstone is interstratified with the limestones of the Dry fork of Clear creek; but these sandstones are older than the productal sandstone of Burrowsville, in Van Buren county.

The pink limestones are more earthy than the limestones occupying the same geological horizon in the central portion of Van Buren county.

NEWTON COUNTY.

No. 9—ROUND-TOP PEAK OF THE JUDAH MOUNTAIN OF THE BOSTON RANGE, TAKEN FROM JASPER, THE COUNTY SEAT OF NEWTON COUNTY.

This is one of the most mountainous counties of Arkansas. Several of the most conspicuous peaks of the Boston range attain here an elevation of more than 1,000 feet above the general drainage of the country.

The wood-cut sketch at the head of this section, represents one of these peaks as seen from Jasper, the county seat of Newton county, and known under the name of the Round-top peak of the Judah mountain of the Boston range.

On the 21st of June, 1858, I set out with the intention of measuring the elevation of this peak above the Hudson fork of Buffalo, but was prevented from accomplishing my object by a violent thunderstom, which I encountered about one-third of the distance up this mountain, and my limited time induced me to postpone its further ascent until the detailed survey was undertaken. The encrinital and marble limestones are well exposed in the bed of the Dry branch, near the foot of the Judah peak, north of Jasper.

The strata exposed immediately on the banks of the Hudson fork of Buffalo, below Jasper, are alternations of limestone and sandstone. The sandstone has a peculiar porous or honey-comb structure; on this rests a light bluish grey limestone. Near the mouth of this stream, a high escarpment of sandstone and limestone forms a prominent feature in the landscape; most of the ledges are probably of lower silurian date, but the perpendicular nature of this cliff, prevented a critical examination of the individual members at this point.

Further down Buffalo fork, at the mouth of Cave creek, rocks still lower in the series, but belonging to the same group, are exposed; indeed, if the hard quartzose sandstone, which forms the base of the bluffs at this place belongs, as there is reason to believe, to the age of the Potsdam sandstone of the New York system, then there is, at this point, a greater elevation of the geological formations than at any locality in northern Arkansas; and we must look here for one of the principal anticlinal axes of Searcy county.

By reference to a map of Arkansas, it will be perceived that the two main branches of White river take their rise amongst these high peaks of Newton and Madison counties; the longest branch, deflected around this great axis of upheaval, pursues a circuitous course, through the latter county into Benton county, and thence making a great sweep to the north, traverses Barry and Taney counties, in Missouri, before it again waters the State of Arkansas, in the north-east corner of Carroll; while the smaller branch, taking a more direct course to the north-east, through deep gorges of the mountains, empties into the main fork in the south-west corner of Fulton. The geographical features of the country are thus strongly impressed by geological forces, that date back to a period long previous to the existence of the water courses, which now conform to the contour of this disturbed country.

Lead ore has been found in several places in Newton county, as on Big creek and other branches of the Buffalo and Hudson forks of White river; but the only attempt at tracing this ore to its origin in the rock formations, was undertaken near the line between sections 1 and 2, of township 15 north, range 19 west, not far from the mouth of Cave creek, adjoining Hill's mill-tract. At this place Jesse Gunt explored for lead ore, and finally sunk a shaft of forty-five feet. He obtained some 60 to 70 pounds of lead ore, but finally abandoned the prospect. He might have been more successful, had he made search in the calcareous rocks that lie higher in the adjacent hills, instead of prospecting, as he did, over the platform of sandstone which forms the base of the bluffs on this part of the Buffalo fork of White river, as will appear from the two following sections taken near the mouth of Cave creek:

Heights above the Buffalo fork of White river.

545. Top of chert slope.
500. Slope with chert.
440. Loose grey chert in continuation of slope.
430. Reddish grey sandstone.
415. Reddish sandstone with chert segregations.
400. Reddish sandstone with stalactitic structure.
370. Chert masses.
335. Bench of yellowish white sandstone.
300. Rolled blocks of sandstone under the above bench.
270. Obscure ledges of sandstone.
255. Hard grey siliceous sandstone.
250. " " " "
200. " " " " in loose blocks in slope.
130. Hard grey sandstone.
90. Hard, white quartzose sandstone, rusty in the joints, but white internally in the substance of the mass.
50. Hard, white, quartzose sandstone.
25. " " " "
15. " " " "
6. Grey siliceous (?) limestone.
1. Hard, white, quartzose sandstone, possessing a sub-oolitic structure.

In this section very little limestone appears, though some ledges may be concealed in the slope, since about half a mile north-west of the mouth of Cave creek, the following section was obtained above the main platform of hard, quartzose sandstone, which forms an escarpment on the north side of Buffalo:

340. Slope with chert masses of 40 feet.
200. Bench of brown, ferruginous sandstone.
290. Encrinital chert and sandstone.
270. Bench of white sandstone 6 feet exposed.
250. Slope with chert.
235. Reddish grey siliceous limestone.
215. Grey " "
180. Checkered calcareous sandstone.

The chert slope at 340 feet in this section is nearly on a level with the chert slope of the previous section. This formation seems to cap generally the subordinate ridges from 500 to 550 feet above Buffalo, but there are other ridges, off to the south, which must be nearly double this height.

The rocks which constitute the preceding sections, have the lithological aspect and chemical composition of the rocks which form the hills on both sides of the Upper Mississippi, between the mouth of the Chippewa and Black river, and around Lake Pepin, referrible to the age of the Potsdam sandstone and calciferous sand-rock of the New York system.

Geology being decidedly a science of comparison and analogy, I may venture to predict, in the absence of all systematic mining operations, from my former experience in other similarly constructed countries of the north-west, as well as from what has already been observed in Marion and Carroll counties, in Arkansas, that lead ore will be found, to some extent, in the rocks of Newton county; but, in all probability, somewhat irregularly disseminated in "pockets," "crevices," "strings," and horizontal openings through the rocks, rather than in regular bodies; hence, mining operations will be attended with some uncertainty, and considerable labor and expense; still, where the surface indications are encouraging, and the calcareous rocks predominate over the sandstones, they may be undertaken by those having the necessary experience in rocks of this description, with considerable prospect of success, so soon as the district is supplied with furnaces for smelting the ore; but not with as much profit to the miner as in a cherty limestone, a member of the subcarboniferous formation, which we shall have occasion to mention hereafter.

In consequence of the southerly dip of the rocks, most of the strata of the preceding sections disappear in succession beneath the waters of Cave creek, as we ascend that stream.

On the waters of Cave creek, about six miles above its mouth, a liver-colored marble-limestone forms the base of a cliff, at an elevation of 10 to 20 feet above the bed of Cave creek, overlaid by cherty limestone. Several nitre-caves have been formed by the disintegration of the liver-colored marble limestone under the cherty limestone. The principal nitre-cave is on the property of J. S. Thompson, on section 27, township 15 north, range 19 west.

The dark brown nitre-earth, which forms the floor of this cave, is rich in salts of nitric acid, owing, no doubt, to the large quantity of organic matter incorporated with the earth. The nitre-earth has been traced for 50 to 60 yards back into the cave, and for 7 to 8 feet in depth, mixed with tumbled rock.

Time has permitted, as yet, only a partial qualitative examination o this salt-petre earth, which shows it to be rich in nitre-salts, associated with abundance of sulphate of lime.

From a hopper of this earth, containing about 200 bushels, 1,000 pounds of salt-petre have been obtained, after being treated with lye, and crystallized by evaporation in kettles, in a very rude manner. This would be equal to about 5 pounds to the bushel. But it is estimated, that there must have been a loss of at least one-third from leakage, overflow of the receiving trough during rainy weather, and other causes.

When the quantitative analysis of this earth shall have been completed, we shall be able to give a more precise estimate of the per centage of nitre-salts which it actually contains.

It appears that this cave must have been once the habitation of the aborigines, since not only bones of men, animals, and birds, such as the buffalo, deer, and turkey, have been found, on removing the earth; but even the entire skeleton of an infant, enveloped in rags, and lying in a willow-basket. The bones are frequently found under a bed of ashes. A polished ivory breast-dirk, with three holes in it, for the attachment of a handle, and a long piece of rope, were also found in this cave, together with a broken sea-shell (*Pyrula.*)

There is reason to believe, too, from these and other relics and appearances in the cave, that it has been worked, to a limited extent, for nitre, in the early settlement of the country.

The accumulation of organic matter, mixed with the earth of this cave, is so profuse that it emits a strong ammoniacal odor, wherever it has been stirred up and recently exposed by excavations. I infer, from the presence of animal exuviæ—one of the chief requisites for the formation of nitre-salts—as well as from the approximate results obtained by the rude method hitherto employed in the manufacture of salt-petre on Cave creek, that the earth of the Thompson salt-petre cave contains a larger per centage of nitre-salts than any of the nitre-earths hitherto reported on; at least, that part accumulated within 150 feet of the mouth of the cave.

Beyond this, where the cave becomes low and contracted in its dimensions, for a limited distance, the earth will, probably, not be found as strongly impregnated with organic matter, and, therefore, proportionally less productive in salt-petre.

This cave has several branches, which have been followed for some hundred yards; these may also contain some nitre-earth; but as the floor is covered with large blocks of tumbled rock, the underlying earths are not accessible without considerable labor.

A peculiar fatty or oily principle seems to be extracted with the nitre-salts, during the leaching of the earth, which, according to J. S. Thompson, rises in the form of a greasy scum to the surface, during the progress of the evaporation, and is capable of saponification with alkalies.

The quantity of organic matter was too small, in the amount of earth subjected to qualitative examination in the laboratory, to be appreciable; we are, therefore, still left to conjecture, from the accounts given of the nature of this substance, what it may prove to be. If it is capable of forming a soap with lye, as represented, we should suppose it to be one of the oily acids; but, as these are insoluble in water, they could not be taken up by the water used to extract the soluble salts from the earth in their uncombined state, as this fatty principle seems to have been; nor do we understand how it could be so readily washed off the hand by simple water, as we understand the substance in question to have been. Glycerine, it is true, is a component of many fats, which, when set free, is miscible with water; but this is a basic, organic compound, which does not form true soaps; neither has it the greasy feel which the substance contained in the nitre-earth is said to have. It is more probable that it may be some combination of one of the known oily acids, with ammonia, which is soluble in water, as a kind of ammoniacal soap; from this, when subsequently decomposed by the addition of lye, the ammonia may be set free, while the stronger alkali, taking its place, combines with the fatty acid to form a soap, which finally rises to the surface, when the liquor becomes sufficiently concentrated. This is rendered more probable, since by the addition of caustic lye to this earth, ammonia is evolved.

It seems likely that the animal matters, present in this earth, may undergo a gradual change in their native bed, similar to that which produces adipocere, but resulting in the combination of margaric, or some of the other oily acids, with ammonia, which is more soluble in water than that substance.

We have several pounds of this earth still on hand, and may be able, hereafter, to determine the nature of this organic principle, if it exists in sufficient quantity to be separable, so that it can be subjected to the necessary tests for its determination; if not, we must trouble Mr. Thompson to collect, the next time he has occasion to make salt-petre, some of this substance from his kettles, for future special investigation.

About a mile below J. S. Thompson's, an escarpment of silico-calcareous beds runs along the western borders of Cave creek, the lower layers of which, decaying faster than the superincumbent mass, have formed a deep recess beneath overhanging ledges. One of the early settlers in this part of Newton county, has taken advantage of this natural rock-house, to make it serve as a roof, back, and part of the side walls to a house; closing in the south front with pine slabs, on either side of a stone chimney, and cutting two doors and windows, he has managed to construct, at little expense and labor, a long narrow room, about 8 by 30 feet, in which I found two families numbering 8 to 10 persons residing at the time of my visit. Though somewhat contracted in the back part of the apartment, from the sloping nature of the ceiling to the north; still as the overhanging ledges are sound and impervious to water, this half-natural and half-artificial dwelling, I found far more comfortable, than many log cabins met with in the western states.

Plate No. 10, is a sketch of this rock-house dwelling, taken from the south-east.

The primeval forest and vegetation surmounting the entablature of the vestibule, reminded me forcibly of some of those remarkable habitations exhumed by the enterprise of Stephens, in Yucatan, which have been so interestingly and ably discribed by him, and beautifully depicted by the artist Catherwood. Many of these, it will be remembered, had large trees growing on the roof, and were often so completely concealed by dense gungle, that they were only disclosed by the use of the machete, axe and shovel.

CARROLL COUNTY—Continued.

The marble limestone is well developed in the south-east corner of Carroll county, as well as in adjacent sections of land in Newton, Searcy, and Marion counties. On Marshalls creek it is underlaid by a sandstone mostly white, soft, and possessing the saccharoidal character of the sandstone observed under the cavernous limestones of Lafferty creek, in the north-western part of Independence county, and, no doubt, occupies the same geological horizon as the sandstone represented in plate 4, overlying the lead-bearing rocks of the eastern part of this county, and the western part of Marion.

The block of marble sent from Arkansas, to be placed in the national Washington monument, was quarried near the corner of Carroll and Newton counties.

At a tan-yard on Davis' creek, I saw a slab of this rock eight feet by two and a half, which had been got out for a currier's table. The predominating color of this rock is grey, mottled and clouded, with liver-colored spots and stains. This slab was dressed smooth, but not polished; when wet it exhibited, however, the hues and appearance which it would possess, if polished, and gave one a better idea of its tints and the variegated aspect of its surface, than could be obtained from an inspection of the rock in its native bed. The coloring matter is due to oxide of iron, irregularly distributed in the mass, and in that high state of oxidation and allotropic condition in which it is but little disposed to unite with nitric acid, even at a boiling temperature. At a future period, we intend submitting a chemical analysis of this marble limestone, which will give the per centage of metallic oxide, that enters as a coloring principle into the composition of this rock, which may be regarded as one of the most valuable mineral productions of this part of Arkansas.

It had been supposed, that oxide of manganese entered into the composition of this material, but the specimen submitted to a qualitative chemical examination for this metallic oxide, gave no indication of its presence, although the test applied is so extremely delicate, that it will distinctly indicate even the minute trace of manganese found in some specimens of white Carrara marble.

The conspicuous range of hills, lying partly in Carroll and partly in Newton county, whose northern terminus bounds the Marshall prairie, on the south, is composed of two flanking peaks, and central flat-topped ridge.

The most southerly of these conical peaks, is known by the name of the "Pilot mountain;" the northern one is called the "Stack mountain," while the middle ridge has received the name of the "Boat mountain," from its fancied resemblance to a boat, rising out of the adjacent prairie, like some gigantic water-craft resting on the ocean.

The view represented by wood-cut No. 12, was taken on the edge of the Marshall prairie, near the corner of the three counties of Carroll, Newton and Searcy, and exhibits the Boat mountain in the back ground, flanked on the left by Pilot mountain, and on the right by the Stack mountain.

The indistinct terrace seen towards the summit of the Boat mountain, is formed by cliffs of conglomerate, partly concealed by trees and vegetation, and forms the highest bench of prominent sandstone in this mountain.

The Boat mountain rises to the height of 844 feet above Marshall's prairie, at the foot of the principal ascent, and 1244 feet above our encampment of the 23d of June, on Marshall's creek. By computation, its summit must be about 1,527 feet above Little Red river, at Clinton.

Black, bituminous shale is in great force at the base of the mountain, extending 70 feet up the slope, resting on light-grey limestone, with segregations or intercalations of chert.

No. 12---Marshall's Prairie, with the Boat, Pilot and Stack mountains in the distance, near the corner of Benton, Newton and Washington counties.

The black shale has a slight dip to the north-east, which will reduce the thickness from 70 feet—the height from its base to its highest observed out-crop—to 40 or 50 feet of actual thickness. It has concretions of septaria, both calcareous and ferruginous, disseminated especially through its upper part, some of which contain a considerable per centage of iron. There are also saline exudations of sulphate of alumina and sulphate of iron, with, perhaps, some chloride of sodium or common salt; these attract the game and stock of the country, which resort to it as a "lick."

The space between the shale and the millstone grit, that forms the top of the mountain, is chiefly occupied by alternations of sandstones and limestone belonging to the upper division of the subcarboniferous group.

The following section exhibits the succession, and relative approximate thickness, of the principal rock formations of which the Boat mountain is composed.

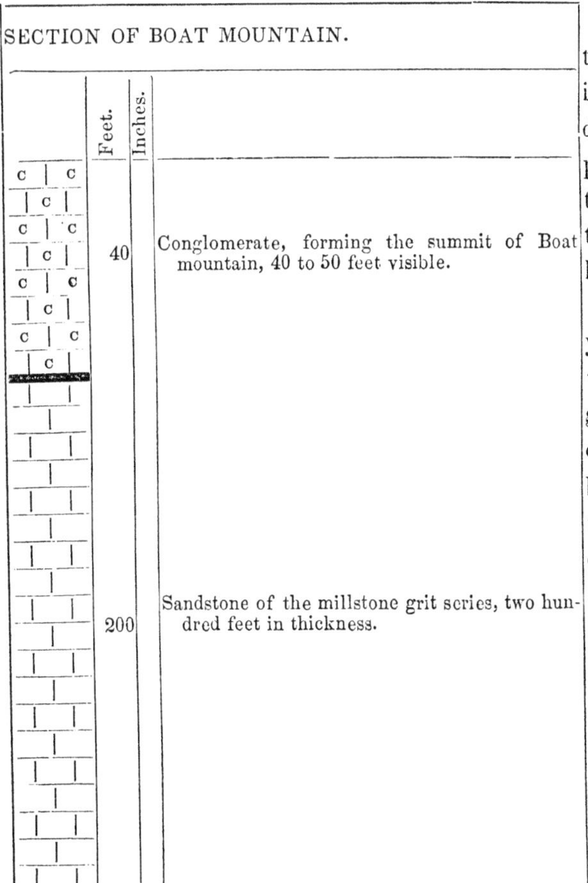

The upper member of the millstone grit series is here pebbly, and underlaid by grits without pebbles; all the members together occupying a thickness of nearly two hundred and fifty feet.

These repose upon the yellow upper strata of the subcarboniferous group, including the Archimedes and pentrimital beds which are, however, mostly concealed by forest and vegetation; in all, about one hundred and sixty feet in thickness.

Beneath these, are coarser - textured, and subcrystalline members of the same group, occupying a space of three hundred and ten feet.

These coarse-textured, subcarboniferous lime-

SECTION OF BOAT MOUNTAIN—CONTINUED.

	Feet.	Inches.	
			Sandstone of the millstone grit series, two hundred feet in thickness—Continued.
	160		Upper yellowish subcarboniferous limestone, including the Archimedes and encrinital limestones with alternations of shale; one hundred and sixty feet in thickness.

stones are underlaid by sixty feet of sandstone, which reposes on the black bituminous shales with calcareous and ferruginous segregations and septaria, which occupy a space along the slope of the base of the mountain, of sixty or seventy feet. The correction for dip will, however, probably reduce its actual thickness to forty or fifty feet. This black shale reposes on the light-grey cherty limestone, that constitutes the base rock of Marshall's prairie, which is probably referrible to the subcarboniferous era, being a part of the cherty limestone group overlying the marble limestone on Cave creek, and elsewhere, in Newton and Searcy counties. It is probable,that all the high ranges of hills, constituting the Boston mountain range of Newton county, have a geological structure analogous to the section here presented of the Boat mountain, with, probably, some local variations in the relative thickness of the different members; since, in

SECTION OF BOAT MOUNTAIN—CONTINUED.

	Feet.	
	310	Coarse-textured, and subcrystalline members of the subcarboniferous group; three hundred and ten feet in thickness.

many instances, conglomerate sandstone has been found, either in place, or in loose blocks on the slopes and at the foot of the mountains; detached masses have, evidently, rolled either from the summit of the adjacent hills, or, at least, from elevated positions on their flanks.

The black slate is, perhaps, not everywhere present as an important member of the subcarboniferous group, since it has not everywhere been found at the base of these hills; but, being prone to crumble to clay, and being, no doubt, sometimes locally reduced in thickness to a few feet, it is then, generally, completely concealed by debris, and thus frequently overlooked.

The scenery in Carroll county, in the vicinity of the Boat mountain, as shown in the wood-cut No. 12, of Marshall's prairie, has much of the same character as the prairie landscapes in Wisconsin and Iowa. It is, decidedly, a fine agricultural district. The distant hills, and the roll-

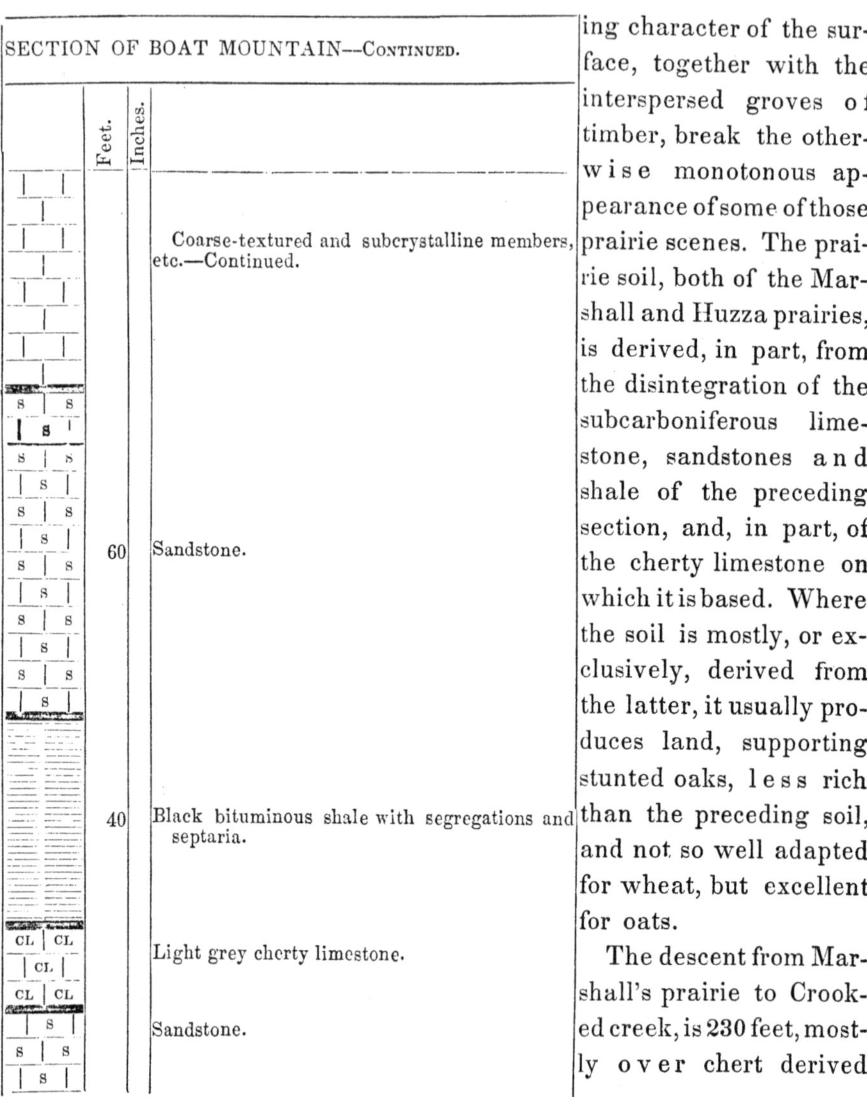

SECTION OF BOAT MOUNTAIN—Continued.

	Feet.	Inches.	
			Coarse-textured and subcrystalline members, etc.—Continued.
	60		Sandstone.
	40		Black bituminous shale with segregations and septaria.
			Light grey cherty limestone.
			Sandstone.

ing character of the surface, together with the interspersed groves of timber, break the otherwise monotonous appearance of some of those prairie scenes. The prairie soil, both of the Marshall and Huzza prairies, is derived, in part, from the disintegration of the subcarboniferous limestone, sandstones and shale of the preceding section, and, in part, of the cherty limestone on which it is based. Where the soil is mostly, or exclusively, derived from the latter, it usually produces land, supporting stunted oaks, less rich than the preceding soil, and not so well adapted for wheat, but excellent for oats.

The descent from Marshall's prairie to Crooked creek, is 230 feet, mostly over chert derived from the equivalent of the light-grey cherty limestone, that underlies the black bituminous shale, at the base of the Boat mountain. Between Marshall's and the Huzza prairies, 100 to 200 feet of sandstone was passed over, interstratified amongst the limestone.

The ascent from the Big spring, on Crooked creek, to the Baker prairie, is 270 feet. The light-grey limestone is here again exposed with segregations of chert, and with some *encrinites* imbedded; but the species were not distinguishable.

One and a half miles south-east of Charles Hutchison's farm, the following succession was observed in a ravine:

1. Sandstone.
2. Chert.
3. Light-grey limestone.

The Pilot Knob, near Charles Hutchison's, has the same general geological structure as the Boat mountain.

Four and a half miles from Carrollton, the Archimedes limestone was observed with remains of a dark shale over it. Under this limestone comes in a sandstone, which has much the appearance of that over the grey limestone on Crooked creek; it is not likely that they can occupy the same geological horizon, unless there has been a great thinning away of the measures that form the base of the Boat mountain.

Some loose pieces of conglomerate were also seen between four and six miles from Carrollton.

The descent to Terrapin and Long creeks, is about 390 feet; in the bed of the former creek, entrochital, cherty limestone was found.

Along with some yellow pyrites, which was submitted to me for examination by the citizens of Carrollton, there were some specimens of a bluish-black scoriaceous ore, in some of which I detected a notable quantity of copper. This ore was said to have been obtained in the Childer's mountain, about seven miles west of Carrollton, on the waters of Cornelius or Dry creek. This ore has the appearance of some of the Ducktown copper ores of Tennessee; and, as I found samples of that variety of Tennessee copper ore in the hands of the brother of the individual, who brought the ore into town, I thought it probable that this might be a sample of Tennessee ore, which, from inadvertency, had been mixed and confounded with the pyritiferous ores of the Childer's mountain. On this account, and as the locality of this ore was then only known to the individual who collected it, and he was from home, I concluded, as my proposed route through Carroll county lay north-west, to request the Hon. W. W. Watkins, as soon as it was convenient for him, to visit the locality on Childer's mountain in company with the discoverer of the ore. This he afterwards did, and subsequently addressed a letter to me, dated the 6th of July last, in which he states that there was no mistake as to the ore having come from the locality, since he had now obtained specimens from the mines himself, viz: on south-west quarter of section 31, township 19 north, range 23 west, and had forwarded some specimens to await my arrival at Little Rock. These specimens I received at Little Rock, and have now had an opportunity of testing them for copper, in my laboratory, by the application of the reagents considered most delicate for the detection of that metal, without obtaining any copper reaction. If copper is to be found amongst these ores, in the Childer's mountain, it can be only sparingly and locally disseminated.

Most of this ore sent to me, from this mountain, is a white iron pyrites, associated with a hydrated oxide of iron, in which yellow iron pyrites is diffused.

Where the Berryville road crosses the Childers' range of mountains, it is elevated about 370 feet above Terapin creek. The surface rock, at this elevation, is sandstone, overlying cherty limestone.

In the gap of the Osage mountain, the sandstone must be at least 130 feet in thickness.

About 11 miles north-west of Carrollton, and three and a half miles from W. Jones', on the divide between Scott's prairie and Prairie township, magnesian limestones, probably of lower silurian date, crop out, which are separated from the limestone and sandstone of the Osage mountain, by crisp chert. The upper beds of this lower formation have the same earthy character and checkered appearance on the surface, as the strata which form the lower portion of the hills in township 19 north, range 17 west; and on Fallen-timber creek, in Marion county, and are, no doubt, of the same age. Some of these limestones probably possess hydraulic properties. This change in the formations is accompanied by a corresponding change in the growth, which consists of small oaks, interspersed in groves on the hillside, with a thick undergrowth of sumach and blackberries.

Here, as in Marion county, numerous springs of water issue from amongst these earthy, magnesian limestones, and, flowing down the slopes, rendering the roads wet and miry.

The crisp chert, which occurs on this side of Scott's prairie, has a different lithological appearance from that associated with the subcarboniferous rocks on the south-east side af the same prairie, and occupies probably a lower geological position.

The hills about W. Jones' are composed of the same description of magnesian limestones, and crisp chert, with some associate sandstone. About midway of the hills, the so-called "cotton rock" is found: a white, close-textured variety of magnesian limestone, which is used for underpinning the houses and building the *external* walls of chimneys. If placed exposed to the direct heat of the fire, it is apt to crack and give way; therefore, for the inside lining of fire-places, another bed is preferred which lies higher in the hills; this is, however, judging from its external appearance, a purer limestone, and, though it may not be so liable to crack by heat, it will certainly be more easily burnt to lime. Hereafter an analysis of these rocks will be made.

Several intercalated bands of sandstone occur in the hills in this part of Carroll county; most of them are below the level of the "cotton rock."

The formations here appear to be of the same character and age as those in the lead region of the eastern part of this county, and the western part of Marion, already described in the first part of this Report; it is probable, from this analogy in the two regions, that lead ore will be found, to some extent, disseminated in pockets in the calcareous members, in the same manner as it occurs in the Coka and Mitchell diggings.

Four of the most conspicuous hills of the Osage range, in the north-west part of Carroll county, in sight of Berryville, have received the names of the "Sister," "Grandfather," and "Indigo" knobs. The Sister hill, nearest to Berryville, gave a height of 370 feet above the Berryville branch of King's river. The summit rocks on this hill are the red, variegated, and encrinital marble limestones; but most of the layers on this hill appear to be too earthy, and too prone to decomposition for ornamental outside work.

The "Fire-stone" was found in place about 15 feet from the top, and the "Cotton-rock" towards the base of the principal ascent, at an elevation of about 70 to 80 feet above the branch from which the levels were taken.

In sighting with the level, across from the Sister to the Grand-father knob, a bench of rock was observed, cropping out about 80 or 100 feet from the top, corresponding, in level and position, to the red, variegated, and encrinital limestones that crown the Sister-hill. By computation, the Grandfather-peak must be nearly 100 feet higher than the Sister-hill.

The succession of the different beds of rock, forming the hills in Prairie township, as far as they have yet been observed, is as follows:

1. Subcarboniferous chert.
2. Sandstone.
3. Light-grey, subcarboniferous limestone.
4. Chert.
5. Encrinital, pink and red limestones; the place of the marble rock.
6. Sandstone; about 70 feet in thickness.
7. Chert.
8. Magnesian limestone and sandstone.
9. "Cotton-rock," a variety of magnesian limestone.
10. Magnesian limestones, some of which, probably, possess hydraulic properties.

Three or four pounds of lead ore are reported to have been found adjacent to the town of Berryville, on land owned by Berry. The remarks previously made in regard to the lead region of the eastern part of Carroll county, will apply also to Prairie township.

Five miles north-west of Berryville, on the Osage, is a locality worthy the attention of the iron manufacturer. Iron is found here in quantities which might be sufficient to supply a smelting furnace. An attempt was made, in this vicinity, to establish iron works; but, in consequence of the death of Belcher, one of the principal parties interested, the enterprise was never fully carried out.

In the high ridge dividing the waters of the Osage fork of King's river from Piney, the succession was as follows:

1. Cherty sandstone.
2. Encrinital limestones.
3. A great mass of chert, replaced sometimes by sandstone.
4. Magnesian limestones, interstratified with some sandstone.

At Stevens' mill, on Piney creek, the encrinital limestone is underlaid by 60 to 80 feet of sandstone.

The soil, derived from the cherty sandstone, forming the summit of the above "divide," supports a growth of pine.

On the ridge between Piney creek and the Dry fork of King's river, the strata of the preceding section appear to have dipped considerably towards the south-west, so that they lie lower in the ridges, and are capped with white, subcarboniferous limestone and sandstone, overlying the cherty sandstone of the preceding section.

In descending from these strata to the Howard farm, on the Dry fork of King's river, a great mass of chert was passed over.

No black shale was visible in any of the sections in this part of Carroll county.

The rock in the bed of the Dry fork of King's river, at Howard's farm, is light-grey limestone and chert, at least 50 feet in thickness, and apparently of subcarboniferous date; but, if so, there must be a rapid dip of the strata between the Piney and Dry forks of King's river.

Some lead ore is said to have been plowed up in Howard's field.

A large spirifer was found in the limestone of the Dry fork, allied to *Spirifer striatus*, and casts of *Orthis crinistria* in the overlying chert, both of which species belong to the subcarboniferous era, and, therefore indicate the age of these rocks.

In passing from the Dry fork to the main branch of King's river, a ridge of about 330 feet in height was passed over. At the base of this ridge, is the aforementioned light-grey limestone, 50 feet or more in thickness; over this is a slope of chert, containing casts of *Orthis crinistria*, surmounted by sandstone, which forms the top of the ridge, where we passed over it into Madison county.

MADISON COUNTY.

The continuance of the south-west dip, brings in still higher members of the subcarboniferous group on the Main fork of King's river.

Five miles below the forks of King's river, there are alternations of limestones and sandstones, with some shaly partings, all belonging to the upper division of the subcarboniferous group. Fifty feet above the highest bed of limestone observed at this locality, there are some thirty feet of shale shown in a section in a ravine. The lower part of this shale is black and bituminous, and exhibits, in splitting, curious, conchoidal impressions, in which, however, no organic structure is discerned; the upper part is light-grey and encloses flattened concretions of clay ironstone. This shale is overlaid by sandstones belonging to the millstone grit series.

Ascending the valley of King's river towards the forks, masses of conglomerate sandstone are encountered, which have fallen from the cliffs above. From the forks of King's river, a high bluff is seen to the east, with vertical cliffs of conglomerate and millstone grit, overhanging the shales, under which are the sandstones, Archimedes, and encrinital limestones of the upper subcarboniferous group.

The soil of the valley of King's river is black and rich, from the washings it receives from the limestones and bituminous shales of the adjacent slopes; but the same cause has operated to produce a miry road, liable to be washed into deep holes, which makes the traveling disagreeable.

Both the ascent of the valley, and the southerly dip, contribute to bring the Archimedes limestone and millstone grits gradually lower in the hills as you proceed up King's river.

In the ridge, which divides the waters of King's river from those of War Eagle and Richland creek, on or near Samuel Rags' farm, and about a quarter of a mile to the end of the Clarksville road, a small branch makes a perpendicular fall over twelve feet of overhanging conglomerate sandstone; beneath this are about eighteen inches of shale, including six inches of coal. I traveled fifteen miles from my câmp on King's river, to see this coal, in the hopes that it might prove to be a workable bed, but was disappointed in finding it so thin; because a good bed of coal would be of infinite service to this country, remote from a navigable stream, if for no other purpose than that of blacksmith's use.* At considerable labor a few hundred pounds of this coal were obtained, by taking advan-

*So necessary do blacksmiths find coal in their business, that they often go great distances and haul a small supply to their shops, although it may be of inferior quality.

tage of the cavernous opening made by nature, beneath the cliff of conglomerate: already the bed is so difficult of access, back in the recesses of the cliff, that even with all the height, obtainable by the removal of the whole thickness of the shale, a space of only from 18 to 24 inches is cleared between the hard sills of sandstone, to work in, and it has become therefore necessary, in order to obtain any coal, that the workman should lie on his side and work his pick in this uncomfortable position.

By computation, the coal under this conglomerate is at least 400 feet above the valley of King's river. It is underlaid by millstone grit, succeeded, in the descending order, by a great thickness of marly shales, under which are the Archimedes, and encrinital limestone and associate sandstone. No continuous section was obtained where the relative thickness of the different members could be measured.

In summits of the highest ridges, near the head of King's river, about 200 feet of red and variegated shales and sandstone come in over the conglomerate. In this space, coals of workable thickness are more likely to occur than under the conglomerate; and the inhabitants of Madison county would do well to make diligent search for outcrops of coal, in these higher measures. As yet, however, no symptoms of coal have been discovered amongst these superior shales, in the south-eastern part of Madison county.

Some pieces of lead ore are reported to have been picked up in the valley of King's river, viz: in the Basham and Roebuck settlement on Dry creek, three miles above Kingston; also by Burney, higher up the valley, near the head of King's river. At the latter locality, the rocks being mostly conglomerate sandstones and shales, which have not retained that openness of fissure requisite for the retention of metallic insinuations, it is not likely that productive lodes should occur, accessible to any reasonable amount of shafting; at the former, where the underlying limestone formations are nearer the surface, the prospect is somewhat more favorable; but still I do not consider the geological indications, in the south-east part of Madison county, as encouraging for mining operations as in the northern part of this county, where the barren and cavernous cherty limestones immediately underlie the country; the reason for this conclusion will appear more fully when treating of Benton county.

From the forks of King's river, we ascended for several miles on the western branches of that stream, and then rose 460 feet to the divide between King's river and Warton's creek. In this ridge, the Archimedes, pentremital, encrinital, and other members of the upper division of the subcarboniferous limestone group were found in force, with intercalations and partings of shale and marl, with some alternations of ferruginous sandstone, especially on the western declivity, descending to Warton's creek.

At Dotson's farm, on that stream, underneath these formations, a black, bituminous, sheety shale crops out, similar to the shale of Wiley's Cove, in Searcy county, of which 15 feet can be seen exposed on the west bank of the creek. This shale dips at an angle of 5 or 6 deg. down stream, and is soon lost to view under flagstones, these again dip under argillaceous shales, including a ferruginous, calcareous band, charged with the remains of *producta* and *chonetes*, of which the *P. elegans* is the most abundant.

The ridge dividing Warton's creek and War Eagle, is 290 feet above the former stream. On the top of this ridge, some 60 to 80 feet of conglomerate overlies subcarboniferous limestones, shales, and sandstones.

The succession on Warton's creek and War Eagle, is as follows:

1. Ferruginous and argillaceous shales.
2. Conglomerate sandstone.
3. Shales, both black and ferruginous.
4. Millstone grit and shaly sandstones.
5. Shales.
6. Archimedes and pentremital limestones.
7. Black shale, thin.
8. Grey shales, including band of productal calcareous rock.
9. Flagstones.
10. Dotson black sheety shale.

No. 10, the Dotson black shale, is the lowest bed visible in this part of Madison county.

Five miles above Huntsville, concretionary and schistose beds of Archimedes limestone form the bed of War Eagle, and a rugged bench of harder layers of the same rock borders for some distance its north bank, like an artificial wall. Some dark shales are intercolated amongst these upper subcarboniferous limestones on this stream. Here the dip is southeasterly, so that the flagstones and dark shales soon rise from beneath the aforementioned limestones, in a north-west course.

The surface of some of the slabs, both of the flagstones and harder shaly strata, is covered with cylindrical and conical impressions, often in high relief, some of which are in semi-lunar whorls or coils. These are, probably, referrible to various species of fossil *fucoides*, or sea weeds; but the structure is so obscure that the inference of their origin is, at present, rather problematical.

All the ridges passed over between King's river and War Eagle, had a capping of conglomerate, which is separated from the Archimedes limestone by ferruginous shales; these are, however, not as thick as in the valley of King's river. The conglomerate has, also, a considerable mass of ferruginous shale overlying it; and the associate sandstones of the millstone grit series are also charged with oxide of iron; indeed, some of these ferruginous layers appear to contain iron enough to be entitled to rank as ores, and were they not too siliceous, might be profitably reduced to iron.

A few miles south of Huntsville, the road is in many places strewed with white water-worn quartzy pebbles, derived from the disintegration of the conglomerate rock which lies in the hill above.

The soil here is generally red, from the quantity of iron washed into it from the shales and ferruginous sandstones of the adjacent hillsides.

About 15 feet of black shale are exposed in the banks of the spring branch of War Eagle, two miles below Huntsville. This shale encloses hard and heavy kidney-shaped masses of carbonate of iron, in the center of which particles of white iron pyrites are found, which have been mistaken for silver ore. Here, a considerable quantity of good iron ore could be obtained, though not enough, by itself, to supply a furnace; but, no doubt, other localities of the same ore can be disclosed, which, together, might afford sufficient. In fact, the symptoms of the presence of iron are so general in the rocks of this vicinity, under the conglomerate, as to render it a locality well worthy the attention of the iron master and the owners of property. This mass of shale is covered with flaggy sandstone, and is, most likely, the equivalent of the Dotson black shale and flagstone of Warton's creek. The strata dip, here, to the south-east.

A qualitative analysis of the water obtained at the head of Kimble's creek, 4 miles from Huntsville, was made, and gave, as its principal constituents:

Bi-carbonate of lime.

Bi-carbonate of magnesia.

Bi-carbonate of the oxide of iron.

Chloride of sodium.

Chloride of magnesium.

Small quantities of sulphate of soda.

It is a weak, saline chalybeate, possessing mild laxative, and tonic properties.

At our encampment on Holman's creek, 2 miles north-west of Huntsville, the Archimedes limestone occurs in ledges on its banks, underlaid by black shales.

The same limestone, with its accompanying shales, occurs two or three miles from Phillips' on the road to Osage spring.

A few inches of coal are said to have been discovered some distance up Holman's creek, associated with this black shale. The rocks, along this branch, lie too low in the geological formations to contain any workable beds of coal.

On this same stream, about nine miles north-west of Huntsville, the road leads, for half a mile, through barrens with a sandy soil, followed by prairie in which sandstone crops out about 10 miles from Huntsville. This prairie is bounded by wooded hills off to the south-west.

Proceeding towards the north-west, the Archimedes limestone and associate shale are succeeded by chert and cherty limestone on the edge of the barrens; after which comes sandstone in the prairie. In the former, casts of *Orthis crinistria?* were found about four or five miles from Holman's creek.

This cherty limestone, which belongs, doubtless, to the lower division of the subcarboniferous group, has a considerable area in the northern part of Madison county, and possesses the peculiar lithological character of the most productive lead-bearing rocks of the adjacent part of south-western Missouri.

Some lead ore has been found in the Moudey settlement, about four miles north of Huntsville; if it had its origin in this formation, it is a locality which should claim the attention of the miner, as will appear more fully in the next section, when treating of Benton county.

This cherty limestone, containing a few *entrochites*, underlies the Brush creek barrens, and the spring at C. Fitches', on the edge of these barrens, and close to the line between this county and Washington, wells up through the same description of rocks; these are analogous, and most probably cotemporaneous with, the geological formation that underlies the barrens of Kentucky.

BENTON COUNTY.

In the extreme south-east corner of this county, along the bluffs of White river, the barren limestone formation, of which we had occasion to speak in the previous section, under the head of Madison county, forms conspicuous cliffs near the crossing of the road from Huntsville to Bentonville. On section 24,? township 18 north, range 19 west, (if this road is correctly laid down on the maps,) a hard, sheety black shale comes in under this limestone, having the appearance of the black shale of Wiley's Cove, in Searcy county; but, probably, occupying a rather lower geological position in the subcarboniferous group; since that shale underlies the Archimedes and encrinital limestones in the upper division of the subcarboniferous group, while this succeeds, in the descending order, the barren cherty limestone of the lower division. From 30 to 35 feet of this shale are seen in section, not only along the bluffs of White river, but also on Hickory creek, about a mile to the west. At both localities, the shale is overlaid by the barren limestone, which, on White river, forms cliffs of 80 to 100 feet.

I have never seen, in any of my previous surveys in the western states, amongst the subcarboniferous rocks, shales possessing the solidity and hardness of the shales of Wiley's cove, or those of the south-east part of Benton county, which may be almost entitled to the appellation of slates, though not durable enough for roofing purposes; in this respect, these shales resemble, in lithological character, the hard, black, sheety shale or slate of the Salt river valley, in Kentucky, and at the base of the knobs of Floyd county, Indiana, belonging to the devonian period; which slates are the representatives, probably, of the "Gennessee slate" of the New York Reports. The superposition and association will undoubtedly place both the shales of Wiley's Cove and Hickory creek, in Benton county, as members of the subcarboniferous group. The fossils found, as yet, in these shales, are too imperfect, and too few, to enable one to judge, from them alone, of the age of these Arkansas shales; we are, therefore, obliged to resort, for the present, to order of superposition for a solution of the problem.

The ascent from White river, up the ridge, on the west side is 310 feet; the road runs over chert, derived from the disintegration of the cherty limestones, overlying the aforementioned black shale. In this chert are found some of the disjointed disks of oval-shaped stems of *platycrinus;* and at the Osage spring, the fountain head of Osage creek, it contains *Productus punctatus*, and the same species of reticulated, fossil corallines which characterize the cherty limestone in the barrens of Kentucky and Tennessee.

The lands between White river and Bentonville, are mostly oak barrens, interspersed with prairie.

Samples of soil were taken from Benton county, for future chemical analysis, from the Hon. A. B. Greenwood's farm, near the town of Bentonville.

The oak and hickory timber which has now sprung up on the borders of the present prairie, is mostly of a growth as recent as the settlement of the country; since the greater portion of this part of Benton county was, before that time, open prairie, with, here and there, thickets of low bushes. West of Bentonville, there is a mulatto soil, somewhat different in its character from that immediately around Bentonville, and very productive, as most soils of this color proved to be in the analyses of Kentucky soils.

Water is generally obtained, in these prairies, at the depth of 20 to 25 feet, after passing through chert and red clay, such as underlies a considerable area of this county. This underclay will, no doubt, be found an excellent fertilizer of land; and entering, as it does, largely into the subsoils of this country, and therefore accessible by subsoiling, will be a permanent store of agricultural wealth to the country.

In the valley of Sugar creek, the black shale is again seen under the limestone, and is in view at intervals along this stream, all the way to the northern boundary of the state.

At Squires' mill, 16 feet of black shale is well exposed, with 6 or 8 inches of marly earth between it and the overlying limestone.

The stripe of the geological formations appears, therefore, to run diagonally through Benton county, from Hickory creek, in the south-east corner, to where Sugar creek crosses the state line into Missouri.

Two and a half miles south of the state line, the limestone, over the black slate, contains large *Spirifer striatus?*

The succession in Benton county, so far as yet ascertained, is:

1. Productive and coralline chert, at the head of the Osage and elsewhere.
2. Cherty limestone of the barren limestone group, forming cliffs on White river and elsewhere.
3. Black slate of Hickory and Sugar creeks.

The first and second members of the preceding section, are of the same age and composition as the lead-bearing formations of the Granby lead mines, in Newton county, Missouri; and there is every reason to believe, from analogy of structure, both in the rocks and general surface of the country, that here, in Benton county, as well as in the northern parts of Madison, Washington, and western part of Carroll county, discoveries may be made of lead deposits, similar to those of the Granby mines, in Missouri; therefore, it may be well, in this connection, to record some of the facts connected with the mode of occurrence of the lead ores in these mines, which is, in many respects, peculiar, and particularly worthy the attention of the inhabitants of north-western Arkansas; since it may be the means of leading to discoveries that may not only enrich the owner of the land, but develop the mineral resources of the country.

At the Granby lead mines, the lead ore has not generally been found, as usual, in fissures and veins, with a more or less perpendicular hade, but rather running in horizontal sheets between the stratification of the rocks, and generally beneath the great mass of overlying heterogeneous chert deposits, where it rests on the underlying limestone, which often possesses oolitic structure, close to the rich deposits of sulphuret of lead.

The depth at which this junction of chert and limestone takes place, is from 30 to 80 feet. The average depth of the shafts, before reaching the main deposits of ore, may be put down at 65 feet. After the shaft has reached the level of the "*Sheet mineral*," a barrier is often found, which has to be penetrated before reaching the heaviest beds of ore, known, technically, by the name of the "bar rocks;" this is usually from 15 to 30 feet through; it seems to be composed of porous calcareous matter, in which some sulphuret of lead, sulphuret of zinc, (black-jack), and bitter spar, (magnesian limestone), is disseminated. After this barrier is broken through, the miner reaches the "sheet mineral," lying, not perfectly level, but waving somewhat with the irregular, corroded surface of the rock on which it has been deposited, and mixed, more or less, with a "tallow clay," either red or white, which is a tenaceous, unctuous clay, sometimes ferruginous, in certain states of dryness cuts like tallow or soap. There are, also, various minerals, either amorphous (i. e. without any regular geometrical forms), or crystallized; such as pearlspar, bitter spar, carbonate of lead, carbonate and silicate of zinc, sulphuret of zinc, with occasionally crystals of sulphate and phosphate of lead, disseminated with the calc-spar, the principal vein-stone accompanying the galena. The so-called "black-jack rock," (i. e. a rock in which sulphuret of zinc is largely disseminated), is considered a good indication of lead ore.

The material passed through in sinking the shaft, is mostly white chert in displaced and confused masses. This chert is often light and porous—almost possessing the structure of pumice.

Three tiers of sheet-ore have been successively passed through; that at an average depth of 65 feet from the "grass," has proved, as yet, the most productive. Ore has been reached, however, within 10 and 20 feet of the surface.

The horizontal sheets of lead ore vary in thickness from a fraction of an inch to 2 feet, and even, in some extraordinary instances, to 3 feet. The average thickness may be put down at 6 to 10 inches. They are often so rich that it is not uncommon, after a shaft has been fairly sunk to the level of the ore, for two men to raise from 1,000 to 2,000 pounds, and even sometimes 3,000 to 4,000 pounds, in six or eight hours. 30,000 to 50,000 pounds have been raised out of the Hopkins mine by 20 men, each man averaging from 400 to 300 pounds a day.

At the Frazer shaft, from a quarter acre lot, 10,000 pounds were taken out; and, from all the Frazer claims, up to the present time, comprising 10 acres, 400,000 pounds of lead ore have been raised. The total amount of ore raised in the last two years is about 800,000 pounds.

The ore, as has been said, lies mostly in horizontal spaces, conformable with the bedding rock; but, nevertheless, there are crevices having a connection with the ore, the bearing of which is nearly north and south, opening occasionally into cavernous spaces, precisely analogous to the ore-bearing veins in other parts of the state, and in Wisconsin and Iowa; but these are either entirely barren of ore or contain only small quantities. My impression is, that the lead ore once occupied these north and south crevices, and was subsequently removed, in part or in whole, into its present bed by a transposition, analogous to that known to minerologists under the name of the pseudomorphous process, by which one mineral is removed, while another takes its place, assuming often the form of the first mineral, instead of the usual form belonging to itself. The term "analogous" is used, because the lead ore here cannot exactly be considered to occur in a *false* form, or one belonging to another mineral; in this instance, I believe, it only took the place of the amorphous rock; therefore it was not infiltrated into a pre-existing geometrical mould, if I may so express it, but had freedom of space sufficient to assume its usual cuboidal structure. That it should be deposited like a limestone or sandstone, is altogether improbable and contrary to the usual nature of such ponderous and difficultly soluble minerals.

The lead-bearing rock is not very fossiliferous, but there can be distinguished the *Orthis crinistria*, *Productus cora*, and other fossils of the cherty barren limestone division of the subcarboniferous group; not, however, belonging to the Archimedes and pentremital group, as has been suggested.

Though the profitable discoveries of lead ore at the Granby mines, have hitherto been confined to about one mile square; still, they attracted a population, in two years, of 3,000 people, to a section of land before almost neglected, even by the farmer, and which now, with the unfavorable circumstance under which the mining claims are held, (being part of a tract conditionally ceded to one of the proposed Pacific railroad routes), has, nevertheless, in that short space of time, converted a wild prairie into a populous town, full of enterprise and industry.

It should be observed, too, that the snrface indications were no more encouraging, at the time the mines were started, than they are in many localities that may be pointed out in the above counties in Arkansas, where the same formation exists and where the cherty materials, thrown out from excavations for wells, cannot be distinguished from the rubbish rock at the mouth of the Granby shafts. I may add, too, that, in all these counties, surface ore has occasionally been found under circumstances similar to that in which they were first discovered in Newton county. But still the search after lead ore may be precarious, and lead to many disappointments; since ore is only *locally* and not *universally* distributed through the rock; hence it requires not only a general knowledge of minerals, but special experience in this particular rock formation, to sink a shaft successfully on ore, even though the miner may have surface indications to guide him.

If the ore should be found in sheets, as in Missouri, the thickness of the lead-bearing rock is not a matter of so much moment; but if it should occur in veins or lodes, then that question assumes importance.

In the north-west part of Arkansas I did not find, at any one place, more than one hundred feet of the cherty, barren limestone exposed; but this is, probably, not its entire thickness. In Searcy county, solid cliffs of more than 200 feet of this rock have been observed. In following vertical veins through this rock, the black shales of Hickory and Sugar creeks will be encountered; in this rock it is not likely that ore will be found in sufficient quantities to be profitable to work; but this shale is of no great thickness; 38 feet is the greatest number of feet I have seen exposed, and it is not likely that the whole mass will exceed 50 feet. This passed through, solid limestones will be again entered, in which the veins may also prove productive.

The chances, then, are favorable for the occurrence of productive lead mines in the north-west part of Arkansas, north of the boundary line of the millstone grit and its underlying shales. This boundary line will be hereafter described, and ultimately indicated by a colored geological map, if the survey be hereafter carried through in detail.

Near the north-east corner of the State of Arkansas, in Benton county, on Butler creek, black slate, the equivalent of that on Hickory and Sugar creeks, makes its appearance on the hillsides in the barrens, under a low cliff of white sub-crystalline limestone. These cliffs are surmounted by cherty limestone, chert, and cherty sandstone, which underlie the flat woods of Spavinaw, like those between Indian creek and Oliver's prairie, in Missouri, south-west of the Granby lead mines.

A sulphur spring was reported to me on Butler creek, about five miles east of Maysville; but not until I had passed half a day's travel to the south of it, so that I had no opportunity of testing it.

Beatty's prairie, north-east of Maysville, is a perfect counterpart of Oliver's prairie in Newton county, Missouri; the gently undulating surface, fringed, like it, with groves of oak, small hickory, is also dotted with low mounds, bearing tofts of rank weeds, and made up of isolated heaps of chert gravel. These mounds are so uniform in appearance that they convey the idea of an artificial origin.

In riding over this prairie, about 3 miles from Maysville, the ground sounded hollow under the horses feet, marking, no doubt, the roof of some cavernous space in the underlying limestone. It is not improbable that this spot may be on the line of some crevice, and, if within the sphere of action that produced the metalliferous deposits of Newton county, Missouri, might lead to sources of cotemporaneous ore beds. The apparent west north-west bearing of the lead mines of south-western Missouri would, however, rather indicate their course north of this locality.

The cavernous nature of the limestone, of this part of Benton county, is also indicated by the sinking of a branch of the Corner spring, that runs by the Burrow farm, beneath the surface, a few hundred yards below the house on this farm.

The white, soft, decomposing chert of the barrens south of Beatty's prairie, has casts and impressions of reticulated corallines, similar to those of the corresponding formations in Kentucky and Tennessee. These fossils were also observed, in greater abundance and perfection, near the centre of township 18 north, range 32 west, in the materials thrown out of a well.

The soil of this part of Benton county appears to be well adapted for wheat, and, having a substratum of red clay, which, no doubt, will be found to have fertilizing effects, the productiveness of the surface-soil, by judicious management, need not be materially impaired, even by continuous culture. This country is well watered by fine springs, that issue from the south-west slopes of the cherty limestone.

The greater part of Benton county is, therefore, based on this member of the subcarboniferous group, except in the higher grounds, where the flat oak woods prevail; there the barren limestone and chert is overlaid by shaly rocks and a kind of buhrstone and cherty sandstone.

WASHINGTON COUNTY.

The geology of the northern townships of this county is very analagous to that of Benton county. The southern extension of the cherty barren limestone is here, as there, the base rock of the country, the underlying shales only showing themselves in the deepest cuts, in the extreme north-east corner of the county, on White river, near Van Winkle's mill, and near Blackburn's mill, on War Eagle. At the former of these localities, the limestone is cavernous. Close to the Washington county line, but probably in the south-east corner of Benton county, a salt-petre cave is reported which I have not yet seen.

One of the most interesting features of the northern part of Washington county, consists in the noble springs, which gush forth amongst the ledges of limestone, in such volume and force as to afford water-powers for small mills, even at their very source. The Elm springs, forming the head of one of the branches of the Clear-fork of the Illinois river, are one of the most remarkable of these springs. They are, no doubt, due to the fissured and cavernous nature of the barren limestone, reposing on its underlying impermeable shale. Atmospheric water, filtering with facility through the cavities and rents of the limestone, is arrested by the impervious shale beneath, and flows out along the slope of the southerly dip. Besides affording convenient and permanent water powers, these springs, no doubt, contribute greatly to the fertility of the lands in the adjacent valleys, not alone by their irrigating effects, but by reason of the large amount of carbonic acid and lime with which they are charged, which must, undoubtedly, give a remarkable impetus to vegetation; since they are two of the most essential fertilizers in all manures. One of them, carbonic acid, is, in fact, the great solvent, or vehicle, which carries nourishment to the plant.

In township 17 and the southern part of 18 north, range 29 west, the succession of the different beds of the subcarboniferous group is approximately as follows:

	Feet.	Inches.	
S	200?		White, yellow and brown sandstones, some of which have a cellular structure.
	40?		Ferruginous and dark shales.
CH	40?		Chert and cherty barren limestone.
L	35		
	40?		Black cherty shale.

The first and highest member of this section—the sandstone formation—occupies the summit of the ranges of hills adjacent to White river, above and below the mouth of Brush creek, and will, doubtless, be found capping many of the isolated peaks, which rise in various directions out of the barrens and prairies, on both sides of the Missouri road leading to Springfield. The second member underlies more immediately those south-east sections of land, bordering on White river, that are elevated 150 to 200 feet above that stream, while the underlying chert and cherty limestone form cliffs on White river, near the mouth of Brush creek, and become the surface rocks in the north-west part of the county, in consequence of the rise of the geological formations in that direction.

This latter rock is, no doubt, for reasons already advanced in the preceding section, the source of the pieces of lead ore which, according to the statements of many citizens, have been occasionally picked up in this township and along some of those branches, forming the heads of the Illinois river, which take their rise in the northern part of this county. This inference is further corroborated by the statement of William Ray, that he had dug out a wagon-bed full of lead ore, somewhere in township 17 north, range 29 west, 6 to 8 miles north-east of Fayetteville.

Three miles north-west from the mouth of Brush creek, considerable iron ore of the limonite variety of mineralogists was discovered towards the base of the sandstone formation—the first member of the preceding section. Most of this ore seen on the surface, in connection with the sandstones, was too siliceous to make good iron; but it is not improbable, that better ore may be found amongst the underlying shales of the second member; strata which, being argillaceous in their composition, are more favorable for the retention of segregated iron ore, free from sand. These shales, seen in the slope of the road leading to the ford on White river, at the mouth of Brush creek, have a ferruginous appearance, favorable for the presence of ores of iron.

The soil east of the Missouri road is more sandy than that west, in consequence of having received debris and washings from the adjacent main sandstone ridge lying to the east.

It is not improbable, when the highest points of this range of hills come to be explored in detail, that some of the members of the upper subcarboniferous group may be found, or even part of the millstone grit series.

Where chert materials prevail, harder and more durable than the rest of the formation, they have resisted decomposition for a longer period of time than the surrounding parts, and given rise to those isolated mounds which rise conspicuously, in all directions, out of the prairie, when viewed from some elevated position in the neighboring hills.

The low ridges bordering the northern limits of township 18 north, range 29 and 30 west, are composed of chert—the third member of the section previously given—while the farming lands in the valleys, which join them on the south, are based on the calcareo-siliceous member; i. e. the barren limestone formation. The low ridges, 140 feet above the Clear fork and the black-jack barrens, in the centre of township 17 north, range 30 west, adjacent to the Fayetteville road, are of the same formation.

Near the line between township 16 and 17 north, range 30 west, sandstone ledges, belonging to the first division of the section, are in place, resting on the underlying ferruginous shale. In the latter, some iron ore was observed.

Approaching the town of Fayetteville, these strata dip rapidly under the upper members of the subcarboniferous group.

Immediately adjacent to Fayetteville, on the north, ferruginous shales are seen, dipping at an angle of 20 deg. to the south-west, underlaid by a kind of amygdaloidal sandstone belonging to the millstone grit series.

One mile west of Fayetteville, on the head of the Trace branch of Wild Cat creek, black shale is exposed, containing abundance of good carbonate of iron, which, with other localities, will go far towards supplying the wants of a furnace for the reduction of iron. Over the black shale, with iron ore, is a variegated shale, on the exposed surface of which numerous crystals of selenite or sulphate of lime are forming, no doubt, from the mutual action of protosulphate of iron and bi-carbonate of lime; giving rise to sulphate of lime and protocarbonate of iron. This may be the origin, too, of this latter mineral, so abundantly found in the underlying black shale. The production of the protosulphate of iron, implicated in this mutual decomposition, is evidently to be accounted for, at this locality, by the gradual oxidation of sulphur and iron, the elements of iron pyrites, abundant, even now, in these shales, and, no doubt, more so at a former period, before the production of the above minerals.

This gypsiferous shale would, undoubtedly, prove to be a valuable mineral manure, applied to some of the siliceous soils, overlying the sandstone formations of this county, as well as to those located at the base of the sandstone ridges, which have received the sandy debris washed from their flanks.

The strata concealed in the slope above these shales, exposed both at the Lick and on the Town branch, are, most probably, a continuation of similar shales, underlying the Archimedes limestones, such as were afterwards seen under that rock elsewhere in the county, as will appear in the subsequent part of this section.

The shale beds, partly exposed in the drain below Cato's spring, probably overlie the Archimedes limestone; this member includes a seam of coal of one or two inches of no practical value. The eight inch coal, which has been partially opened for the use of the blacksmiths, lies higher up in the hills, in shales, above the pentrimital limestone, at Cato's spring, over which is the main body of sandstone, forming the upper part of the ridge southeast of Fayetteville, including one or more calcareous bands.

On the Town branch, on section 20, township 16 north, range 30 west, about 20 feet of black shale are exposed, similar to that at the Lick, one mile west of Fayetteville; the former shale contains large septaria, both of carbonate of lime, and carbonate of iron.

Feet.	Inches.	
100?		Sandstone of the millstone grit series.
		Calcareous bands.
125?		Sandstone of the millstone grit series, cellular, and carbonaceous.
	8	Shales, including eight inches of coal.

The subjoined is an approximate section of the order of superposition of the different beds from the sandstones, in the ridge south-east of Fayetteville, to the black shale, with carbonate of iron, at the Lick, 1 mile west of town. The exact thickness of each of the members I am unable to give, until more accurate measurements and levels are taken to the outcrop of the different members, and correction for dip calculated; for the present, most of the thicknesses are given by computation from observations at different localities, rather than from actual measurements at one locality. But, we hope, hereafter, to have an opportunity of submitting a more complete section, in detail, with the absolute thickness of the beds.

The sandstones, that form the upper portion of this section, contain some remarkable and very curious impressions, composed of subcylindrical branches, radiating from a centre, bearing a distant resemblance to some fossil

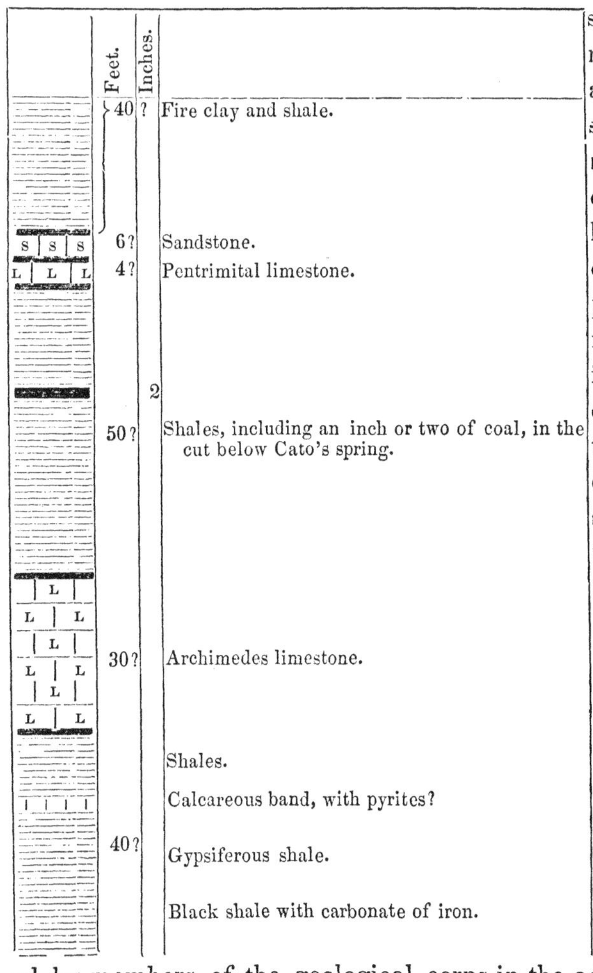

sponges; but less symmetrical, and without any apparent porous structure. They are, most likely, of vegetable origin, and may, perhaps, be referrible to that obscure order of marine plants, known under the name of fucoides; but, if so, are entirely different in form from anything of the kind I have ever observed before, or seen described in any of the works on fossil botany.

In the collection of W. Washburn, I saw some fine specimens of lepidodendrons, which have weathered out of some of the higher sandstones of the preceding section; and imperfect specimens of the same fossil plant were observed by members of the geological corps in the adjacent sandstone ridges. This is a plant which occurs in the millstone grit, but more abundantly at the base of the coal measures.

It is a question of interest and importance, to determine whether any portion of the upper sandstones and shales of Washington county can be referred to the true coal measures; since, in that case, there would be hope of finding thicker and more valuable beds of coal in this county than have yet been discovered. At present no coal beds are known of more than 18 or 20 inches; except one, with a clay parting, in Mountain township, on the head of the Illinois river, 6 or 7 miles east of Boonsboro, which is about two feet thick; and those beds, at present known, in the immediate vicinity of Fayetteville, in shales under the millstone grit, do not exceed one foot.

On section 18, township 15 north, range 29 west, 30 to 35 feet of shale are exposed, on the banks of Wood's branch, near Orion Rieffs' house. In this shale, and 11 to 12 feet above the bed of the creek, a band of dark grey fossiliferous limestone occurs, in which a greyish yellow iron pyrites is disseminated, that has attracted no small attention in the neighborhood, and has been quarried to some extent, in the hopes that it might prove to be an ore of silver. Those who had taken the trouble and labor to extract this ore, were much disappointed that I could give them no encouragement to prosecute further their silver-mining operations. The Wood's branch shale underlies the Archimedes, cavernous limestone of the adjacent ridges with, perhaps, some interstratified layers of sandstone, and occupies, in all probability, a geological position corresponding to that of the shale in the Town branch, and at the Lick, one mile west of Fayetteville.

The dark grey, pyritiferous, fossiliferous limestone, contains *bellerophon*, *Productus cora;* also a *nucula* and *euomphalus*, the species of which have not yet been determined. This rock would take a polish, but from the large quantity of sulphuret and protoxide of iron, which it contains, would be liable to rust and stain, if exposed to atmospheric agencies.

The succession on Wood's branch of the Middle fork of White river, on township 15 north, range 29 west, is as follows:

1. Brown sandstone with amygdaloidal cavities.
2. Space concealed with shales?
3. Archimedes cavernous limestone.
4. Grey and black shales, with perhaps some interstratified sandstone, and including, near its base, a band of dark, fossiliferous, pyritiferous limestone, and segregations of carbonate of iron.

The carbonate of iron is quite abundant in the lower part of this shale, in the sections both of the Middle and West fork of White river, so much so, that I believe sufficient ore can be obtained from the various localities of its outcrop, to supply a furnace, in connection with ores of the limonite variety, which can, probably, be found higher up over the limestone.

The caverns in the vicinity of Orion Rieffs, have been formed by the disintegration of the concretionary beds of the Archimedes limestone. They are low and difficult of access. From one of these caverns, some earth was collected for the purpose of examining it for nitre; time has not yet permitted an analysis of this earth, but its appearance does not indicate a large per centage of salt-petre.

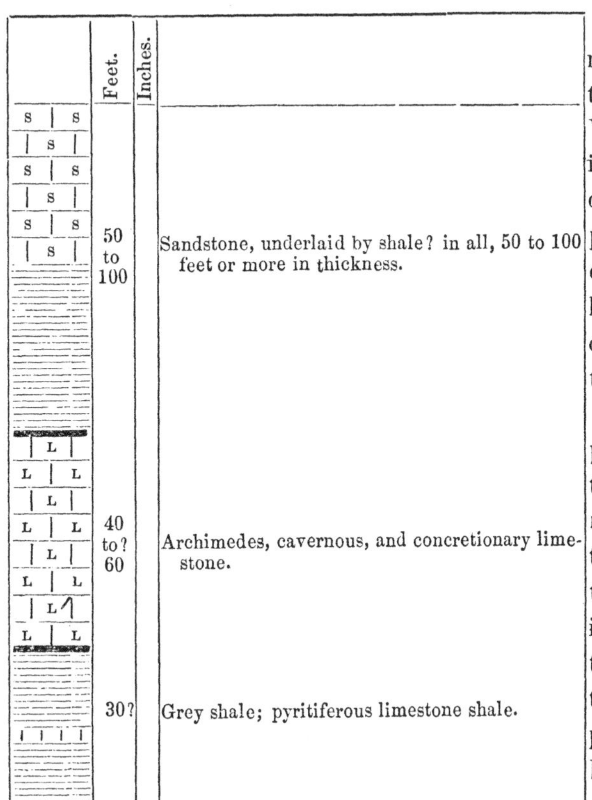

	Feet.	Inches.	
	50 to 100		Sandstone, underlaid by shale? in all, 50 to 100 feet or more in thickness.
	40 to? 60		Archimedes, cavernous, and concretionary limestone.
	30?		Grey shale; pyritiferous limestone shale.

The succession of the rocks on the waters of the Middle Fork of White river, is exhibited in the accompanying diagram, in which the position of the bed of dark grey, pyritiferous limestone is shown, included in the shales at the base of the section.

Several so-called "sulphur springs," rise through the black bituminous shales, at the bottom of the sections, in the central part of Washington county. The water of one, which was obtained from John May's place, one mile south of Fayetteville, was found by the application of chemical reagents, to contain, as its principal constituents:

Sulphate of magnesia, (epsom salts).
Sulphate of alumina, a trace.
Sulphate of iron, a trace.
Bi-carbonate of lime.
Bi-carbonate of magnesia.

This water will act as a mild laxative.

County surveyor Ross informed me that there has been some difficulty in running lines with the compass, in the valleys and along the spurs of some of the hills, with what is considered the true variation in this part of the state, of 8 deg. 30 min. The iron ores which I have seen on the surface, viz: limonite ores and protocarbonate of iron, do not affect the magnetic needle; neither have ores of lead any influence on it; it is only native iron, iron ores containing a combination of peroxide and protoxide, in the proportion of about 69 per cent. of the former, and 31 of the latter, and magnetic iron pyrites, containing about 40 per cent. of sulphur and 60 of iron, that attract the needle. Those localities will require, therefore to be examined hereafter for such ores, when the survey of Washington is made in detail.

Samples of the red upland soil of this county were collected, for future chemical analysis, from John Rieffs' farm, on section 31, township 16 north, range 30 west, where the growth is white-oak, hickory, overcup oak, hackberry, walnut, box-elder, slippery-elm, black-ash, dogwood, and black locust, with an undergrowth of papaw, spice, and large grape vines.

This soil is a good sample of the red uplands of the centre of Washington county; it resembles the Cane-hill land, but is less siliceous; it overlies, and has been mostly derived from, the Archimedes limestone and its associate shales.

The ridge that divides the waters of the West fork of White river from those of the Illinois river, is composed of the same series of shales, limestone, and sandstone, as already described, at Orion Rieffs, on Wood's branch. Here, however, the junction of the shale with the limestone can be seen better than at that locality.

Near the bed of the branch, that runs by Bryant's house, a pyritiferous dark limestone is interstratified in the shale, similar to that on Wood's branch. Twenty feet over this is the base of the limestone, which is about 25 feet in thickness. Eighty feet higher is the top of the sandstone, but this level does not represent its true thickness, since the limestone rises so rapidly to the north-west that it reaches the surface under John Tennyson's farm on the top of the hill, not half a mile from Bryant's.

A bed of coal of six to seven inches, is reported by Bryant, on the Davis place, on the waters of the Illinois; one a foot thick at J. Phillips', on the waters of the West fork; a bed of 1 foot to 18 inches on the west side of the Davis ridge, south of Henry Ross's, and also on Morrison's place; and a 6 to 8 inches seam at Curlis's, low down in the Boston range of mountains. The outcrop on the Morrison place is generally considered the best coal for blacksmiths' use, in this part of Washington county.

Some of the upper layers of limestone, at A. Byrants', contain a considerable per centage of oxide of iron, and might come under the denomination of *Eisenkalkstein* of the Germans. A black bed of limestone is also interstratified in the mass of limestones, besides the band included in the underlying shale.

Near the line between township 15 and 16, where the Cane Hill road crosses the head of a branch, a locality was pointed out to me where copper ore has been supposed to exist. I could see no surface indications to corroberate this opinion, neither do I consider the rock, which forms the surface, at all favorable for metalliferous veins. A much more likely thing to be discovered in the rocks of this part of Washington county, where they form synclinal folds or troughs, is salt. By boring a few hundred feet, in some favorable position, it is highly probable a productive brine might be reached. Such a place is the Clay lick, on the property of Maj. John Billingsley, on the east prong of the Illinois river, near where the mountain road crosses that stream. I tested water which oozes up in this lick, and found it to contain a notable quantity of chloride of sodium, or common salt, some chloride of magnesium, and only a trace of sulphates.

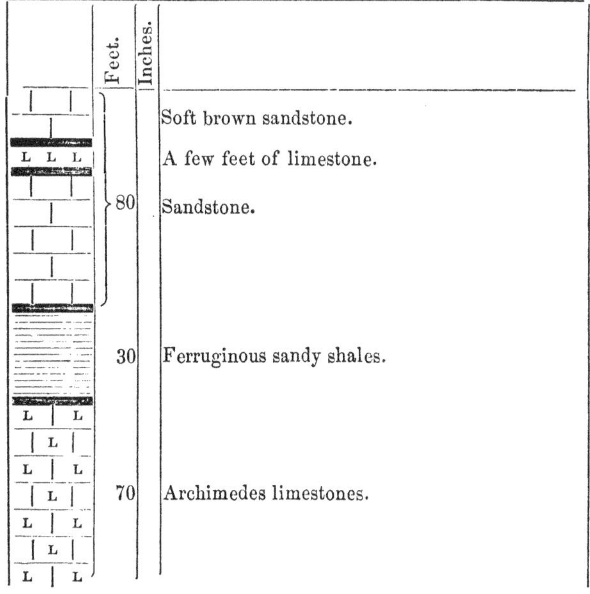

The succession, in the ridge south-west of where the road crosses the East fork of the Illinois river, is represented in the annexed diagram, the levels commencing in the bed of the East fork of the Illinois river, and extending to the top of the ridge, over which the road passes.

On the waters of the same branch of the Illinois river, on Dr. Kuykendall's place, a fine chalybeate spring issues from the bed of ferruginous sandstone of the millstone grit series. This water has a powerful deoxidizing effect, instantly blackening a silver solution, even without the addition of ammonia; from this fact and the comparative small amount of carbonic acid present, it is probable that the protoxide of iron present, is held in solution by some organic acid. This water will probably be found to have valuable alterative and tonic effects combined.

About a quarter of a mile from Dr. Kuykendall's, there is also a sulphur spring, which I tested and found it to contain, as its principal constituents:

Free sulphuretted hydrogen.
Chloride of sodium.
Chloride of magnesium.
Only a trace of sulphates.
Bi-carbonate of lime.
Bi-carbonate of magnesia.

This water, having more saline matter (particularly chlorides) than the water tested at Thomas', 2 miles from Fayetteville, will be found more laxative in its effects; but it is doubtful whether its alterative effects will be as decided, since the proportion of sulphur appears to be less. As iodides are usually an accompaniment of chlorides, this water will probably be found useful in reducing glandular swellings.

At the blacksmith's shop, near the sulphur spring, I saw several specimens of coal, found in this county, and obtained information in regard to the localities of others; viz: the Morrow coal, 14 inches thick, considered to be the best for blacksmith's use; the Dyer coal, 12 inches thick, found on the second bench of the Boston mountain, which is a heavier coal than the former, but contains impurities; Barnet's bank, about 11 inches thick, on the waters of Cove creek; and Store's bank, three quarters of a mile beyond, and about the same thickness as that at Barnet's.

On Cane hill, close by James Mitchell's house, the Archimedes limestone is well exposed, and is quite cavernous. One cave, near Wm. Mitchell's house, is about 180 feet long, and seems to have been the resort of bears and other wild animals, in former times. It occupies precisely the same position as the one which I visited near Orion Rieffs. The succession of the rocks on Cane hill is only a modification of the preceding section.

1. Fine grained sandstone, 15 to 20 feet.
2. Limestone, a few feet.
3. Coarse yellow sandstone, 40 feet.
4. Greenish grindstone grit, 45 to 70 feet.
5. Archimedes limestone, 60 feet.
6. Marly shales in the bed of the branch.

The blacksmiths of Boonsboro obtain a coal from section 16, township 14 north, range 32 west, about three quarters of a mile from town; it is 6 or 8 inches thick: this is the most westerly outcrop of coal known in this county.

Some iron ore is reported in Vineyard township, which I have not yet examined.

A bold spring issues at Boonsboro, from under a bench of Archimedes limestone, 45 feet in thickness. The new college has been built on a commanding point on the shaly sandstones that occupy the hill, immediately above the platform of limestone. Beneath these are dark shales, succeeded, in the descending order, by an even-bedded, brown freestone, very suitable for building purposes. The road to the Barren fork of the Illinois river, passes for several miles on this building stone, which, being often disjoined and displaced from the giving way of the underlying shale, renders the road exceedingly rough. This underlying shale is of no great thickness, and overlies chert and cherty limestone, which forms a mural escarpment on the north bank of the Barren fork, extending down to the bed of that stream.

The different beds and their order of superposition, from the schistose sandstone of College hill, to the cherty limestone of the Barren fork of the Illinois river, are shown in the annexed section:

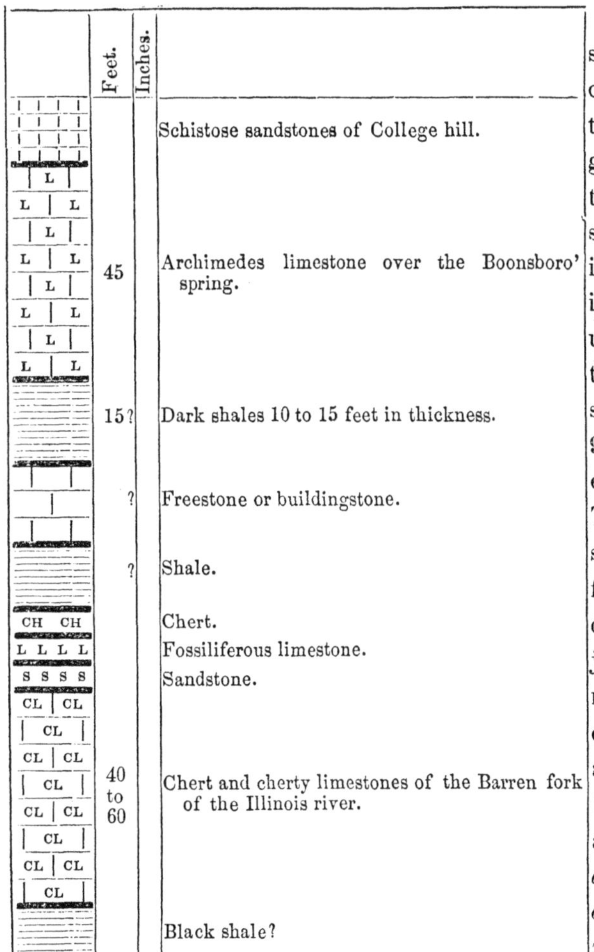

A modification is observable in this section, causing it to differ from those sections previously given of the strata under the Archimedes limestone: it consists in the introduction of the building stone amongst the underlying shales. Near the Barren fork, the strata have a strong dip, 9 to 13 deg. north north-east and north-east. The fossiliferous limestone lies in pavement form, with a regular and deeply marked system of joints, having a course north-west and south-east. The most abundant fossils in this rock are *Terebratula plano-sulcata* and *planum-bona; Productus cora* and a *Productus* allied to *P. semi-reticulatus;* a *favosite* resembling the *basaltica*, but so deeply imbedded and firmly attached in the substance of the rock that they could not be properly examined in place, nor detached without defacing them in such a manner that the disposition of the rows of connecting pores could not be seen so as to determine their specific character.

Both *Productus cora* and *Terebratula plano-sulcata* were found, also, in the overlying chert.

This limestone has marly and shaly partings.

The rock which forms the immediate cliff on the Barren fork, above Morrow's house, and extends down to the bed of that stream, is a very rugged and cherty limestone.

Some loose pieces of lead ore having been found in the bed of the Barren fork, some shallow pits and shafts were sunk in the bluff above, into this cherty limestone, and about 100 pounds of lead ore taken out from amongst the red clay and loose chert, some of which will yield 70 to 80 per cent of lead. Here we have a further confirmation of the lead bearing character of this barren cherty limestone formation.

This rock does not appear to be as thick here as further to the north, since shale has been struck in Morrow's well beneath this rock.

Some "gravel mineral" has also been found in the bed of the Barren fork of the Illinois, near the mill, six miles from Evansville.

The fossiliferous limestone was again seen, three and a half miles from Evansville, overlaying dark ferruginous, and light colored chert.

The succession in Vineyard township is, therefore, approximately as follows:

1. Fine grained siliceous rock, approaching to the texture of whetstones in its character.
2. Limestone.
3. Shale?
4. Yellowish coarse sandstone.
5. Finer grained schistose sandstone of the character of grindstone grit.
6. Archimedes or other limestones.
7. Dark shale rocks.
8. Brown freestone.
9. Shale.
10. Fossiliferous chert.
11. Fossiliferous limestone with marly and shaly partings.
12. Chert and
13. Cherty limestone.
14. Black shale.

All of these strata belong to the millstone grit and underlying subcarboniferous group.

Soon after leaving Evansville, we ascended a high ridge, 550 feet above the Barren fork, in the gap through which the road passes.

On the north-west slope of this spur of the Boston mountain range, the outcropping ledges of rock are mostly sandstone and subcarboniferous limestone, with some alternations of shale. In this side the Archimedes limestone was observed at an elevation of 240 feet. On the south-east slope of the mountain an immense mass of marly shale makes its appearance, with some intercalated beds of limestone. The top of this marly shale is 230 feet below the summit. It is at least 100 feet in thickness, down to the junction of this shale and an underlying bed of limestone.

The rocks are evidently much disturbed in this mountain. At one point in the descent, a dip of 4 deg. south-west was observed; but a short distance further the dip was reversed.

CRAWFORD COUNTY.

Close to the spring, at the foot of the mountain over which we passed from the Barren fork of the Illinois to Lee's creek, the Archimedes limestone is in place, 260 feet below the level of the principal mass of corresponding limestone, in the section of the north-west slope of the mountain.

There is no doubt a dislocation of the whole of the rocks of the mountain with a subsidence to the south-east, which causes so sudden a depression of this limestone.

Associated with *Archimedes* at the spring, near the foot of the mountain, on Lee's creek, occurs *Agassizocrinus conicus*.

Lee's creek meanders for many miles at the base of high cliffs and slopes of the spurs of the Boston mountain range, which are composed of sandstones, shales and limestone, belonging to the age of the millstone grit and subcarboniferous group, the strata gradually dipping down stream towards the south. No coal has ever yet been discovered on this part of Lee's creek, but near its head, 15 miles above Alfred Smith's place, a bed is represented as occurring and ranging from 10 to 12 inches in thickness.

Half a mile below Alfred Smith's farm, sandstone was observed dipping 10 deg. to the south-east, the Archimedes limestone being no longer visible above the bed of Lee's creek.

One of the most remarkable features in the scenery of north-western Arkansas is the " Natural Dam," represented in the steel plate engraving forming the frontispiece to this volume. It is formed by a solid bed of sandstone, from 6 to 8 feet in thickness, which runs entirely across the bed of Lee's creek, forming a natural barrier to the descent of the water, in consequence of the gradual dip of the rock *up stream* towards the north-east, at an angle of 4 to 5 deg., being just the proper inclination to dam the water back, and throw it to a sluice, that might be solidly and permanently fixed to this rock wall near where it runs into the north-west bank.

The log mill, seen in the frontispiece, is one of the rudest description; hardly capable of grinding 30 to 40 bushels per day; quite insufficient even for the accommodation of the immediate neighbors. The efficiency of this natural dam, running, as it does, from bank to bank, with just the proper inclination and a slightly diagonal direction, across the entire water course; the solidity of its natural masonry, destined to indure for ages; its situation in the midst of a valley, which though contracted in its dimensions by the mountain fastnesses that bound it on both sides, is, nevertheless fertile and capable of supporting a moderate population; all combine to make this natural mill-site an object of great interest, and its many advantages would justify the erection of a substantial building, fitted up with all the modern improvements in the machinery of a well regulated business grist-mill; this would attract customers, not alone from the valleys of the different branches of Lee's creek, but also from the neighboring mountains, and more distant settlements, and contribute, perhaps, more than any improvement that could be introduced into the country, to attract fresh population and render the condition of its present inhabitants independent, comfortable and agreeable. Notwithstanding the continual wear to which this member of the millstone grit series—more durable than its associate beds—is continually subject; not alone from the mechanical force exerted by the running waters of Lee's creek, but from the almost irresistible power of expansion, caused by the alternate thawing and freezing of the water, continually permeating its mass; it stands yet, a monument of ages, bearing testimony to the strength and insolubility of the siliceous cement that binds the particles together, and the stability of the individual grains of which its substance is composed; and it affords, at the same time, a striking example how induring architectural edifices may be made, if constructed of such freestone, judiciously selected, well built, and strongly jointed with good mortar.

The ridge, passed over about two miles from the Natural Dam, is about 390 feet above Lee's creek, and is composed, so far as can be seen, of sandstones and shales of the age of the millstone grit; with, perhaps, a capping of some of the lower members of the overlying coal measures.

It is nearly of the same materials that compose the high range of hills above the town of Van Buren, which has a commanding view over the valley of the Arkansas. From these heights, in a clear day, Fort Smith can be seen, while the bluff opposite to it and the glistening water line, marking the bend of the Arkansas river, where it emerges from Indian territory and sweeps past Fort Smith, can be distinctly seen at all times; also the distant range of hills, running from the Choctaw country towards Sebastian county, including the House and Sugar Loaf mountains; with the small prairie in the middle ground, which is said to be underlaid by coal.* The accompanying wood cut [see p. 127] is engraved from a rapid sketch of this extensive prospect, comprising the various objects above enumerated, taken from the above heights, north-west of the town of Van Buren. At the foot of this hill, and in the cuts of the ravines immediately back of the town of Van Buren, 23 to 25 feet of shale are exposed, the lower portion of which, for ten feet, is black and bituminous. One hundred and ten feet more of shale have been passed through in the well sunk at Pennywit & Scott's mill, including, near the bottom, a small seam of coal, reported 18 inches thick.

The strata immediately exposed, adjacent to the town of Van Buren, are:

Sandstone.

Grey shale and shaly sandstone, with ferruginous segregations, 30 feet.

Black and reddish shales, 15 feet.

Blackish grey shale, with segregations of carbonate of iron, 15 feet.

Shales, including 18 inch coal, passed through in the steam mill well below the town of Van Buren, 110 feet.

These shales lie no doubt at the base of the millstone grit, as we found in the overlying sandstone, 150 or 200 feet above these shales, the same curious impressions of plants (?) which occur in the millstone grit of Van Buren county, near Theodore Goodlow's, showing the great extent and remarkable persistency of this formation, as it extends through the northern counties of Arkansas.

The sandstones and shales seen in section in the Ozark mountains, north of Van Buren, have much the lithological character of the "Barren Coal Measures" of the eastern coal field of Kentucky, in which schistose earthy sandstones predominate; but it is not improbable that they may be all referrible to the millstone grit, which seems to have an enormous expansion, and to occupy great areas in the north-west counties of Arkansas.

Four or five miles north-west of Van Buren, in some of the deep cuts, where red and ferruginous shales are exposed, more or less iron ore was observed, but mostly of a siliceous character.

The shales, at the base of the hills bordering on the Arkansas river, noted in the preceding sections, seem to underlie a great extent of country not only in this county, but for a great distance down the valley of the Arkansas river, in a south-east direction.

As limestone is a very scarce article in this county, it may be well to take note that there is a dark-grey, ferruginous, calcareous bed that crops out, not only near the sulphur springs in the bed of the Sulphur branch of

* This country, south of the Arkansas river has not yet been explored.

Webber's creek, but on Baker's hill, 2 miles from the springs, and on a hillside, 7 miles north-west of Van Buren and 1 mile from the Dripping springs. This rock will doubtless burn to lime, and yield an article which, though dark, will probably make a good mortar for building purposes.

It is very probable that this ferruginous, fossiliferous limestone may be found about one-third of the distance up the high hill back of Van Buren; for, being encrusted with a rusty external coating, it is difficult to distinguish it, in its native bed, from the associate sandstones. This limestone varies from 3 to 8 inches in thickness.

The Pennywit sulphur water was tested at the fountain head. Its principal constituents are:

Bi-carbonate of lime.

Bi-carbonate of magnesia.

Chloride of sodium, or common salt.

Chloride of magnesium.

Trace of sulphate of soda, (glauber-salts.)

Trace of sulphate of magnesia, (epsom-salts.)

A trace of free sulphuretted hydrogen.

The taste of this water, and the small, white fibrous sediment, formed in the gum log through which it rises, favor the view that there is some sulphur in this water, combined either with some organic principle, or other substance. It will be observed that this water contains a notable quantity of common salt; this fact, taken in connection with the formation through which it wells up, and the cellular nature of the sandstones in the vicinity of the springs, renders it probable that, if the Sulphur branch of the Webber fork of Lee's creek flows in a synclinal trough, (as it very likely does, from the dip of the strata being reversed towards the valley of the Arkansas river), a good, profitable brine might be reached by putting down a systematic boring in the neighborhood of these springs.

For further remarks on this county, see the Report of the Assistant Geologist.

No. 14----View across the Arkansas river into Sebastian county, from the heights above Van Buren, in Crawford county, the House and Sugar-loaf mountains in the distance; the site of Fort Smith in the middle ground on the right.

JOHNSON COUNTY.

My own observations in this county have been confined, as yet, to the coal region of the Spadra.*

The best locality for the examination of the Spadra coal, is a few hundred yards above the confluence of Spadra creek with the Arkansas river, on the property of E. B. Alston. An opening has been made there into this coal, a foot or two above low water, where it can be seen under a high bank of dark shales and over flagstones, which appear in the bed of Spadra creek, with, probably, some intervening fire-clay which could not, however, be seen, in consequence of the water that had collected in the drift. This coal is three feet thick, including a clay parting of 3 to 4 inches, one foot from the bottom of the bed. The underlying flagstones, in the bed of Spadra, dip from 3 to 5 deg. to the north, in which dip the coal is doubtless implicated; but the state of the opening prevented me from making an observation for dip in the drift.

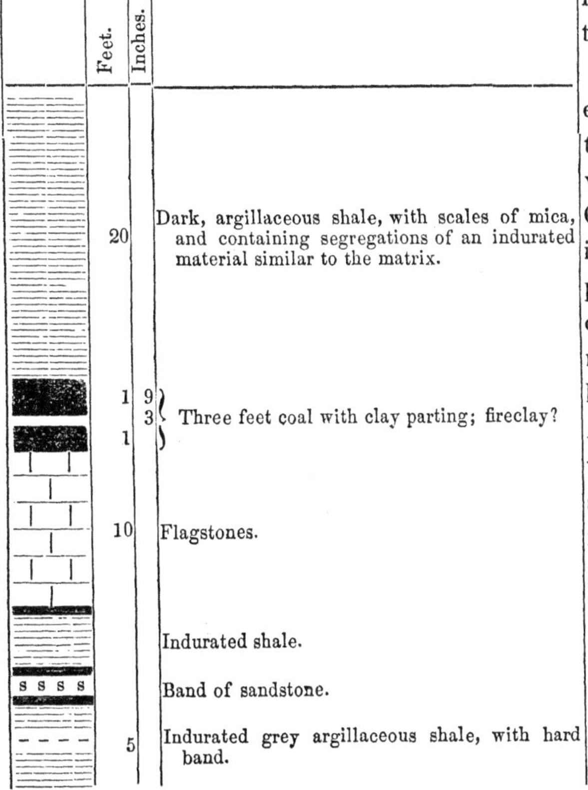

The annexed section exhibits the position of this coal, and its relation with the associate beds. On Spadra creek, nothing lower than the upper layers of flagstones can be seen; but, on the north bank of the Arkansas river, under E. B. Alston's house, the continuation of these flagstones can be observed, resting on indurated, argillaceous shale, with hard bands of sandstone, extending down to low water of that stream, as shown in the lower part of the preceding section.

*For further remarks on this county, see the Report of the Assistant Geologist.

9

The shale that forms the roof of the coal, is considerably indurated and of an argillo-siliceous composition, with disseminated scales of mica, and includes segregations of a material not very different from its matrix, but harder and heavier. Some obscure stems and long slender leaves or glumes of some plant can be discovered, by splitting up the shale; but their specific and even generic characters are difficult to make out. The dark shales, forming the roof of this coal, are visible in sections at several bends of Spadra creek, for more than a mile above its mouth. From the dip of the rock, there is no doubt that this coal could be reached by shafts of reasonable depth, sunk in or near the town of Clarksville.

The character of this coal is worthy of especial notice. The approximate chemical analysis here given shows it to be a semi-anthracite, rich in carbon, and containing a small proportion of ochre-colored ashes; with only 8.4 per cent. of volatile matter, including moisture expelled at 300 deg. of Fahrenheit's thermometer. Its specific gravity is 1,335.

The approximate analysis gives:

Volatile matters	8.4	Moisture	0.5
		Volatile combustible gases	7.9
Coke	91.6	Fixed carbon	85.6
		Ashes (ochre yellow)	6.0
	100.0		100.0

This coal contains a far higher per centage of fixed carbon than any western coal that has ever been analyzed in my labaratory, except some coals* which I received from Arkansas some years before the commencement of the survey.

In this respect, the Spadra coal resembles the coals of the Shamokin basin, of Pennsylvania; especially the Zerbe's run semi-anthracite; containing, in fact, 1.35 per cent. more fixed carbon than that coal, and nearly 1 per cent. less ashes. Its gaseous matter is chiefly hydrogen, as its luminous property is so feeble as hardly to be distinguishable by daylight, when this coal is exposed to a red heat in an open spoon. The existence of a semi-anthracite coal in the west is the more surprising, since the for-

* One of the specimens of coal was said to be from White county, and most probably from the bed mentioned in the section of that county. It had a specific gravity of 1.39, and gave by analysis

Volatile matters, including moisture	10
Fixed carbon in coke	86
Ashes	4
	100

Another specimen said to be from the Petite Jean mountain yielded:

Volatile matters, including moisture	8.5
Coke, including ashes	91.5
	100.0

mation, in which it occurs, is comparatively level, undisturbed, and bearing little evidence of metamorphism or change by internal heat; while the coals of similar composition in Pennsylvania occur, as we are informed by Hayes and Rogers, only in coal fields and isolated patches, in the most disturbed portions of the Apalachian chain, and are associated with some of the boldest flexures and greatest dislocations of the whole coal region of that State. The nearest rock of undoubted igneous origin to this coal, at present known to me in Arkansas, is situated in Hot Spring county,* some sixty miles, in a direct line, south of the Spadra; yet, here we have a coal, possessing all the chemical properties of the semi-anthracites, that are usually found in the midst of the most striking evidence of decided igneous action. The inference which I draw from these facts, is that, though granite and other hypogene (nether-born) rocks do not actually reach the surface in Johnson county, as far as at present known, they must be near enough the surface to have exerted an igneous action, sufficient to have permeated the strata, now found on Spadra creek, with heated vapors or gases, that have expelled the greater portion of the gaseous matter; or else this coal has been subject to some extraordinary chemical agency, by which carburetted hydrogen has been removed. It is hardly possible that the Spadra coal can owe its present composition to any difference in the vegetation from which it was originally produced; since it would be, in that case, a strange exception to anything previously observed in the bituminous coal fields in any of the states west of the Alleghany mountains. But the peculiar fissured structure of the Spadra coal favors the idea, that the volatile matter has been expelled by a process more rapid than can be attributed to slow chemical changes, unaided by an elevation of temperature; since the escape of the volatile matter by heat causes an expansion of the particles, and that severing the coal, gives it a friable tendence. The Spadra coal, in common with the semi-anthracites of the Shamokin coal field of Pennsylvania, possesses this peculiar subdivision into cuboidal lumps, indicative of a quicker escape of the expansible gases than would take place under prolonged chemical evolution.

This question of a former subterranean igneous action is interesting, not only in its relation to the influence it may have exerted upon the coals of the Arkansas valley, but, also, in its important bearing upon the metalliferous character of the underlying geological formations; since it is a matter of experience, that rocks are more apt to be intersected by metallic veins in districts adjacent to axes of dislocation; and these are a frequent accompaniment of subterranean, igneous action.

* It is likely that granite or some other igneous rock may be found in Montgomery connty.

From the insight obtained into the chemical composition of this coal, by an approximate chemical analysis, I am led to believe that the valuable properties of this coal have hitherto been overlooked.

The experiments of Johnson, De la Beche, Playfair, Hayes and Rogers, on different coals, as well as the experience in the east, go to prove that, though the semi-anthracites may not be the best adapted for some purposes, they have far higher heating and considerably more reducing powers than the best bituminous coals; and, besides, the semi-anthracites will evaporate, in a given time, from 15 to 20 per cent. more pounds of water than bituminous coals. It has been shown, moreover, by Hayes and Rogers, that the efficiency of the semi-anthracites in these operations is due to the total amount of carbon that enters into the composition of both coke and volatile combustible matter, but principally to the amount of *fixed* carbon to be found in the coke alone; for it appears that the volatile carbon, i. e. the carbon which escapes as gas in the form of carburetted hydrogen, contributes but little to the actual heating effect, since the greater part of the caloric, generated by the combustion of this gas, becomes latent or absorbed by its change of state, from the solid or condensed condition in which it exists in the coal, into the elastic gaseous form it assumes during combustion.

Now, the analysis of the Spadra coal proves it to contain 25 to 30 per cent. more fixed carbon in the coke than the best bituminous coals* of Europe or America; and it even exceeds, by 1.35 per cent, that of the richest semi-anthracites of Pennsylvania; it has 3.83 per cent. more fixed carbon in the coke than the celebrated "Parker vein," of George creek valley, Maryland.

Of the forty-three coals reported on by Johnson, in his work on American coals, the semi-anthracite of Lyken's valley approaches nearest in composition to the Spadra coal, as will be seen by comparing the following approximate analyses of these two coals:

	Spadra.	*Lyken valley.*
Volatile combustible matter	7.9	6.88
Fixed carbon	85.6	83.84
Ashes	6.0	9.25

The composition of the Spadra coal approaches so nearly to that of the Lyken valley coal of Pennsylvania, that we may assume the practical

* A sample of Pittsburg coal, analyzed by Johnson, gave 54.93 fixed carbon. A specimen, analyzed by Dr. Robert Peter, 65.30 fixed carbon in coke. A specimen of Youghiogheny coal, analyzed by myself, gave 60.14 fixed carbon in coke. Johnson's specimen must have been an inferior specimen, for the best Pittsburg coals always give a larger per centage of fixed carbon in the coke than 54.93.

properties observed by experiments on this coal by Johnson, to be very nearly the same as those that would be found in the Spadra coal, if subjected to the same tests; I, therefore, subjoin some of the most important characters representing the efficiency of that coal, compared with Pittsburg coal: one of the best known and most generally useful of our western bituminous coals.

While one part of Pittsburg bituminous coal will generate 8.2 pounds of steam at a temperature of 212 deg., the same quantity of Lyken valley semi-anthracite, will generate 9.46 pounds of steam at 212 deg.

While one cubic foot of Pittsburg coal will generate 384 pounds of steam, one cubic foot of Lyken valley semi-anthracite will generate 459 pounds of steam.

The reducing powers of semi-anthracites is considerably greater than that of bituminous coal; as is shown by the relative amounts of litharge reduced to lead by these same coals: 28.89 parts being reduced by Pittsburgh coal, while 32.6 are reduced by the same quantity of Lyken valley semi-anthracite.

The Spadra coal resembles still more closely the Zerbe's Run coal of the Shaneokin coal field of Pennsylvania, as will be seen by the annexed comparative approximate analyses:

	Spadra.	*Zerbe's Run.*
Volatile combustible matter............	7.90	7.31
Fixed carbon.........................	85.6	84.25
Ashes................................	6.0	6.11

Hayes and Rogers estimate the water evaporated at 212 deg., by 1 pound Zerbe's Run coal, at 9.58 pounds. The rate of evaporation per hour, to one square foot of grate, is 88.92, while the average for bituminous coal is 70.92, under the same circumstances.

The combined evaporative power and speed for the Zerbe's Run semi-anthracite are represented by the numbers 4777.4, while taking equal bulks of the averages of bituminous coals, under the same circumstances, the numbers would be 3456.0.

These semi-anthracites burn after the manner of the natural coke of Virginia, throwing out, when fully ignited, an intense heat, accompanied by a blue flame.

They require, it is true, a tolerably strong draft to bring them into full combustion, and, therefore, are perhaps not so suitable for open grates as the more inflamable bituminous coals, requiring usually the addition of blowers to increase the current of air passing through the grate, until the fire is fairly started; and this is probably the reason why these coals, when first introduced into the eastern cities, were rejected as altogether unmanageable and impracticable. Now, even the harder anthracites are in common use in Philadelphia and New York for heating apartments, and sometimes in open grates, with temporary blowers; and it is now universally admitted that, for forges, rolling mills, and blast furnaces for the manufacture of iron, the semi-anthracites are unsurpassed.

No. 11—PART OF THE BOSTON MOUNTAIN RANGE, NEWTON COUNTY.

GENERAL SUMMARY, INFERENCES, AND REMARKS IN CONCLUSION.

The three leading formations of the northern counties of Arkansas, west of Black river to the Indian boundary, and north of the Arkansas river, are:

First. The millstone grit, with its associate shales, and conglomerate.

Second. The subcarboniferous limestone, and its associate chert, shales, and sandstones.

Third. The magnesian limestones, and their associate sandstones, calciferous sandrocks and chert, belonging to the lower silurian period.

The formation known in Kentucky, Indiana, and Tennessee, under the name of the knob sandstone, is absent, or only very obscurely represented. It is doubtful, too, whether the grey and black bituminous shales and slates, belonging to the devonian period, are to be found in Arkansas. There are a few encrinital and variegated limestones and associated chert, which intervene between the magnesian limestones of lower silurian date and the subcarboniferous chert and limestones; these may belong to the devonian era, but, as yet, I have no positive evidence to decide fully this question.

No rocks have yet come under observation which I have been able to refer unequivocally to the upper silurian period, such as occur in Jefferson county, Kentucky, Clarke county, Indiana, and elsewhere in these states, under the coralline beds of the falls of the Ohio.

East of Black river, in Greene, Poinsett, and Randolph counties, incoherent sands, loose and cemented gravel, and clays of quaternary date, prevail.

No crystalline* or hypogene rocks, i. e., no rocks which have been protruded from beneath, as mountain masses, dykes or veins, possessing the structure of granite or syenite, have been observed, as yet, by the geological corps, *north* of the Arkansas river: i. e., *in the part of the state on which I am now reporting.*

*A red granite is reported on Spavinaw creek, near the Cherokee line. Whether this be correct information I am, at present, unable to say, as I have not examined the locality.

Arkansas is destined, I believe, to take the lead of all the western states, in her resources in ores of zinc and manganese.

The magnesian limestone, belonging to the lower silurian period, seems to be the great repository of the zinc ore, of which there are three principal varieties: the pure carbonate of zinc—the calamine or smithsonite of mineralogists—the silicate of zinc or electric calamine—and the sulphuret of zinc or blende, (black-jack of the miner).

The analyses of these ores prove them to be at least as rich as, if not richer and purer than, the zinc ores of the most noted localities in Europe; and there is no reason why they should not be worked with profit to the miner and smelter, as well as with benefit to the State of Arkansas in particular, and to the United States in general.

The manganese ores have, chiefly, been found in the cavernous subcarboniferous limestones. These ores appear to be very abundant. A compact variety allied to psilomelane, is the kind which I found most common on the surface, but there are other softer varieties, which have proved, on analysis, to compare favorably with those of Thuringia, the most celebrated European locality.

Arkansas promises, also, to afford considerable lead ore, which occurs both in the magnesian limestones of lower silurian date, and in the subcarboniferous limestones; also in the slates of the base of the millstone grit, where these border on the confines of the granite region of Pulaski county.

The lead ore in this latter position is rich in silver, probably more so than the argentiferous galena of Europe, which have been wrought to any extent. The only ore, which has been cupelled in my laboratory, that surpasses it in the per centage of contained silver, is some of the steel-grey, finely crystalline argentiferous galena from Villeport, near Lozere, in France.

Fragments of a porous lead ore, picked up among the rubbish at the mouth of one of the shafts in Pulaski county, yielded by cupellation from the reduced lead, at the rate of 224 ounces from the ton of 2,000 pounds; and a specimen of a bright, steel-grey ore, finely crystalline in its structure, from the same mines, obtained in Little Rock, gave as much as 339.2 ounces to the ton of 2,000 pounds.

The cherty limestone, which underlies the barrens and prairies of the north-west part of the state, promises to afford rich deposits of lead ore, as the geological formation is a complete counterpart of that around the already famous lead mines of Granby, in Newton county, Missouri.

The lead region in the lower magnesian limestones, bears more of the character of those in Taney county, Missouri.

Iron ore promises to be abundant in all the three leading formations; especially in Pope, Pulaski, Randolph, Lawrence, Madison, Washington, and Benton.

Near the junction of the subcarboniferous limestones and the saccharoidal sandstone, overlying the lower magnesian limestones, there are encrinital, mottled and variegated limestones, which take a good polish, and will make, at many localities, a fine marble rock, particularly near the corner of Carroll, Newton, and Searcy counties.

The best and thickest coal, which I have yet seen in Arkansas, is the Spadra coal of Johnson county. It is a semi-anthracite, even richer in fixed carbon than the celebrated Zerbe's run coal of the Shamokin coal field of Pennsylvania, and is superior, for manufacturing purposes, to any western coal at present known, where durability, intense heat and reduction are required. Its thickness is three feet. It crops out close to the Arkansas river above the mouth of Spadra creek, and extends back into the interior of Johnson county.

During the geological survey of northern Arkansas, I have been strongly impressed with two facts: one is the vast extent, both vertically and superficially, of the millstone grits and the associate shales. There are eight whole counties that are already known to be almost entirely occupied by this formation; besides a large portion of six other counties: the other is the immense quantity of silex in the shape of chert, buhrstone, and chalcedonic flint, irregularly mixed and segregated amongst the rocks, especially the limestones; or diffused as quartz, in veins, amongst the sandstones. I have traveled for days and weeks upon these siliceous formations, both amongst the rocks of subcarboniferous and lower silurian date.

It remains for me to define approximately the general boundary between the millstone grit and the subcarboniferous limestones, since it is north and west of that line that the lead and zinc ores are accessible for mining, within reasonable depths, excepting, indeed, those deposits in Pulaski county which border on the region of the igneous rocks.

Commencing on White river, on Shield's bluff, where the old Cherokee boundary line strikes that stream, it runs nearly west, through the southern tier of townships in Izard county; thence, it preserves the same westerly course through the northern tier of townships, in Van Buren county, bearing more to the north-west; thence it meanders with the highest ranges of the Boston mountain, in the southern part of Newton and the central part of Madison county, towards Fayetteville, in Washington county;

thence diverging to the south, it reaches the Indian boundary line, in the south-west corner of that county.

Its southern limits cannot yet be defined, since this formation extends south of the Arkansas river, beyond the range of our present geological reconnoissance.

All the accessible veins and deposits of lead, zinc, and manganese ores, at present known, are situated to the north of this line; they doubtless extend beneath a portion of the area occupied by the millstone grit; but, probably, are too deeply seated in the midst of the high mountainous district, south of this line, to be reached by the miner, except near the valley of the Arkansas river, in Pulaski county.

The coal beds interstratified amongst the beds of the millstone grit, are too thin to be worked profitably by drifts.

Where the porous sandstones of the millstone grit form synclinal troughs under the drainage of the country, there are favorable positions for reaching productive brines by boring. Several of these saline troughs seem to exist, six to twelve miles north of the Arkansas river, in Crawford, Franklin, Johnson, and Conway counties.

Large quantities of iron are disseminated amongst the beds of the millstone grit; when associated with the sandstones of that formation, it is generally too sandy to be smelted with profit and advantage; but the underlying ferruginous shale in many places offers encouragement for the search of the iron manufacturer, as for instance, at the Dwight Old Mission, in Pope county; on War Eagle, in Madison county; and the centre of Washington county. The bog iron ore of Pulaski county, 8 miles north-east of Little Rock, promises to be sufficiently extensive to supply a furnace, according to the report of the Assistant Geologist.

The time allotted for working up and reporting on the materials, which have been collected during the field work of this and the preceding season, has been too short to admit of the full digest, due consideration, and minute analysis of all the subjects and specimens now on record, and in the office of the Arkansas survey; we have, in fact, only been able to make a commencement towards a thorough investigation of even the resources now within our reach. If the means are provided, we hope, hereafter to be able to complete this important, interesting and useful work, begun under such favorable auspices.

If the survey is continued, it would be desirable to put at least three corps in the field, in order to carry forward the work as rapidly as possible. For that purpose, the geological appropriation should be equal to that in Missouri; that is, twelve thousand dollars ($12,000) per annum.

With this amount, the geological reconnoissance of the rest of the state could be completed in the next two years, and considerable progress made, at the same time, towards surveying the mineral districts in detail.

As one of the great ulterior objects of the geological survey of the state, is the construction of a geological map, in which the areas of the geological formations can be distinctly laid down, and their boundaries accurately defined, it will become necessary, particularly through the country bordering on the confines of two geological formations, as well as in the mineral districts, to define the ridges, hills, and mountain ranges, on sectional maps, since the limits of formations often conform to, and are intimately connected with, the relief and topography of the country. The law authorizing a geological survey of the state, in detail, should, therefore, provide that the geologist have access to all sectional, county, and other maps; records and profiles of railroads and other surveys, so as to afford him every facility in laying down such topographical and geographical details, as may be necessary for the accurate exhibition of the geology of the state. It may become necessary, too, at the same time, to run a judicious system of levels in connection with lines of odometer measurements over parts of the country, in order to define with accuracy the elements of dip, the thickness of the formations and their individual members, and to form a basis of calculation for identifying equivalent beds, estimating the depth or height at which any known bed of coal, iron ore, or other valuable mineral deposit can be found, when concealed by debris, or carried by the inclination of the strata beneath the water courses.

This can all be done if adequate means are furnished, and it is only by the adoption of such a system of operations, that a *complete detailed* survey of the state can be made.

I may add, in this connection, that, without exceeding the appropriation above named, and with very little additional expense over and above what must necessarily be expended, otherwise, in the various geological departments, a botanical survey of the state could be instituted, if considered advisable, without organizing a corps for that branch alone; and many useful items could, in the same way, be gathered in other departments of the natural history of the state of Arkansas.

The chemical department is already well organized, so that, if the continuance of the survey be provided for, the chemical work can be carried forward, with despatch, upon the same plan as heretofore provided for.

In carrying out such an important work as this, the palæontological department must, of course, not be neglected; that is, the collection of the organic remains or fossils of the different rocks, and the ultimate determination of their generic and specific characters; in fact, without attention to this, the geologist would dispense with one of his principal aids in drawing important practical inferences and proofs corroborative of his assertions. This branch of the survey might appear to some, without due reflection, a matter of little importance; but when we consider that it is the surest and safest guide to the identification of all the formations of sedimentary origin, and even of the individual members of such formations, as for instance, the beds of coal, we discover that it is the index, the criterion, the sign, the "divining rod," if I may so express it, which is to lead the geologist in his search after mineral wealth.

I cannot present the practical importance, as well as the interest connected with the study of these relics of by-gone ages, in a stronger light than by inserting here an extract from my report of the surveys made in behalf of the United States, some years since, in the north-west:

"The study of the organic remains of rocks is, indeed, a most beautiful, a most fascinating research. What can be more extraordinary: that we, the generation of the nineteenth century, should exhume from out the hard substance of the solid rocks, the delicate forms of organic beings of by-gone ages, and display to the wondering eye of the naturalist, even their minute anatomical details? And this, not alone, of races which inhabited this earth in times immediately preceding the human epoch; we are even permitted to contemplate, and restore to our perceptions, the very fishes, molusks, and corals, that swarmed in the carboniferous seas millions of ages ago. The animal matter composing their tissues and bones, is indeed gone, but the simultaneous mineral infiltrations preserve a perfect counterpart. We can depict those remarkable and elegant forms of vegetation which constituted the forests, that fringed the shores of that same treacherous and overwhelming ocean. We seize them in the very act of uncoiling their frond, and unfold to the admiring gaze of the botanist, that luxuriant canopy of foliage that once waved in the sea breeze nurturing their stems. We accomplish even more than this: we can read the records of myriads of the lower orders of animals, that date their existence yet further back than the times that gave growth to trees, now stored up as mineral fuel in the bowels of the earth—to times at least as long prior to the coal formation, as that geological era is antecedent to the present time; we can assign to each its place in the zoological systems, and fill up the gaps in the existing orders of the animal and vegetable kingdoms.

To think that we, at this day, can demonstrate the structure of the eye of some of these—the most ancient races—and even count the lenses by which light was concentrated to the optic nerve, is truly astonishing! Is it then surprising that it should engage the attention of the closest philosopher, and awaken the enthusiasm of the enterprising explorer?

But palæontology is not a study of mere curious, scientic inquiry; it has also its practical inferences, and these of the most important character, with their direct matter-of-fact bearings. In illustration of this view of the subject, permit me, in this connection, to direct the attention of the reader to Figs. 1, 5, and 6, of Table IV.* The fossil corals represented in these engravings, are found imbedded in the subcarboniferous limestones, and near the top of the series; always under the true productive coal bearing beds; never above these, or included in them; and no where else. This geological fact holds good, not only in Iowa, but through the entire range of the subcarboniferous limestones in Indiana, Illinois, Kentucky, and Tennessee. In not a single instance, from the range of the Cumberland mountains, on the east, to the interior of Iowa, on the west, has a workable bed of coal been discovered in a position beneath the strata of limestone containing these corals. In these organic remains, then, we find the surest, the most unerring guide in the search after this valuable article of commerce, that warms our houses, that drives our steam engines, by which we navigate our rivers, lakes, and oceans; that propels the machinery by which we weave our fabrics; that reduces our iron, by which we cultivate our soil, and carry on every conceivable mechanical operation; that refines our metals, that contributes to the production of both the necessaries and luxuries of life, and by which we transmit intelligence with the swiftness of lightning, to stations the most remote. Without the knowledge of this fact, millions of dollars might be expended—have been expended—in fruitless and hopeless mining operations after geological incompatibilities.

All the figures on Table V, A and B,* are equally persistent in their undeviating geological position, quite below the productive coal measures, as well as beneath these same coral bearing beds.

In strategraphical palæontology we have, then, the safest and the most trustworthy index to direct our explorations after mineral treasures in the fossiliferous strata."

* See Geological Report of Wisconsin, Iowa, and Minnesota, 1852.

CHEMICAL REPORT

OF THE

ORES, ROCKS, AND MINERAL WATERS

OF

ARKANSAS,

BY

WILLIAM ELDERHORST, M. D.,

CHEMICAL ASSISTANT TO THE GEOLOGICAL SURVEY.

INTRODUCTORY LETTER.

---o---

CHEMICAL LABORATORY OF THE GEOLOGICAL SURVEY,
New Harmony, Indiana, September, 1858.

DR. DAVID DALE OWEN,
State Geologist of Arkansas:

SIR—In conformity with your instructions, I herewith transmit to you the Chemical Report of the Geological Survey of Arkansas, containing the chemical analyses of such ores, rocks, etc., as you deemed most important for incorporation into this volume.

The analyses have all been performed in the chemical laboratory of the survey, with the exception of the qualitative examinations of the natural waters, which were executed in the field. Among the valuable mineral productions, in which the northern counties of Arkansas abound, special attention has been paid to the ores of zinc. Specimens of the ores from all the principal localities which were visited by us in the first field excursion in the fall of 1857, have been subjected to analysis, and I should not neglect to state, that I have endeavored, by a careful selection of average specimens, to give to those, more directly interested in those mines, a correct idea of the *average value* of these ores. I am happy to say, that the results of my examinations even surpass the favorable opinion which I formed of their value in the field; and there remains no doubt, in my opinion, that with judicious management, the working of these mines and smelting of the ores, extracted therefrom, will prove not only very remunerative to the enterprising miner and smelter, but highly beneficial to that portion of the state in which these mines are situated. Much, however, remains yet to be done with regard to the development of the mineral riches of these counties: analyses ought to be made of the *different kinds* of ore taken from the old mines, as well as of specimens from the newly discovered mines*; all the rocks associated with the ores, ought

*Mr. E. T. Cox collected specimens of ore from new localities during the field-excursion in the spring of 1858, but from some unaccountable reason, the boxes containing them, have not yet arrived.

to be carefully examined (the analyses of a few of them you will find detailed on p. 176, etc.), in order to establish a rational connexion between the general geological features of the country and the mineral deposits, and to discover, if possible, the hidden cause which occasioned the formation of such extensive deposits, and exercised so powerful a pseudomorphic action as is evidenced in that part of the state.

I beg leave to call your attention, in the next place, to the analyses of the ores of manganese. You will perceive, by a glance at the table on p. 166, that the analytical results here are also very favorable; the ores are valuable to the bleacher, the paper and the glass manufacturer, and I confidently believe, that by pursuing a rational system of mining, and examining carefully the neighborhood of the veins on Lafferty creek, an ore still more valuable, the "pyrolusite" of the mineralogists will be discovered, an opinion based on the observation: that the last mentioned mineral almost invariably occurs associated with psilomelane and braunite, the minerals already found. I have endeavored, on p. 167, etc., to establish rational formulas for the composition of these ores, in the expectation of throwing some light on the mutual chemical relation which the various, so closely connected minerals, bear towards each other; I hope that the continuance of the survey may enable me, by an additional series of analyses, to draw some general conclusions as to their formation, mutual relation, and probable origin.

As to the remaining portion of my Report, no further remarks appear necessary: the analyses speak for themselves.

The reasons which prompted me to append a chapter on the "methods of analysis," I have given below.

All which is respectfully submitted,

WILLIAM ELDERHORST,

Chemical Assistant.

ORES OF ZINC.

———o———

The ores from two counties only have as yet been subjected to analysis, viz: those from Lawrence county and Marion county; [one from Independence county, see "Appendix."]

A.—ORES OF ZINC FROM LAWRENCE COUNTY.

Ores, containing zinc, especially in the shape of carbonate of zinc, have been found at numerous localities in this county. The richest diggings are situated in the vicinity of Calamine, and at the time of our visit, the deepest excavations had been made at the localities, designated, respectively, as the Hoppe mine, Bath mine, and Koch mine. Specimens of the ore taken from these three mines, were subjected to analysis. The ore occurs in cavities (pockets and veins) in dolomite, and in most cases, is found imbedded in a stiff, red, feruginous clay. Both, the dolomite and the clay, contain small quantities of zinc, (compare analyses Nos. 32, 34 and 35.) In some cases, however, the ore is closely connected with the dolomite, either adhering to its surface, or filling small cavities in the rock, or traversing the dolomite in small veins, rarely more than a quarter of an inch in diameter.

A.—Ore from the Hoppe mine.

By far the greater quantity of the ore found at this mine, is a massive, amorphous, hydrous carbonate of zinc, of pale grayish-yellow color; soft; breaks easily; powder of a pale cream color; small pieces dissolve readily in dilute hydrochloric acid, with effervescence. The composition of this mineral is given below, No. 1; the analysis may be considered to represent the composition of a fair average-specimen of the whole of the ore brought out from this mine. The ore No. 1, contains, occasionally, cavities in which small yellow crystals of blende (sulphuret of zinc) are found.

Although of comparatively rare occurrence at this locality, large crystals of blende are occasionally met with, sometimes imbedded in dolomite and surrounded by masses of flesh-colored, crystallized smithsonite, (carbonate of zinc), and pearlspar. Crystals of smithsonite are abundant; they are either found in the small veins traversing the dolomite (No. 32), or forming the outer layer of irregular masses of ore, imbedded in red clay; the crystals are of pale yellow, pale red, or flesh-color, rough on the exterior, frequently possessing curved faces. A few hand-specimens presented the appearance of a brecciated rock; here, angular fragments of a light reddish-gray, very close-textured dolomite (?) of splintery fracture, were imbedded in a matrix of greenish-gray, coarser grained dolomite, intermixed with flesh-colored crystals of smithsonite.

The great mass of the ore occurs imbedded in red, feruginous clay, in more or less rounded, irregular pieces. These pieces frequently consist of three distinct layers: the outer one is formed of well-developed crystals of pure smithsonite; then follows a layer of amorphous smithsonite, possessing the physical properties of the above described ore, No. 1, which passes gradually into a very soft amorphous mass of the composition given in No. 2, and which is nothing but the same mineral constituting the second layer, intermixed with some clay and other impurities. Its color is from cream-color to brownish-yellow; it is easily scraped with a knife, yielding a cream-colored powder.

No. 1. Massive, amorphous, carbonate of zinc.

Composition dried at 230 deg. F:

Clay, and silicia	18.805
Carbonate of zinc	75.474
" " lime	0.364
" " magnesia	trace
Peroxide of iron, and alumina	1.771
Water, and loss	3.586
	100.000

The air-dried ore lost 0.69 per cent. of moisture at 230 deg. F.

The carbonic acid in the carbonates of zinc and lime amounts to 26.685 per cent.; a separate experiment, on treating the pulverized mineral with hydrochloric acid in a carbonic acid apparatus, gave 26.881 per cent. Some of the iron was probably in the state of proto-carbonate.

75.474 per cent. of carbonate of zinc, are equal to 48.95 per cent. of oxide of zinc, or to 39.30 per cent. of metallic zinc.

No. 2. Same as No. 1, impure.

Composition, dried at 230 deg. F:

Clay, and silica	31.069
Carbonate of zinc	51.111
" " lime	8.114
" " magnesia	4.417
Peroxide of iron, with traces of alumina and manganese	4.800
	99.191

The air-dried mineral lost 1.29 per cent. of moisture at 230 deg. F.

51.111 per cent. of carbonate of zinc are equal to 33.149 per cent. of oxide of zinc, or to 26.60 per cent. of metallic zinc.

B.—Ore from the Bath mine.

The prevailing ore at this locality is a massive, brownish-yellow, cellular smithsonite; the cavities are clad out with botryoidal incrustations of grayish-white smithsonite, and occasional buff-colored crystals of the same mineral. The surface of the ore is covered with a thin crust of yellowish-red clay. Several pieces of the ore were crushed, well mixed, and from the mixture two samples taken for analysis, (No. 3 and No. 4).

At this mine occurs also the light-colored, soft variety of carbonate of zinc, partly amorphous, partly sub-crystalline, pieces of about a cubic inch of which are cemented together by the dark brownish-gray or brownish-yellow cellular smithsonite above described; the dark-gray cellular masses often consist of concentric layers, the outer layers being generally of a much lighter color, and contain occasionally crystals of brown blende.

The dolomite containing the ore at this locality, abounds with small veins of pearlspar, and with amygdaloidal cavities, sometimes an inch wide and two and a half inches long, which are filled with crystals of pearlspar and blende.

No. 3. Brownish-yellow, cellular, smithsonite.

Composition, dried at 250 deg. F:

Clay, and silica	8.831
Carbonate of zinc	86.490
" " lime	0.742
" " magnesia	trace

Alumina, sesquioxides of iron and manganese,	4.389
Oxide of lead	trace
" " copper	trace
	100.452

The air-dried ore lost 0.50 per cent. of moisture at 250 deg. F.

86.49 per cent. of carbonate of zinc are equal to 56.099 per cent. of oxide of zinc, or to 45.045 per cent. of metallic zinc.

No. 4. Same as No. 3; different specimen.

The analysis of this sample was executed by igniting the ore, and extracting the oxide of zinc with a mixture of ammonia and carbonate of ammonia, (compare "methods of analysis," below.)

Composition of air-dried ore:

Carbonic acid and water	32.150
Silica, clay, iron, lime, etc	14.519
Oxide of zinc	53.331
	100.000

53.331 per cent. of oxide of zinc are equal to 42.822 per cent. of metallic zinc.

The residue, left after the treatment with ammonia, etc., and which consists essentially of clay, was found, on examination, to contain some oxide of zinc, showing that a small portion of this oxide must exist in the ore in combination with silica, forming silicate of zinc, a compound insoluble in ammonia. On comparing analysis No. 4 with No. 3, it appears that about 3 per cent. of oxide of zinc are combined with silica.

C.—Ore from the Koch mine.

The principal ore from this mine is a cellular, subcrystalline mass of brownish-white and grayish-white color; within the cavities, the surface of the smithsonite is botryoidal and usually covered with a very thin layer of red clay; this mineral is intimately associated and intermixed with an amorphous, grayish-yellow, massive variety of carbonate of zinc, resembling ore No. 1, from the Hoppe mine. Its powder has a pale cream color.

Three different specimens of this ore were analyzed; of the first specimen a complete analysis was made, showing the total amount of oxide of zinc present, and the quantitative relation of the impurities. The other two specimens were analyzed after the method employed for No. 4, showing only the amount of oxide of zinc that is contained in the ore in the state of carbonate or hydrate.

No. 5. Brownish-white, cellular smithsonite.

Composition, dried at 250 deg. F:

Silica	0.501
Oxide of zinc	61.753
Peroxide of iron	0.552
Alumina	0.097
Lime	1.338
Magnesia	trace.
Carbonic acid, water, and loss	35.759
	100.000

The air-dried ore lost 0.14 per cent. of moisture at 250 deg. F.

61.753 per cent. of oxide of zinc are equal to 49.59 per cent of metallic zinc.

No. 6. Same as No. 5; different specimen.

Composition of air-dried ore:

Carbonic acid and water	35.911
Insoluble residue (silica, iron, lime, etc.,)	6.839
Oxide of zinc	57.250
	100.000

No. 7. Same as No. 5; different specimen.

Composition of air-dried ore:

Carbonic acid and water	35.267
Insoluble residue (silica, iron, lime, etc,,)	8.298
Oxide of zinc	56.445
	100.000

The mean of analyses Nos. 6 and 7, shows 56.847 per cent. of oxide of zinc, combined with carbonic acid or water, which is equal to 45.65 per cent. of metallic zinc. In both cases, the residue from the treatment with ammonia, was found to contain zinc, whence the presence of a small quantity of silicate of zinc may be inferred.

B.—ORES OF ZINC FROM MARION COUNTY.

In this county, the only locality from which specimens of ores of zinc were obtained, is known as " Wood's mine," situated, section 13, township 19 north, range 17 west, on the west branch of George creek. The ore occurs here, as in Lawrence county, in pockets or veins in dolomite (the analysis of which is given in No. 34,) and is in most cases found imbedded in ferruginous clay. The most valuable ore is a compact, cellular, sub-crystalline smithsonite, of brownish-white and grayish-white color, surface botryoidal, resembling, in its general appearance, the principal ore from the Koch mine, (analysis No. 5); the cavities are partially filled with clay. The subjoined analysis, No. 8, represents the composition of this ore. The sample has been carefully selected, so as to approach as near as possible to the composition of a fair average-specimen.

Well developed crystals of smithsonite, abundant in the mines of Lawrence county, appear to be entirely wanting, as are also the thin veins of pearlspar, traversing the dolomite. In their stead, the dolomite is frequently found incrusted with a compact mass of a pale brownish-white, or greenish-white carbonate of zinc, with botryoidal surface, consisting of a succession of concentric layers, the whole deposit having sometimes a thickness of upwards of half an inch. Its hardness is between 4 and 5; streak white; translucent; brittle; fracture splintery; heated in a glass-tube, closed at one end, gives no water, but turns opaque and yellow, after cooling opaque and white; on charcoal before the blowpipe, gives the reactions of oxide of zinc. Its composition is given in No. 9. Intervening between this mineral and the dolomite, a thin layer of crystallized quartz, of brownish color, is frequently met with; the quartz in the subjoined analysis (No. 9), is probably derived from an intermixture of this layer with the carbonate of zinc.

No. 8. Brownish-white, cellular, smithsonite.

Composition, dried at 212 deg. F:

Clay, sand, and silica	7.523
Oxide of zinc	59.770
Peroxide of iron, with trace of manganese	3.507
Oxide of cadmium	0.486
" " lead	0.066
" " copper	trace
Lime	0.466
Magnesia	trace
Carbonic acid, water, and loss	28.182
	100.000

The air-dried ore lost 1.84 per cent. of moisture at 212 deg. F.

59.77 per cent. of oxide of zinc are equal to 47.97 per cent. of metallic zinc.

The iron has been represented as peroxide, because the greater part of it has certainly been derived from the red clay, filling the cavities of the ore.

No. 9. Compact smithsonite, incrusting dolomite.

Composition, dried at 212 deg. F:

Quartz	1.512
Oxide of zinc	65.967
" iron	trace
Lime	1.067
Magnesia	trace
Carbonic acid, and loss	31.454
	100.000

The air-dried mineral lost 0.116 per cent. of moisture at 212 deg. F.

From the high per centage of oxide of zinc in this mineral, it would appear to be a basic carbonate of zinc, but as no direct carbonic acid determination was made, it is not, at present, possible to construct a formula for its composition.

Rounded pieces of dark-gray, subcrystalline dolomite appear, sometimes, as if cemented by carbonate of zinc, which surrounds the fragments in concentric, incrusting layers. The carbonate of zinc is of grayish, brownish, or reddish color; between its layers, but mostly between the dolomite and the carbonate of zinc, a white mineral is occasionally observed, whose properties and composition are given in No. 10.

No. 10. Marionite, a new hydrous carbonate of zinc.

Occurs in concentric and contorted laminæ, also, in botryoidal and mammilated incrustations; amorphous; earthy; color milk-white; hardness 2.5; easily reduced to powder; powder milk-white.

Dissolves readily, and completely, in cold dilute hydrochloric acid, with effervescence; also, when pulverized, in ammonia; in both solutions, sulphydrate of ammonia produces a white precipitate. Heated in a matrass, yields water and turns yellow; heated before the blowpipe with a solution of nitrate of cobalt, assumes a bright green color; on charcoal, behaves like oxide of zinc.

On being ignited in a platina capsule, the mineral lost 26.818 per cent; the residue, dissolved in hydrochloric acid, and the solution precipitated with carbonate of soda, gave 73.262 per cent. of oxide of zinc.

Carbonic acid and water	26.818
Oxide of zinc	73.262
	100.080

The water was determined by heating the mineral in a small glass retort, the neck of which was connected with a chloride of calcium tube. The experiment gave 11.808 per cent. of water; this deducted from the total loss by ignition gives the carbonic acid; hence, the composition is:

Oxide of zinc	73.262
Water	11.808
Carbonic acid	15.010
	100.080

The only mineral known consisting of oxide of zinc, carbonic acid, and water, is Smithson's "zinc-bloom," for which the formula 3 $ZnO.CO^2 + 3 HO$ has been constructed. This formula requires: *

		Found by Smithson.
Oxide of zinc	71.28	69.38
Carbonic acid	12.89	13.50
Water	15.83	15.10
	100.00	97.98

Von Kobell § constructed for this mineral the formula 3 [2 $ZnO.CO^2$] + 2 [ZnO.3HO], which does not agree with Smithson's analysis, and which, therefore, cannot be considered as expressing the composition of zinc-bloom. But Von Kobell's formula agrees very well with the analytical results obtained by me for the above-described mineral, which has to be considered a new species, or at least a new variety of zinc-bloom, and for which I propose the name of "*Marionite.*" †

		In 100	Found
8 Zn O	324.24	72.99	73.262
3 CO^2	66.00	14.86	15.010
6 HO	54.00	12.15	11.808
	444.24	100.00	100.080

Blende (sulphuret of zinc), occurs abundantly at Wood's mine. It is mostly of dark brown color, and large crystals are frequently found cemented by irregular masses of impure smithsonite. In some specimens the blende presents a cellular appearance, as if acted upon by a dissolving liquid; the cavities are generally coated with a layer of minutely crystalline carbonate of zinc, of gray or reddish color.

* v. Dana's mineralogy, 4th ed. p. 460.

§ v. Rammelsberg's Handworterbuch, etc., vol. 2, p. 295.

Want of material prevented a repetition of the analysis.

The blende is very pure, though occasionally small particles of iron pyrites and copper pyrites are visible. Fragments of a large crystal, of brownish-yellow color, were found, on examination, to be pure sulphuret of zinc, with only 0.47 per cent. of sulphuret of cadmium, and a trace of copper. The qualitative examination of another specimen showed the presence of a small amount of cadmium, with traces of copper and iron.

———o———

The subjoined table will furnish a comprehensive view of the composition of the ores from the various localities; the numbers in the column "carbonic acid and water," have mostly been obtained by subtracting from 100 the sum of the directly determined constituents. Thinking it a matter of some interest, to compare the ores of Arkansas with those of other countries, I have added a few analyses of the ores of Upper Silesia, where about one-half of all the manufactured zinc is produced, and some other localities, and it will be seen, on comparison, that the Arkansas ores are inferior to none, and superior even to the famous Silesian ores.

1 to 9 correspond to Nos. 1 to 9 of the Report; 10, analysis of a white compact smithsonite from the "Planet-Grube," near Tarnowitz, Upper Silesia; 11, analysis of a compact smithsonite from the "Marie Grube," near Miechowitz, Upper Silesia; 12, analysis of a red compact smithsonite from same locality; 13, analysis of a white compact smithsonite from the "Scharley-Grube," near Beuthen, Upper Silesia; 14, analysis of a red compact smithsonite from Polonia; 15, analysis of a compact, brownish, smithsonite from the "Busbacher Berg," near Aachen, Prussia; 16, 17, and 18, crystallized smithsonites from Altenberg, near Aachen; 19 and 20, crystallized, green smithsonite from the "Herrenberg," near Aachen; 21, crystallized smithsonite from Moresnet, Belgium. 10 to 14 have been analyzed by G. Von Gellhorn, [*Chem. pharm. Centralblatt*, 1853]; 15 to 20 by Monheim, [*Chem. pharm. Centralblatt*, 1850, and *Dana, system of mineralogy, 4th ed.*]; 21, by Schmidt, [*Rammelsberg, 5th supplement.*]

	Oxide of zinc.	Carbonic acid and water.	Silica and insoluble silicates.	Peroxide of iron.	Alumina, lime, magnesia, etc.
1	48·950	30·271	18·805	1·974	
2	33·149	23·612	31·069	11·361	
3	56·099	30·717	8·831	4·805	
4	53·331	32·150		14·519	
5	61·753	35·759	0·501	1·987	
6	57·250	35·911		6·839	
7	56·445	39·267		8·298	
8	59·770	28·182	7·523	3·507	1·018
9	65·967	31·451	1·512	trace	1·067
10	49·77	31·22		20·48	
11	27·02	26·63	16·58	10·86	19·79
12	39·15	30·36	0·35	17·40	12·74
13	42·12	30·35	8·42	1·49	17·60
14	48·07	33·49		18·03	
15	60·97	10·32	18·79	9·52	1·67
16	39·11		62·00		
17	36·22		62·28		
18	55·04		44·54		
19	55·59		45·56		
20	48·23		50·69		
21	63·06	35·06	1·58	0·34	

The smelting of zinc from these ores, although not quite as simple a process as the smelting of lead from galena, offers no difficulties: the ore, reduced to a proper size, is simply mixed with a sufficient quantity of coal, and heated, in a closed vessel, to a temperature high enough to cause the reduction of the oxide; the metal, being volatile, distills over and is collected in a receiver. The execution of the process varies somewhat in practice; at present, three methods are principally in use, known as the English, the Belgian, and the Silesian method, each possessed of its peculiar advantages and disadvantages.

The only preliminary operation which the ores are subjected to, besides the necessary sorting and bruising, is the calcination, (and even this operation is sometimes omitted in England). The calcination is generally performed in reverberatory furnaces, and has the object of removing carbonic acid and water, and lessening the cohesion of the ore; it is a necessary operation if the carbonate of zinc contains blende, to convert the latter into oxide of zinc; in this case, a small proportion of coal must be added.

Where fuel is cheap, the calcination is advantageously performed in heaps. The heaps are formed by alternate layers of wood and carbonate of zinc; fire is set to the lowest layer of wood, and the ore left to the influence of heat and air; by this means the water is removed, but not the carbonic acid, and the state of cohesion lessened.

In the English process, the calcined ore is mixed with about one-seventh of its weight of coal, and filled into large crucibles or pots. These pots are made of fire-clay, and cement of old pounds finely ground; they are covered with a lid, through an orifice of which the charge is introduced, and are provided, at the bottom, with an aperture; to this aperture a long sheet iron pipe is joined, which dips, at its end, into a vessel filled with water. On heat being applied, the oxide of zinc becomes reduced, the metal is vaporized, passes through the iron pipe, and collects in drops in the water vessel. From 6 to 8 pots are placed in a furnace; a furnace will work up from 6 to 10 tons of ore in 14 days, consuming from 22 to 24 tons of coal, and yielding 2 tons of zinc, on an average. A pot lasts about four months.

In the Belgian process, the reduction furnace is filled with long, horizontal earthen tubes, from 3 to 4 feet long, and from 4 to 5 inches in diameter; 22 tubes in each furnace; the tubes are filled with a mixture of ground ore and coal, (1 volume of ore to $\frac{1}{3}$ to $\frac{2}{3}$ volumes of coke or charcoal, broken to pieces the size of nuts); to each tube a conical piece of cast-iron is attached, in a slightly slanting position; these conical pipes serve as receivers and condensers of the vaporized zinc, and are raked out every two hours. Each earthen tube holds 40 lbs of the mixture of ore and coal; the distillation is completed in 12 hours, and each furnace yields every 12 hours, 100 lbs. of crude zinc; on being remelted and cast into moulds, the crude zinc loses 10 per cent. For every pound of zinc, about 28 lbs. of coal are used.

In the Silesian process, the small earthen tubes are replaced by muffles, made of fire-clay mixed with ground potsherds; the muffles are from 3 to 4 feet long, and have a diameter of from 14 to 18 inches. The number of muffles in a furnace varies from 5 to 10; in Upper Silesia, double furnaces, holding 20 muffles, are in use. The charge consists of calcined ore mixed with an equal volume (about one-fifth by weight) of cinders. A single muffle will produce from 40 to 50 lbs. of zinc daily. A muffle will last several months.

The crude zinc obtained by any of the above described processes has to be remelted; in this operation the heat must not rise above a low red-heat, and the surface covered with a layer of charcoal. Experience has shown that, with careful management, 100 lbs. of crude zinc will yield from 92 to 94 lbs. of purified zinc, and from 12 to 16 lbs of a scoria, containing nearly 50 per cent. of zinc.

The preceding data I have collected from the most reliable works on metallurgy which I had at my command. They would be more valuable if I could have added a calculation of the probable expense at which a furnace can be worked, and also of the probable expense of erection; but the prices of building material, fuel, etc., the wages of workmen, and all other contingent expenses being so extremely variable, the conditions under which the mining and smelting of the ore are carried on in Europe being so little comparable to the circumstances which would surround similar enterprises in Arkansas, I very much doubt whether a calculation of that kind, even if it could have been made with some approach to accuracy, would have benefited any one anxious to get information on the subject. The above data teach how much metallic zinc can be produced in a certain time, with a furnace of a certain construction and size, how much fuel will be consumed in the operation, and how much of the crude ore is probably required to effect the result; this is all that science can teach—commerce and political economy must furnish the rest of the desired information. To one point, however, I wish to call particular attention, viz: the richness of the Arkansas ores; in all calculations respecting the probable success of active mining and smelting operations, this circumstance ought to enter as an important item, since, from it, we must reasonably expect a comparative large yield of metal, and, therefore, larger returns than ordinary, other circumstances being equal.

ORES OF LEAD.

Galena, or sulphuret of lead, is the only ore of lead as yet found in the northern counties of the state. The different kinds of galena which were subjected to analysis, occur all in dolomite, either in pockets or veins; they are all distinctly crystalline, forming, for the most part, large cubes, with perfect cubical cleavage.

They are almost pure sulphuret of lead (containg 13.4 parts of sulphur to 86.6 parts of lead), being perfectly free from zinc, antimony, and copper; only three of them contain appreciable quantities of iron. All the ores contain some silver, though probably only one of them (No. 14) a sufficient quantity to be profitable for working. For the method employed in determining the amount of iron and silver, compare "methods of analysis," below.

A.—GALENA FROM MARION COUNTY.

No. 11. Galena, from Wood's mine, section 13, township 19 north, range 17 west, west branch of George creek:

Occurs in the dolomite No. 34. Is pure sulphuret of lead without any impurity but a trace of silver. The lead, smelted from the ore, contains 0.00624 per cent. of silver, equal to 1.67 ounces of silver in the ton of galena (1 ton=2,000 ℔s).

No. 12. Galena, from the New York company's diggings:

Is pure sulphuret of lead, with a little sulphuret of iron, corresponding to 0.103 per cent. of metallic iron. The lead, smelted from the ore, contains 0.01066 per cent. of silver, equal to 2.88 ounces of silver in the ton of galena.

No. 13. Galena, from Molton's diggings, one mile above the fork of Jemmy's creek:

Is pure sulphuret of lead with a little sulphuret of iron, corresponding to 0.16 per cent. of metallic iron. The lead, smelted from the ore, contains 0.00294 per cent. of silver, equal to 0.784 ounces of silver in the ton of galena.

No. 14. Galena, from Seawell's diggings:

Is pure sulphuret of lead, without any impurities but a small quantity of silver. The lead, smelted from the ore, contains 0.14014 per cent. of silver, equal to 37.44 ounces of silver in the ton of galena.

No. 15. Galena, from Hudson's diggings:

Is pure sulphuret of lead with only traces of iron and silver. The lead, smelted from the ore, contains 0.00746 per cent. of silver, equal to 2 ounces of silver in the ton of galena.

No. 16. Galena, from McCarty's diggings:

Is pure sulphuret of lead, without any impurities but a trace of silver. The lead, smelted from the ore, contains 0.00825 per cent. of silver, equal to 2.25 ounces of silver in the ton of galena.

No. 17. Galena, from Jemmy's creek diggings, near the forks:

Is pure sulphuret of lead, with a little sulphuret of iron, corresponding to 0.1 per cent. of metallic iron, and a trace of silver. The lead, smelted from the ore, contains 0.019 per cent. of silver, equal to 5 ounces of silver in the ton of galena.

B.—GALENA FROM LAWRENCE COUNTY.

No. 18. Galena, from E. W. Haughton's diggings:

Occurs associated with a light, ochre-yellow, argillaceous rock, containing oxide of zinc (v. No. 37).

Is pure sulphuret of lead, with only traces of iron and silver. The lead, smelted from the ore, contains 0.00292 per cent. of silver, equal to 0.78 ounces of silver in the ton of galena.

C.—GALENA FROM CARROLL COUNTY.

No. 19. Galena, from Coka and Mitchell's diggings:

Is pure sulphuret of lead, with only traces of iron and silver. The lead, smelted from the ore, contains 0.01083 per cent. of silver, equal to 2.9 ounces of silver in the ton of galena.

TABULAR VIEW—*Of the composition of the different kinds of galena from the counties of Marion, Lawrence, and Carroll.*

LOCALITY.	Contain in 100 parts, 86.6 parts of lead, with		Am't of silver in a ton (2000 ℔) of galena.
	Iron.	Silver.	
No. 11, from Wood's mine	none	0.00624	1·67
No. 12, from New York company's diggings	0.103	0.01066	2·88
No. 13, from Molton's diggings	0.160	0.00294	0·784
No. 14, from Seawell's diggings	none	0.14014	37·44
No. 15, from Hudson's diggings	trace	0.00746	2·00
No. 16, from McCarty's diggings	none	0.00825	2·25
No. 17, from Jemmy's creek diggings	0.100	0.01900	5·00
No. 18, from E. W. Houghton's diggings	trace	0.00292	0·78
No. 19, from Coka & Mitchell's diggings	trace	0.01083	2·90

Only one of these ores (No. 14) would probably pay for the extraction of the silver; the others are good lead ores. If, by sinking shafts, and ascertaining the extent of the ore-deposit at Seawell's diggings, the presence of a sufficient quantity of the ore can be proved, there is no doubt that, with judicious management, the extraction of silver will prove very remunerative. In England, the average quantity of silver contained in the lead which is worked for silver, is 7 or 8 ounces per ton, or about 6 or 7 ounces per ton of galena.* The galena, from the mines of the "Middletown Silver and Lead Mining and Manufacturing Company," in Connecticut, contains from 25 to 75 oz. of silver to the ton (of 21 cwts) of lead. The galena from the "Washington mine," North Carolina, contains only 7.5 oz. of silver in the ton (average of 200 assays). *

ORES OF MANGANESE.

Of the five specimens of ores of manganese, subjected to analysis, two (Nos. 20 and 21) were collected on the spot; the other three, I received from a gentleman in Batesville, who collected them at the localities below mentioned.

No. 20 Psilomelane, from the main manganese mine, two miles above West fork of Lafferty creek, Independence county:

Massive; lustre submetallic; color between dark steel-gray and iron-black; hardness 5.5; fracture subcrystalline, hackly, somewhat resembling the fracture of cast iron; brittle; strikes fire with steel; powder reddish-brown.

Before the blowpipe, infusible alone; on charcoal in reduction flame becomes reddish-brown; in a matrass, yields water; with fluxes, gives the manganese reactions. Dissolves in hydrochloric acid with evolution of chlorine, leaving a small residue of silica.

Occurs in veins traversing the encrinital beds of the cavernous limestone.

Composition, dried at 250 deg. F:

Manganoso-manganic oxide (Mn^3O^4)	91.367
Silica	2.845
Baryta	0.512
Lime	trace
Water and oxygen, expelled by heat	5.931
	100.655

The air-dried mineral lost 0.53 per cent. of moisture at 250 deg. F.

* See J. D. Whitney's "Metallic Wealth of the United States." Philadelphia, 1854.

The above numbers are the direct result of analysis. In order to ascertain how much of the volatile matter, expelled by heat, is water, and how much oxygen, the pulverized mineral was heated in a platina capsule over the smallest flame of a spirit-lamp with Argand burner, until the weight remained constant; the loss amounted to 1.82 per cent. The heat was then raised and kept for about half an hour, just below redness: the mineral did not suffer any further loss. Assuming the 1.82 per cent. of volatile matter, expelled below red-heat, to be water, we obtain for oxygen 5.931—1.82=4.111 per cent. The 91.367 per cent. of manganoso-manganic oxide consist of 84.995 parts of protoxide of manganese with 6.372 parts of oxygen; these, added to the above 4.111 per cent., give 10.483 per cent. of free oxygen, and the composition of the mineral may, therefore, be expressed thus:

Protoxide of manganese	84.995
Free oxygen	10.483
Silica	2.845
Baryta	0.512
Lime	trace
Water	1.820
	100.655

As a controlling experiment, the amount of free oxygen was determined by Mohr's method [v. "methods of analysis," below], and found to be 10.510 per cent.

No. 21. Psilomelane, from same locality as No. 20.

Massive; close-textured; color bluish steel-gray; hardness 5.5; fracture splintery and subconchoidal; brittle; strikes fire with steel; powder reddish-brown.

Before the blowpipe, and to reagents, behaves like the preceding.

Composition, dried at 250 deg. F:

Manganoso-manganic oxide	88.628
Silica	5.329
Baryta	0.282
Lime	1.178
Magnesia	trace
Water and oxygen, expelled by heat	4.433
	99.850

The air-dried mineral lost 1.02 per cent. of moisture at 250 deg. F.

The amount of free oxygen was determined by Mohr's method to be 10.002 per cent.

Taking into consideration the quantity of free oxygen contained in the 88.628 per cent. of manganoso-manganic oxide, we obtain for water, expelled at a red heat, 0.611 per cent.; hence, the composition of the mineral may be expressed thus:

Protoxide of manganese	82.448
Free oxygen	10.002
Silica	5.329
Baryta	0.282
Lime	1.178
Magnesia	trace
Water	0.611
	99.850

No. 22. Wad, from near the North fork of White river, Izard county.

A brecciated rock; the matrix consists of wad, in which angular pieces of white chert are imbedded. The wad possesses the following physical and chemical properties:

Compact, amorphous; lustre dull, on rounded edges shining; color iron-black; hardness 4; powder dark brownish olive-green.

Heated on charcoal in reduction flame, turns reddish-brown; heated in a matrass, yields water copiously, at a low heat. With fluxes gives the reactions of manganese. Dissolves readily in hydrochloric acid, with evolution of chlorine, and separation of silica.

Having but a small specimen at my disposal, and the siliceous mineral adhering very firmly to the ore, I could not collect enough of the pure wad for the purpose of analysis, but was compelled to analyze the mixture.

The mixed minerals, dried at 220 deg. F., had the following composition:

Manganoso-manganic oxide	51.365
Silica	26.230
Alumina, with trace of iron	6.245
Oxide of cobalt	0.104
Baryta	1.875
Lime	trace
Water and oxygen, expelled by heat	14.889
	100.708

The air-dried mineral lost 2.1 per cent. of moisture at 220 deg. F.

The amount of free oxygen was ascertained by Mohr's method to be 7.82 per cent. Taking into consideration the quantity of free oxygen contained in the manganoso-manganic oxide, we obtain for water expelled at a red heat 10.653 per cent.; hence, the composition of the mineral may be thus expressed:

Protoxide of manganese	47.781
Free oxygen	7.820
Silica	26.230
Alumina, with trace of iron	6.245
Oxide of cobalt	0.104
Baryta	1.875
Lime	trace
Water	10.653
	100.708

Subtracting silica and alumina, as adventitious intermixtures, and calculating the remaining constituents for 100 parts, we obtain for the wad the following composition:

Protoxide of manganese	70.03
Free oxygen	11.46
Oxide of cobalt	0.15
Baryta	2.75
Lime	trace
Water	15.61
	100.00

No. 23. Braunite (?), from Poke bayou, Marion county.

Massive; texture finely granular; lustre submetallic; color dark steel gray; hardness 5.5; strikes fire with steel; powder grayish-black; much more easily reduced to powder, than the two preceding minerals; weathered surface shows brown spots of hydrate of peroxide of iron.

Before the blowpipe, infusible; on charcoal in reduction flame, becomes pale reddish-gray at the point of contact with the charcoal; in a matrass, yields a little water; with fluxes, gives the manganese reactions.

Dissolves in hydrochloric acid with evolution of chlorine, leaving a residue of silica.

Composition dried at 220 deg. F:

Protoxide of manganese	75.386
Free oxygen	7.979

Silica	9.968
Peroxide of iron	3.523
Oxide of cobalt	trace
Lime	1.833
Magnesia	0.192
Water	1.295
	100.176

The air-dried mineral lost 0.1 per cent. of moisture at 220 deg. F.

The free oxygen was determined by Mohr's method. The 1.295 per cent. of water were determined by the loss which the mineral suffered on ignition; the volatile matter was not collected; hence, it remains uncertain whether it consisted of water, or of water and oxygen; but if any oxygen had been driven out by heat, it is difficult to conceive why the weight, after repeated ignitions, remained constant, and why not the whole of the oxygen beyond the composition Mn^3O^4 was removed, amounting to 2.328 per cent. For this reason the loss on ignition has been stated as water.

No. 24. Psilomelane, six miles north of Batesville, on Poke bayou.

Massive; lustre submetallic; color iron-black; fracture uneven, platy; hardness 5.5; powder reddish-brown.

Before the blowpipe, infusible; on charcoal in reduction flame, becomes brown; in a matrass, yields a little water; with fluxes gives the manganese reactions.

Dissolves in hydrochloric acid with evolution of chlorine, leaving a very slight residue of silica.

The mineral was only partially analyzed. It lost at 250 deg. F. 0.452 per cent. of moisture; heated higher, but below redness, the dried mineral lost 1.124 per cent., probably water; and on ignition lost, additionally, 5.185 per cent., which must have been oxygen. The free oxygen was determined, after Mohr's method, to be 11.700 per cent.

The qualitative examination proved the presence of small quantities of cobalt, baryta, lime, magnesia, and silica.

Commercial value of the Ores of Manganese.

The ores of manganese are used in the arts principally for the purpose of bleaching, where they serve, in conjunction with common salt and sulphuric acid, to produce chlorine, the bleaching agent, and in the manufacture of glass, for the purpose of correcting the tinge imparted to the glass by iron. In both cases, their value entirely depends on the amount of free oxygen which they contain, that is: the quantity of oxygen more than sufficient to form with the whole of the metallic manganese the lowest degree of oxidation, the protoxide; for the purpose of the glass manufacturer, they ought also to be as free from iron as possible. Of the various compounds of manganese, the ore containing the largest proportion of free oxygen is the peroxide, commonly known as "black oxide of manganese," a compound which occurs native as a mineral, called "pyrolusite;" it contains 18.36 per cent. of free oxygen.

In order to ascertain, as near as possible, the market value of the Arkansas ores, I procured from a New York firm a sample of what is sold in that city as "black oxide of manganese" at the rate of three and a half cents per pound, by the hundred weight, in the ground state; on analysis, I found this sample to contain 9.246 per cent. of free oxygen, corresponding to 50.35 per cent. of pure peroxide of manganese; it contained a large proportion of silica, a circumstance which probably makes the ore very difficult to grind. In the Hartz mountains, a famous European locality for the ores of manganese, three qualities of the ore are sold, the price varying with the amount of free oxygen; the

First quality contains 12.60 per cent. of free oxygen.
Second " " 10.00 " " " "
Third " " 7.36 " " " "

(See *Bruno Kerl*, in *Chem. Centralblatt for* 1853.)

The ores of Arkansas contain

NUMBER OF SPECIMEN.	Per cent. of free oxygen.	100 parts of ore correspond to pure MnO_2	Peroxide of iron.
No. 20	10.483	57.24	none
No. 21	10.002	54.47	none
No. 22, crude	7.820	42.59	trace
No. 22, freed from gangue	11.460	62.42	
No. 23	7.979	43.46	3.523
No. 24	11.700	63.72	?
Ore from New York	9.246	50.35	?

The ores Nos. 20, 21, 24, and 22 when freed from its gangue, are, as seen by the table, superior to the ore procured from New York, and ought to command, therefore, a higher price; they contain, on the average 10.911 per cent. of free oxygen, which places them intermediate between the 1st and 2d quality of the German ore.

Chemical constitution of the ores of Manganese.

The constitution of the manganese-minerals which do not occur in the crystallized state, has been a point of some discussion amongst mineralogists. As long as their rational formulæ are not indubitably established, every new analysis may be expected to throw some light on the subject. Although the foregoing analyses were principally executed with a view to ascertain the economical value of the ores, the importance of the subject may serve as an excuse, if I take up a short space for purely theoretical speculations.

It was Rammelsberg, if I mistake not, who first considered psilomelane as a compound of peroxide of manganese with bases of the constitution RO, these bases being principally MnO, BaO, KO, CaO, MgO, and CoO; the peroxide of manganese in these compounds acts the part of the acid. Adopting this view, we have to reject, in the construction of a formula, the silicia and the bases of the constitution R^2O^3, as adventitious constituents; a rejection which, though rather arbitrary,* may be admitted on the e a of expediency. Leaving, therefore, the silica in the analysis of Nos. 20 and 21 out of consideration, and calculating the remaining constituents for 100, we obtain for these minerals the following composition:

	No. 20	No. 21
Protoxide of manganese····	86.898	87.22
Oxygen ··················	10.718	10.58
Baryta ··················	0.523	0.29
Lime·····················	trace	1.27
Water ···················	1.861	0.64
	100.000	100.00

Uniting the free oxygen with a portion of the protoxide of manganese to the formation of peroxide, we have

For No. 20.

Peroxide of manganese········	58.373	contains O		21.4
Protoxide of manganese ·······	39.243	"	8.83	9.53
Baryta·······················	0.523	"	0.05	
Water························	1.861	"	1.65	

* Compare on this subject the observations of Gustav Bischof, in the 2d vol., of his "Elements of chemical and physical geology," p. 85, etc.

For No. 21.

Peroxide of manganese........	57.92	contains O		21.27
Protoxide of manganese	39.88	"	8.97	9.93
Baryta	0.29	"	0.03	
Lime	1.27	"	0.36	
Water......................	0.64	"	0.57	

Rammelsberg does not include water under the bases of the constitution RO; but seeing no objection to its being considered isomorphous with CaO and BaO, and gaining the advantage of a simple formula, I have classed it with these bases. From the above oxygen-ratio, we obtain for the two minerals the general expression:

$$RO.\ MnO^2 + x\ MnO^2$$

in which x MnO^2 stands for the amount of peroxide of manganese which must be considered as mechanically intermixed with the compound $RO.MnO^2$. For the potassa-psilomalane from Ilmenau, Rammelsberg deduced the formula $2\ RO.\ MnO^2 + x\ MnO^2$.

For No. 20 we finally obtain the expression:

$(MnO.\ BaO.\ HO).\ MnO^2 + 6.37$ per cent. of MnO^2 mechanically intermixed.

For No. 21

$(MnO.\ BaO.\ CaO.\ HO).MnO^2 + 3.84$ per cent. of MnO^2 mechanically intermixed.

Uniting in analysis of No. 22, the free oxygen with a portion of the protoxide of manganese to the formation of peroxide, we have:

Peroxide of manganese........	62.41	contains O		22.92
Protoxide of mangauese.......	19.08	"	" 4.29	4.84
Baryta......................	2.75	"	" 0.52	
Oxide of cobalt	0.15	"	" 0.03	
Water......................	15.61	"		13.97
	100.00			

The formula

$$(MnO.\ CoO.\ BaO).\ 2\ MnO^2 + 3\ HO + x\ MnO^2$$

requires

Peroxide of manganese (mixed)	9.61			Oxygen-ratio.
Peroxide of manganese (combined)	52.80	contains O	19.36	4

Protoxide of manganese	19.08	"	"	4.84	1
Baryta	2.75	"	"		
Oxide of cobalt	0.15	"	"		
Water	16.33	"	"	14.52	3
	100.72				

This is the same formula which Rammelsberg established for the composition of the wad from Rubeland (v. *2d supplement, p.* 167).

Proceeding in the same manner with the analysis of No. 22, that is, rejecting silicic acid and peroxide of iron, and calculating the remainder for 100, we have:

Protoxide of manganese	86.96
Oxygen	9.20
Lime	2.12
Magnesia	0.22
Water	1.50
	100.00

86.96 parts of protoxide of manganese consist of 67.41 of manganese and 19.55 of oxygen; hence we have, in toto 67.41 manganese to 28.75 oxygen, corresponding to the ratio 69.68 Mn : 29.72 O;
the compound Mn^2O^3 requires 69.68 Mn : 30.42 O,
so that the mineral may be considered as sesquioxide of manganese, or braunite, under the supposition that we are justified in rejecting lime, magnesia, and water as adventitious. But if these bases have to be taken into consideration, and the free oxygen is united with a portion of the protoxide of manganese to the formation of peroxide, we have:

Peroxide of manganese	50.10	contains O			18.40
Protoxide of manganese	46.06	"	"	10.36	12.37
Lime	2.12	"	"	0.60	
Magnesia	0.22	"	"	0.08	
Water	1.50	"	"	1.33	

Here the oxygen-ratio of RO : MnO^2 is nearly as 4 : 6, which would lead to the formula

$$4\ (MnO.\ CaO.\ MgO.\ HO).\ 3\ MnO^2$$

I am not at present prepared to pronounce in favor of any of these views, but as I am continuing my investigations into the composition of the massive manganese-minerals, I hope to find myself soon enabled to advance some well-founded views on the subject.

ORES OF IRON.

No. 25. Yellow ochre, from the St. Francis side of Crowley's ridge, near David Schultze's, between township 18 and 19, range 8, Greene county.

A loosely aggregated, amorphous, homogeneous rock, of gold-yellow color; very friable; feels gritty between the fingers; becomes brick-red on ignition:

Composition dried at 220 deg. F:

Fine sand	71.081
Sesquioxide of iron	23.640
Alumina	trace
Water	5.094
	99.815

The air-dried substance lost 1.15 per cent. of moisture at 220 deg. F.

This ochre forms only a small deposit in the quarternary rocks of Greene county, and is evidently nothing but a fine sand impregnated with hydrated sesquioxide of iron, which is the coloring principle. The amount of iron (15.55 per cent.) is too small to constitute this ochre an iron ore, even if the deposit should prove to be very extensive; but it may be profitably used as a paint, both in its natural state and calcined, since it is very soft and uniform throughout, and hardly needs any washing in order to remove the coarser particles.

No. 26. Limonite, from Old Jackson, Lawrence county.

The ore consists of contorted, more or less concentric layers of brownish-red, steel-gray, and brownish black color; it contains amygdaloidal cavities filled either with stalactitic, glossy red hematite, or with yellow hydrated peroxide of iron.

Dissolves in hydrochloric acid with evolution of chlorine.

Composition of air-dried ore:

Clay, sand, and silica	15.069
Sesquioxide of iron	58.278
Sesquioxide of manganese	13.843
Alumina	trace
Oxide of cobalt	trace
Carbonate of magnesia	0.664

Carbonate of lime	trace
Water	12.080
	99.934

58.278 parts of peroxide of iron contains 40.79 parts of metallic iron.

No. 27. Limonite, from Dr. Payne's land, Pocahontas, Randolph county.

Massive; reddish-brown, with yellow spots on surface; rather earthy in appearance; evolves argillaceous odor when breathed upon, and adheres to the tongue. Powder dark brownish-red, becoming rather more red on ignition.

Composition of air-dried ore:

Clay and sand	21.100
Sesquioxide of iron	69.036
Sesquioxide of manganese	1.488
Alumina	trace
Carbonate of lime	trace
Water	7.590
	99.214

69.036 parts of sesquioxide of iron contain 48.33 parts of metallic iron.

No. 28. Limonite, from Alfred Bevens & Co., Lawrence county.

Massive; of earthy appearance and yellow color on and near the surface, in the interior brownish-yellow and more compact; evolves strong argillaceous odor when breathed upon; adheres to the tongue. Powder dirty brownish-yellow.

Composition of air-dried ore:

Silica	3.099
Sesquioxide of iron	79.663
Sesquioxide of manganese	trace
Alumina	5.203
Carbonate of lime	0.556
Water	11.397
	99.918

79.663 parts of sesquioxide of iron contain 55.76 parts of metallic iron.

No. 29. Limonite, so-called "pot and kidney ore," from Alfred Bevens & Co., Lawrence county.

Massive; compact, stalactitic and reniform; surface smooth, of reddish-brown and blackish-brown color, with occasional yellow spots; fracture dull, dark reddish-brown; emits argillaceous odor when breathed upon; adheres slightly to the tongue.

Composition of air-dried ore:

Silica and clay	3.090
Sesquioxide of iron	83.920
Sesquioxide of manganese	trace
Alumina	1.710
Lime	trace
Water	11.580
	100.300

83.920 parts of sesquioxide of iron contain 59.74 parts of metallic iron.

No. 30. Limonite, four miles south-west of Imboden's ferry, Randolph county.

Exterior crust dirty reddish-yellow, earthy; in the interior dark bluish-brown, consisting of indistinctly concentric, contorted layers; loosely aggregated; rather soft; evolves strong argillaceous color when breathed upon; strongly adhering to the tongue; powder of a dirty brownish olive-green color, becoming dark reddish-brown on ignition.

Composition of air-dried ore:

Insoluble silicates	7.740
Sesquioxide of iron	66.808
Sesquioxide of manganese	11.472
Alumina	1.295
Lime	trace
Phosphoric acid	trace
Water	13.337
	100.652

66.808 parts of sesquioxide of iron contain 46.76 parts of metallic iron.

No. 31. Limonite, four miles west of Salem, Fulton county.

Massive; very compact; on surface brownish-yellow; on fracture brownish-red, with steel-gray spots and stripes; fracture subconchoidal; evolves argillaceous odor when breathed upon; adheres to the tongue.

Composition of air-dried ore:

Insoluble silicates and sand	20.722
Sesquioxide of iron	68.543
Sesquioxide of manganese	1.221

Alumina	3.590
Lime	trace
Water	8.259
	95.155

68.543 parts of sesquioxide of iron contain 47.98 parts of metallic iron.

———o———

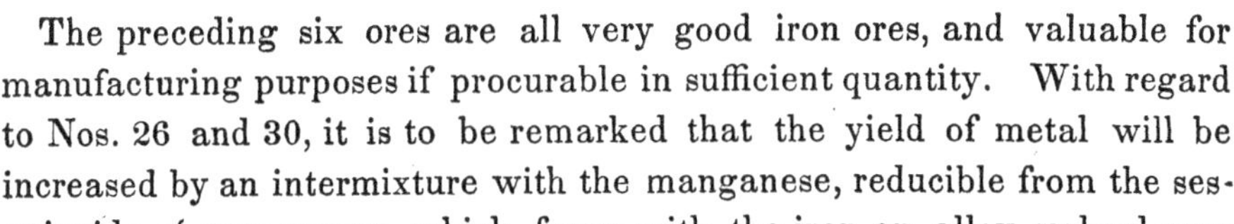

The preceding six ores are all very good iron ores, and valuable for manufacturing purposes if procurable in sufficient quantity. With regard to Nos. 26 and 30, it is to be remarked that the yield of metal will be increased by an intermixture with the manganese, reducible from the sesquioxide of manganese, which forms with the iron an alloy, valued very highly by some iron-men as being particularly adapted for the manufacture of a superior quality of steel.

The following table shows, at a glance, the richness and comparative value of the ores:

100 parts of ore from	Contain		Total.
	Iron.	Manganese.	
Old Jackson, No. 26	40.79	9.64	50.43
Dr. Payne's land, No. 27	48.33	1.04	49.37
Alf. Bevens & Co., No. 28	55.76	trace	55.76
same No. 29	59.74	trace	59.74
Randolph county, No. 30	46.76	7.99	54.75
Fulton county, No. 31	47.98	0.85	48.83

The absence of sulphur and phosphoric acid in these ores is a further recommendation for smelting purposes, as the presence of these impurities is apt to injure the quality of the iron.

ROCKS ASSOCIATED WITH THE ORES OF ZINC AND LEAD.

A careful examination of the rocks in which the ores of zinc and lead occur, and of the substances which are found associated with them in the veins and crevices, will probably throw some light on the origin of these metalliferous deposits, and enable the geologist to form a correct idea of their mode of formation. This was one of the objects we had in view in submitting the below enumerated rocks to chemical analysis. Want of time, however, prevented me from carrying on the investigation to a sufficient extent, and I was obliged to defer to a future period the completion of a sufficient number of analyses to enable us to draw satisfactory conclusions from them.

No. 32. Dolomite, which cuts out the ore at the Hoppe mine, Lawrence county.

A pale yellowish-gray, compact dolomite; fracture subconchoidal; very hard; brittle; powder of a light cream-color.

Composition, dried at 230 deg. F:

Insoluble silicates	6.701
Carbonate of lime	53.998
Carbonate of magnesia	35.059
Carbonate of iron	2.253
Carbonate of zinc	1.978
Potassa	0.106
	100.095

The air-dried rock lost 0.37 per cent. of moisture at 230 deg. F.

No. 33. Dolomite, with and below the zinc-deposit at the Koch mine, Lawrence county.

A dark yellowish-gray dolomite, compact and close-textured; fracture subconchoidal; very brittle; gives out a peculiar bituminous odor when struck with the hammer; powder ash-colored.

Composition, dried at 250 deg. F:

Insoluble silicates	10.935
Iron, alumina, and trace of manganese	1.482

Carbonate of lime	50.975
Carbonate of magnesia	32.487
Potassa	0.136
Organic matter, and loss	4.985
	100.000

The air-dried rock lost 0.16 per cent of moisture at 250 deg. F.

No. 34. Dolomite, in which occur the zinc and lead ores at Wood's mine, Marion county.

A grayish-white, fine-grained dolomite; lustre sub-resinous from minute crystalline, shining particles dispersed through the rock; easily reduced to powder; powder grayish-white.

Composition, dried at 230 deg. F:

Silicia, with a trace of clay	3.191
Alumina, with trace of iron	3.023
Carbonate of lime	50.041
Carbonate of magnesia	42.317
Carbonate of zinc	1.950
Potassa, with trace of soda	0.435
	100.957

The air-dried rock lost 0.23 per cent. of moisture at 230 deg. F.

No. 35. Red clay, occurring in veins and pockets in dolomite and imbedding the zinc ore at the Bath mine, Lawrence county.

A ferruginous clay of dirty yellowish-red color; soft; easily crumbling to powder between the fingers; when burnt, assumes a bright orange-red color.

Composition, dried at 250 deg. F:

Silicates, insoluble in hydrochloric acid	84.616
Sesquioxide of iron	4.303
Sesquioxide of manganese	0.236
Alumina	3.515
Carbonate of zinc	0.380
Carbonate of lime	0.275
Organic matter, and water	6.447
	99.772

The air-dried clay lost 4.32 per cent of moisture at 250 deg. F.

On account of the bright color which the clay assumes on burning, it might become useful as a common paint, though the amount of oxide of iron present is rather small.

No. 36. Argillaceous rock, from the crevices of the New York company's lead mines, Marion county.

Massive, amorphous; color pale yellowish-white and reddish-white; very light and soft; can be cut with a knife like chalk; on the surface, covered with a crust of peroxide of iron; powder of a pale reddish cream color; assumes on ignition a fine pink color.

Composition, dried at 230 deg. F:

Insoluble silicates, mainly a very fine soft clay	96.095
Peroxide of iron, and alumina, with a little phosphoric acid.	1.795
Lime	0.148
Manganese, magnesia, and potassa	traces
Water	2.055
	100.093

The air-dried rock lost 0.73 per cent. of moisture at 230 deg. F.

No. 37. Argillaceous rock, associated with galena, at Houghton's diggings, Lawrence county.

Bears a great resemblance to the preceding rock in general appearance. Its origin is probably the same, occurring, as it does, under similar conditions; but it appears to have come in contact, after its deposition, with liquids containing oxide of zinc in solution. The presence of about 8 per cent. of oxide of zinc in this clay points to the deposition of carbonate of zinc somewhere near Houghton's lead diggings.

Massive, amorphous; color ochre-yellow; light and soft; can be cut with a knife like chalk; covered on the surface with a thin layer of red clay, resembling No. 35; powder of a dirty grayish-yellow color.

Composition, dried at 230 deg. F:

Clay and sand	74.841
Peroxide of iron	2.383
Alumina	8.213
Phosphoric acid	0.214
Oxide of zinc, with trace of manganese	8.262
Carbonate of lime	0.709
Carbonate of magnesia	1.337
Water and carbonic acid (?), expelled by heat	3.844
	99.803

The air-dried clay lost 3.92 per cent. of moisture at 230 deg. F.

As no carbonic acid determination was made, it remains undecided whether the oxide of zinc occurs in the rock as such, or in combination with carbonic acid; most likely as a basic carbonate.

———o———

The foregoing analyses need no comment. Nos. 32, 33, and 34 are true dolomites; the small amount of carbonate of zinc, which occurs in two of them, is by no means surprising if we consider that the deposition of carbonate of zinc in the crevices of the rock was most likely effected by means of liquids containing the salt of zinc in solution; and whether these liquids actually percolated through the dolomite or entered the crevices by some other way, the deposition of a small quantity of the salt in the immediately adjoining rock is equally well explicable. Gustav Bischof mentions several instances of this kind (*Elements of chem. and phys. geology. Engl. edition, vol.* 1, *p.* 165.)

LIGNITES.

Both varieties of lignite, the analyses of which are given below, occur in the same bed, interstratified in the quarternary deposits of Crowley's ridge, Greene county.

No. 38. Lignite, from the Beech-branch of Cache, near Gainesville, Greene county.

Color light brown to blackish-brown; woody structure eminently preserved, laminated; on fracture, partly shining, partly dull; may be cut with a knife, cut surface shining; very brittle; on application of a gentle heat, evolves empyreumatic odor and assumes the appearance of charcoal.

Composition, dried at 212 to 220 deg. F:

Volatile matter	41.030
Fixed carbon (charcoal)	57.405
Ash	1.565
	100.00

The air-dried lignite lost 14.89 per cent. of moisture at 220 deg. F.

A qualitative examination of the ash showed the presence of clay and silica, sulphate of lime, iron, alumina, and potassa.

No. 39. Lignite, from same locality as No. 38.

Color dark grayish-brown; woody structure only partly preserved, indistinctly laminated; fracture dull; may be cut with a knife, cut surface shining.

Composition, dried ot 212 to 220 deg. F:

Volatile matter	31.963
Fixed carbon (charcoal)	53.737
Ash	14.300
	100.000

The air-dried lignite lost 12.774 per cent. of moisture at 220 deg. F.

A qualitative examination of the ash showed the presence of clay (preponderating) and silica, sulphate of lime, iron, alumina, and potassa.

———o———

The small amount of ash which these lignites contain, would make them useful as fuel, if timber were scarce in that part of Arkansas where they occur, or as a substitute for stone-coal, in cases where the use of the latter is preferable to that of wood.

NITRE EARTHS.

Of the samples of nitre earth which were collected on the first geological excursion, I made a complete analysis of only one; two have been analyzed by Dr. Owen,* who determined all the various constituents directly, with the exception of the nitric acid, the quantity of which was estimated by the loss. The importance of the subject made it appear desirable to have a direct determination of this acid in the two samples referred to; they are given in Nos. 41 and 42. For the method employed, see "methods of analysis," p. 190.

No. 40. Nitre earth; labeled "white nitre earth formed from decomposition of bottom rock, Marion county."

A soft, calcareous earth, of pale yellowish-red color, feeling slightly gritty between the fingers; of sandy appearance, containing fragments of

* See Dr. Owen's Report.

soft dolomite, and excrements of bats or birds. It is very easily reduced to a fine powder, which feels soft between the fingers.

Composition dried at 240 deg. F:

Matter insoluble in hydrochloric acid	11.516
Oxide of iron, phosphates of alumina, lime and magnesia	5.908
Lime	22.929
Magnesia	14.884
Potassa	1.106
Chlorine	0.062
Sulphuric acid	1.375
Nitric acid	0.973
Carbonic acid	38.487
Organic matter, and loss	2.790
	100.000

The air-dried earth lost 1.681 per cent. of moisture at 240 deg. F.

Another portion of the air-dried earth was treated with distilled water, until fresh portions of the solvent ceased to take up any fixed matter. The solutions were united, evaporated to dryness, and the residue subjected to analysis. 100 parts of the air-dried earth yielded 3.936 parts of solid, soluble matter, at 220 deg., F., which had the following composition:

Lime	1.013
Magnesia	0.180
Potassa	0.066
Chlorine	0.012
Sulphuric acid	1.338
Nitric acid	0.956
Organic matter and water	0.371
	3.936

Hence it follows, that from 100 ℔s of the air-dried earth 1.791 ℔s of nitre may be obtained, which consist of 0.956 ℔s of nitric acid and 0.835 ℔s of potassa.

No. 41. Nitre-determination, in a nitre earth, labeled "laminated nitre earth from a cave in Marion county."

100 parts of the air-dried earth were found to yield 9.892 parts of solid

matter to the solvent action of water; this extract contained 1.33 parts of anhydrous nitric acid, corresponding to 2.493 parts of nitre.

The air-dried earth lost 7.59 per cent. of moisture at 212 deg. F.

No. 42. Nitre-determination, in a nitre earth, labeled "red nitre earth above and below the laminated nitre earth, same cave."

The watery extract from 100 parts of air-dried earth contains 3.305 parts of anhydrous nitric acid, corresponding to 6.195 parts of nitre.

According to Dr. Owen, the air-dried earth lost 3.15 per cent. of moisture at 300 deg. F.

This nitre-earth is by far the richest of the three, a ton yielding nearly 124 lbs of nitre.

WELL AND RIVER WATER.

The examinations of these waters having been performed in the field, with comparatively limited means, only qualitative analyses could be made, and in these even, regard could only be paid to such constituents as occur in not inconsiderable quantities. I hope to be enabled to report at a future period full quantitative analyses of the water of the principal rivers and mineral springs.

No. 43. Water of the St. Francis river, taken at Chalk Bluffs, Greene county.

The ordinary reagents showed only the presence of
Bi-carbonate of lime, and
Bi-carbonate of magnesia.

No. 44. Water from a well on A. L. Stuart's farm, Greene county.

This water is remarkably pure, containing no lime, and only a small quantity of
Bi-carbonate of magnesia, and a trace of
Chloride of magnesium, or an alkaline chloride.

No. 45. Water from a well on Wm. Lane's farm, Greene county.

This is also a very pure water, containing only minute quantities of
Bi-carbonate of lime, and
Bi-carbonate of magnesia.

No. 46. Water from a well on J. P. Harris' farm, dug through shell-marl of the Loess into gravel below.

Contains a considerable amount of

Bi-carbonate of lime, and

Bi-carbonate of magnesia.

No. 47. Water from a well on Thos. McElrath's farm, sunk in the bottom land, Jackson county.

Contains small quantities of

Bi-carbonate of lime, and

Bi-carbonate of magnesia.

The test with chloride of gold showed the presence of a trace of organic matter.

No. 48. Water of White river, taken at Jacksonport, Jackson county.

The water contains not inconsiderable a quantity of

Bi-carbonate of lime; only traces of

Bi-carbonate of magnesia, and

Chlorides.

No. 49. Water from a well on Mr. Cobb's farm, Oil Trough bottom, 6 miles west of Jacksonport.

Contains small quantities of

Bi-carbonate of lime, and

Bi-carbonate of magnesia, and a comparatively large amount of

Chlorides.

No. 50. Water of North fork of White river, taken at Mr. Ware's mill, Izard county.

Contains considerable quantities of

Bi-carbonate of lime, and

Bi-carbonate of magnesia.

No. 51. Water from a spring, being one of the heads of Big creek, taken near J. Young's farm, Marion county.

Contains a large amount of

Bi-carbonate of lime, and

Bi-carbonate of magnesia.

No. 52. Water of the "Mammoth Spring," head of main Spring river, Fulton county.

Temperature of the spring on the 10th of December, 1857, 57 deg. F., the temperature of the atmosphere being 18 deg. F.

The ordinary reagents showed only the presence of considerable quantities of

Bi-carbonate of lime, and
Bi-carbonate of magnesia.

APPENDIX.

After having brought to a close the foregoing analyses, to be embodied in the present Report, I found time to examine a few more of the specimens collected during our first field-excursion. The results could not be reported in their proper places without re-arranging and in part re-writing the contents of the foregoing pages; I, therefore, give them a place in this appendix.

No. 53. Pearlspar, forming veins in the dolomite (No. 32) of the Hoppe ore-bank.

Crystallized, crystals partly interwoven, the characteristic curved surfaces eminently developed; color white to pale flesh-color; covered on surface with a thin layer of peroxide of iron. Powder, pale reddish-white.

Composition, dried at 220 deg. F:

Silicates, insoluble in hydrochloric acid	0.219
Sesquioxide of iron	1.168
Carbonate of lime	55.052
Carbonate of magnesia	43.560
	99.999

No. 54. Massive smithsonite, from Cury creek diggings, township 15, range 5, sections 35 and 36, Independence county.

The ore consists chiefly of a dirty yellowish-gray and bluish-gray cellular mass, the cells mostly of cubical shape as if formed by the destruction of crystals of galena; they are partly filled with dark-gray smithsonite, forming botryoidal incrustations on the walls of the cells, partly with an amorphous, yellow, soft variety of smithsonite; powder of dirty cream-color.

Occurs in fissures in dolomite.

Composition of air-dried ore:

Silica	2.367
Sesquioxide of iron	2.750
Oxide of zinc	55.238
Sulphuret of zinc	0.328
Lime	2.158
Magnesia	1.065
Carbonic acid and water	34.738
	98.644

55.238 oxide of zinc contain 44.334 metallic zinc. A very good ore for smelting, intermediate between No. 4 and No. 3, of the Bath mine.

No. 55. Massive smithsonite, from Mr. —— Smith's land, township 17, range 2 west, section 10, Lawrence county.

A massive, soft, earthy rock, of white, reddish-white, and pale-yellow color, containing amygdaloidal cavities, which are, in part, filled with incrustations of botryoidal smithsonite; the surface of the latter frequently covered with a thin layer of peroxide of iron. The rock contains crystals of galena imbedded.

Composition of the earthy, air-dried ore:

White sand, and clay (?)	26.454
Sesquioxide of iron, and alumina	2.193
Oxide of zinc	27.600
Sulphuret of lead	0.793
Lime	8.048
Magnesia	3.260
Carbonic acid, water, and loss	31.652
	100.000

27.600 parts of oxide of zinc contains 22.15 parts of metallic zinc. Not a rich ore, but equal to the Silesian ore No. 11, of the table on page 156.

No. 56. Smithsonite, from the Koch mine.

For the subjoined analysis, pieces of the pure, botryoidal smithsonite were taken, which occur as an incrustation on the compact ore.

Concentric incrustation, internal structure semi-fibrous; color yellowish-gray, the outermost layer dirty reddish-gray; hardness between 4 and 5: fracture conchoidal; lustre vitreous; subtranslucent; brittle.

Composition:

Silica	1.449
Oxide of zinc	62.864
Oxide of iron	trace
Lime	1.322
Magnesia	trace
Carbonic acid, (loss on ignition)	34.095
	99.730

The rational composition is, perhaps:

Silicate of zinc	2.748
Carbonate of zinc	94.925
" " lime	2.360
	100.033

which requires 34.398 per cent. of carbonic acid, instead of 34.095, as found.

No. 57. Nitre earth; labeled "average nitre-earth, from J. T. Thompson's nitre-cave on Cave creek, Newton county."

Time did not, at present, permit more than a qualitative examination of the watery extract of this earth. It was found to contain:

A large amount of sulphate of lime;
Nitric acid;
Magnesia;
Potassa;
Chlorine, and a very small quantity of
Phosphoric acid.

As soon as circumstances allow, I shall report a complete analysis of this earth.

METHODS OF ANALYSIS.

---o---

In the following pages, I propose giving a short exposition of the methods employed in the analysis of the ores and rocks described in this Report; not for the purpose of serving as a guide to those engaged in similar investigations, but merely to furnish those who are able to judge with a scale, by which to measure the reliability of the results. For this reason, I shall forbear entering into details, and confine myself to giving a general outline.

SMITHSONITE,

Impurities: insoluble silicates; iron; alumina, lime; magnesia.

I. The pulverized mineral is treated with hydrochloric acid, the solution evaporated to dryness over a water-bath, residue treated with dilute hydrochloric acid, and insoluble silicates collected on filter.

II. The filtrate is oxidized with nitric acid, excess of acid partly removed by evaporation, solution nearly neutralized with carbonate of soda, then iron and alumina precipitated with carbonate of baryta; precipitate collected on filter, dissolved in dilute hydrochloric acid, baryta removed by sulphuric acid, and iron and alumina precipitated with ammonia; the ignited and weighed precipitate is dissolved in hydrochloric acid, the solution reduced with metallic zinc, and the iron determined volumetrically with chamælon mineral.

III. The filtrate from the treatment with carbonate of baryta is precipitated with sulphuric acid, to remove baryta, the solution neutralized with ammonia, and precipitated with sulphhydrate of ammonia; liquid with precipitate allowed to rest (in a well-stoppered bottle) for about 24 hours, sulphuret of zinc collected on filter, washed with water containing sulphhydrate of ammonia, dissolved in hydrochloric acid, and precipitated with a hot solution of carbonate of soda (from the washings, traces of zinc removed by sulphhydrate of ammonia); the carbonate of zinc washed with hot water, and ignited.

IV. The filtrate from the sulphuret of zinc is acidified with hydrochloric acid, the sulphur separated by filtration, the lime precipitated with oxalate of ammonia, and in the filtrate the magnesia determined as phosphate of magnesia-ammonia.

For practical purposes it is unnecessary to ascertain the relative quantities of all the different impurities, and the following method, which was employed in the analysis of Nos. 4, 6, and 7, and which recommends itself by great simplicity, may be advantageously followed:

I. The mineral is ignited, and the amount of carbonic acid and water ascertained by the loss in weight.

II. The ignited substance is digested in a beaker, covered with a watch-glass, with a mixture of ammonia and carbonate of ammonia, the residue collected on a filter, ignited, and weighed. The difference in weight expresses the amount of oxide of zinc extracted.

III. The residue consists of silica, alumina, iron, lime, and magnesia, and also contains silicate of zinc, if this compound was present in the ore. Its presence is easily detected, by treating a portion of the residue before the blowpipe on charcoal.

From the fact that silicate of zinc is insoluble in ammonia, it follows that this mode of analysis is not admissible for ores containing more than a few per cent. of this compound.

Schwarz (see Mohr "*Lehrbuch der Titrirmethode, part I, p.* 231, *and part II, p.* 74,") recommends to precipitate the zinc from the ammoniacal solution (II) by means of sulphhydrate of ammonia, to treat the sulphuret of zinc with sesquichloride of iron which is thus reduced to protochloride, and to determine the amount of the latter with chamæleon mineral; 2 equivalents of iron correspond to 1 equivalent of zinc. I have not succeeded in obtaining satisfactory results by means of this method. The reasons for my failure will appear from the following considerations: It is of the utmost importance that the excess of sulphhydrate of ammonia, employed in precipitating the zinc, be thoroughly removed by washing; if this is neglected, a portion of the sesquichloride of iron will become reduced at the expense of this compound, and the amount of zinc, consequently, be found too high. Now, it is extremely difficult to remove the last trace of the precipitant by washing; even in using boiling water it required *nearly two days' washing*, and I have no doubt that during this time a perceptible quantity of sulphuret of zinc becomes oxidized and passes into the washings as sulphate of zinc. If dilute ammonia is used instead of boiling water, the process proceeds still slower, though the danger of loss consequent on oxidation becomes lessened, and perhaps entirely prevented. At any rate, the length of time required in effecting a thorough washing is a serious inconvenience. I should mention here that I took the precaution of allowing the precipitate to settle before throwing it on a filter. The next step consists in placing the filter with the moist precipitate in a stoppered glass cylinder containing neutral sesquichloride of iron and dilute sulphuric acid [the addition of the latter is required in order to effect a complete decomposition]; in doing so, *I invariably noticed a strong odor of sulphuretted hydrogen;* the escaping gas does, of course, not act on the sesquichloride of iron, and the amount of zinc will be found, proportionally, too low. The method, therefore, is possessed of two sources of error, acting in a contrary sense; the two errors may, perchance, counterbalance each other, and the result *may*, consequently, be the correct one; but the method can hardly be relied upon—at least not as far as my experience goes. For this reason the results, thus obtained, have not been embodied in the Report.

PSILOMELANE,

Containing: water, free oxygen; silica; peroxide of iron, alumina; protoxide of manganese, cobalt, baryta, and lime.

I. To determine the amount of free oxygen, I used the method of Fresenius and Will, with the modification of Mohr; it combines great simplicity with accuracy, and requires but little time. From 1.5 to 2.5 grammes of the dried mineral are introduced into a Florence flask, a measured volume of normal oxalic acid and some concentrated sulphuric acid added, and heated over a spirit lamp until the evolution of gas has ceased; if the ore is decomposable only with difficulty, the liquid is poured off from the dark-colored residue, some more normal oxalic acid and sulphuric acid added, and heated again until the residue appears white, or nearly so; the liquid thus obtained is diluted to 500 cubic centimeters; 100 cub. cent. are taken out with a pipette, largely diluted with water, sulphuric acid added, and the excess of normal oxalic acid determined volumetrically with chamæleon mineral; the same process is repeated with another 100 cub. cent. of the solution; subtracting the undecomposed normal oxalic acid from the amount originally used, we obtain the quantity decomposed by the mineral. 1 cub. cent. of normal oxalic acid is equal to 0.008 grammes of free oxygen.

II. Water and oxygen above the composition Mn^3O^4 are determined by ignition.

III. The mineral is treated with strong hydrochloric acid, solution evaporated to dryness, residue treated with dilute hydrochloric acid, and silica collected on filter.

IV. Filtrate diluted with water, and baryta precipitated with sulphuric acid.

V. Filtrate nearly neutralized with carbonate of soda, and iron and alumina precipitated with carbonate of baryta; separated as described above, in the analysis of smithsonite.

VI. After removal of baryta with sulphuric acid, the filtrate is neutralized with ammonia and precipitated with sulphhydrate of ammonia in a well-closed bottle; the precipitate is allowed to settle, collected on a filter, washed with water containing sulphhydrate of ammonia, and digested with dilute hydrochloric acid [the small quantity of sulphuret of cobalt which remains undissolved is collected on a filter and strongly ignited]; from the solution the manganese is precipitated with carbonate of soda, and the precipitate ignited until the weight remains constant.

VII. In the filtrate from the sulphurets, the lime is determined as usual.

LIMONITE,

Containing: Insoluble silicates; water; sesquioxides of iron and manganese, alumina; phosphoric acid; lime, and magnesia.

I. Water determined by ignition.

II. The pulverized mineral is boiled with strong hydrochloric acid until the residue appears colorless; the whole evaporated to dryness; the dry mass treated with dilute hydrochloric acid, and insoluble silicates collected on filter.

III. The filtrate is diluted to 250 cub. cent.; of these

50 cub. cent. are used for the determination of iron by means of chamæleon mineral.

50 or 100 cub. cent. are used for the determination of phosphoric acid by means of molybdate of ammonia.

100 cub. cent. are nearly neutralized with carbonate of soda, acetate of soda added and heated to ebullition until the liquid appears colorless; the precipitate is collected on a filter, washed, dissolved in hydrochloric acid, and reprecipated with ammonia; it contains all the iron, alumina, and phosphoric acid; the filtrate is treated as in IV.

IV. To the filtrate some hypochlorite of soda is added, and enough acetic acid to produce acid reaction, and allowed to rest for 24 hours; the peroxide of manganese is collected on a filter, and ignited [if the precipitate is considerable, it has to be dissolved in hydrochloric acid and precipitated with carbonate of soda].

V. To the filtrate some hydrochloric acid is added, and heat applied until the odors of chlorine and acetic acid have disappeared; the lime is then precipitated with oxalate of ammonia, and from the filtrate the magnesia with phosphate of soda.

DOLOMITE,

Containing: Insoluble silicates; carbonates of lime, and magnesia; sesquioxide of iron with trace of manganese; alumina, potassa.

I. The mineral is dissolved in hydrochloric acid, solution evaposated to dryness, residue treated with water acidified with hydrochloric acid, and insoluble silicates and silica collected on filter.

II. To the filtrate a little chlorine water is added, to oxidize the manganese, then precipitated with ammonia; the precipitate, containing all the iron, alumina, and manganese, and a little lime and magnesia, is redissolved in hydrochloric acid and again treated as above. This precipitate is free from the alkaline earths. It is dissolved in hydrochloric acid and the solution divided into 2 equal portions:

In the first portion iron plus alumina are determined by ammonia;

In the second portion the iron alone is determined by chamæleon mineral.

III. The two filtrates, and washings, are united, and about ¼th of the liquid used for the determination of lime by oxalate of ammonia, and that of magnesia by phosphate of soda.

IV. For the determination of the alkali a fresh portion of the mineral is treated with repeated portions of boiling acetic acid; the filtrates are united, evaporated, transferred to a platina capsule, and ignited until the empyreumatic odor of decomposing acetic acid disappears; the residue is exhausted with boiling water, the liquid mixed with some oxalic acid, evaporated to dryness, ignited; the residue is again treated with boiling water: the filtrate contains the potassa as carbonate; it is converted into chloride, ignited and weighed.

DETERMINATION OF NITRIC ACID.

To ascertain the quantity of nitric acid in the nitre earths subjected to analysis, I proceeded as follows:

100 grammes of the earth are pulverized, and digested over the water-bath with repeatedly renewed portions of distilled water until all the soluble constituents of the earth are taken up by this liquid. The solution

thus obtained is reduced to a small volume by evaporation, and an aliquot part of the concentrated liquid evaporated to a syrupy consistency in a porcelain crucible, over a water-bath. [It is not possible to evaporate the watery extract to dryness by means of the water-bath; the extract assumes the consistency and appearance of honey, without solidifying].

Some pure, soft iron-wire is then dissolved in strong hydrochloric acid, with the necessary precautions for the exclusion of atmospheric air, and the crucible containing the extract thrown into the solution of protochloride of iron; heat is applied to expel the nitric oxide, the liquid diluted with water, and the amount of unoxidized protoxide of iron determined by chamæleon mineral.

GALENA.

In the different specimens of galena which have been analyzed, the amount of lead was not directly determined; but since it was proved by the qualitative examination of these specimens, that no other impurities, besides iron and silver, were present, the amount of lead can easily be ascertained by subtracting from 100 the sum of these impurities *plus* the amount of sulphur.

For the determination of the silver, the following method was pursued: 50 grammes of the finely pulverized ore are intimately mixed with 50 grammes of carbonate of potassa, 25 grammes of cream of tartar, and 10 grammes of metallic iron (small iron tacks); the mixture is placed in an iron crucible, covered with a layer of borax, the crucible closed with an iron lid, and then exposed to a bright red heat until the mass flows quietly. The contents of the crucible are then poured into a conical iron mould, when the metallic lead falls to the bottom, forming a well-defined metallic button which is easily separated from the slag by a blow with a hammer. The weight of the button of lead varied from 39 to 40 grammes. Of the metal thus obtained, about 5 grammes are subjected to cupellation, and the button of silver is weighed on a very delicate balance.

The iron was determined in the following manner: The finely pulverized galena is oxidized with strong nitric acid; to the mass a few drops of concentrated sulphuric acid are added, and heat applied until the excess of nitric acid is completely removed. The dry mass is treated with water, the insoluble sulphate of lead collected on a filter, and washed with dilute sulphuric acid. To the filtrate a piece of metallic zinc is added, in order to reduce the sesquioxide of iron to protoxide, and the amount of the latter determined by chamæleon mineral.

REPORT

OF A

GEOLOGICAL RECONNOISSANCE

OF A PART OF THE STATE OF

ARKANSAS

MADE DURING THE YEARS 1857 AND 1858

BY

EDWARD T. COX,

ASSISTANT GEOLOGIST.

INTRODUCTORY LETTER.

OFFICE OF THE ARKANSAS SURVEY,
New Harmony, Indiana, October 15th, 1858.

DAVID DALE OWEN, M. D.—

Dear Sir: I herewith submit my Report of a Geological Reconnoissance, made in the State of Arkansas, during the fall of 1857, and summer of 1858; prosecuted in accordance with instructions received from you, at different times, while progressing with the survey.

Allow me, also, to acknowledge here, the many obligations I owe to you for valuable counsel and aid, while carrying forward the survey, under your direction.

Most respectfully yours,

E. T. COX.

INSTRUCTIONS.

The following are instructions received, on different occasions, from Dr. D. D. Owen, Principal Geologist of the State of Arkansas:

Instructions, dated October, 1857.

" After separating from corps No. 1, you will proceed by the most feasible route between Cache and Black rivers, through the north and north-west part of Greene, south-east part of Randolph, the eastern part of Lawrence, and the north part of Jackson county, and make a general geological reconnoissance of those portions of the State of Arkansas.

You will keep your camp on some main route, and make lateral excursions to any points of interest between Black river and the eastern branch of Cache river.

Along the line of your route, you will endeavor to see the gentlemen whose names are in the list herewith furnished, under the head of the counties through which you pass, for the purpose of obtaining information in regard to localities considered of special interest, and make a geological exploration of those which may be considered important.

You will, also, make inquiries in regard to sections of rocks exposed on Black and Cache rivers, and examine the same, in order to obtain a clue to the formations of that part of Arkansas.

I would particularly call your attention to a locality in Randolph county, on Mr. McLaires' land, supposed to contain iron; also, to a locality near Pocahontas, in the same county, which is, perhaps, an extension of the same bed; also, to deposits of black oxide of manganese, supposed to exist in some of the northern counties.

In your descent of the valleys of Black and Cache rivers, you will extend your observations as far south as Jacksonport. If you arrive at this place before corps No. 1, you will encamp at some convenient point, in the vicinity, and wait for further instructions; you will, however, occupy the time, while awaiting my arrival, in making explorations in the vicinity of Jacksonport."

Instructions received at Jacksonport, Jackson county, Ark., Nov. 17th, 1857.

"After crossing Black river, you will proceed to the zinc mines, situated on Reed's creek, in the southern part of Lawrence county, and make a reconnoissance of that part of the country lying between Strawberry and Black rivers, as far north as township 17. You will proceed thence to make a reconnoissance of the country lying between Strawberry and Spring rivers, taking a north-west course towards Salem, in Fulton county, as far north as township 19 or 20. You will then explore Fulton county south of that line, and continue west, through the ranges of township 19; cross White river, and encamp at some suitable point near Yellville, where you will await my arrival and further instructions."

Instructions, dated December 4th, 1857.

"After examining the salt-petre cave, situated in the Horseshoe bend of White river, in Marion county, and collecting samples of the earth for chemical analysis, you will recross White river, and examine that portion of Fulton county south of your previous route, and pass through Cross-plains. Thence you will proceed by 'Evening Shade,' in the south-west corner of Lawrence county, to Cury creek, in Independence county, and examine the prospect for lead ore in that county. After completing your observations in the northern and eastern part of Independence county, you will cross Black river and meet me at Jacksonport."

Instructions, dated May 12th, 1858.

"During the time I shall be absent in Pulaski and Hot Spring counties, you will examine the north-western tier of townships, not previously explored, in Randolph county, and visit Rice's spring on the waters of Muddy creek, take its temperature, and make a qualitative chemical examination of it at the fountain head; you will investigate, also, whatever may be of interest in that vicinity.

From Randolph county, you will proceed through Lawrence county to Batesville, in Independence county, and examine the geological formation on the north side of White river, between that place and the warehouse below the mouth of Laferty creek; and especially ascertain whether there is any evidence of the existence of an outburst of basalt, or other igneous rocks, amongst the subcarboniferous group in that vicinity. You will examine, also, the fossiliferous shale below the town of Batesville.

The manganese locality, a short distance above the mouth of Lafferty creek, was already examined, last season, by corps No. 1; but, as it is desirable to obtain a greater variety of the ores than was then collected, you will either obtain an additional supply from Dr. Smith, former superintendent of the mines, who lives somewhere in the neighborhood, or at the mines. Endeavor, especially, to ascertain whether any of the softer and blacker varieties of this ore occur, and have been taken out; such as are known to mineralogists under the name of "pyrolusite," and "manganite," which are more valuable than the hard, compact "psilomelane" ore, which was found most abundant in the rubbish of the mine last year.

You will write to me from Batesville, and let me know when you will be in Van Buren county, and at what place it will be most convenient for us to meet, either in that county or White county.

From Independence county, you will cross over White river, into White county, and explore the northern townships in that county, as far south as Searcy.

In the counties south of White river, you will especially investigate for coal, as the south-west dip of the rocks from the Oil-trough ridge and Shields' bluff, lead to the inference that coal may soon come in south of these localities."

Instructions dated 21st July, 1858.

"You will proceed to finish the geological reconnoissance of Crawford county, examining those localities in the south-east part not yet explored; especially the coal on Frog bayou, and the sulphur spring on the property of Mr. Herd.

From Crawford county pass into Franklin, and examine the state salt spring, on Mulberry creek, exploring, also, the geological formations on that stream; thence pass down towards Ozark, and take the most feasible route to examine the coal region, on the waters of Horsehead creek, in Johnson county, and the geological position of the rocks, in the northern part of that county.

As I, myself, shall have an opportunity of examining the Spadra coal, it will not be necessary for you to go to that locality in this county.

In your explorations of Pope county, I would especially direct your attention to a locality near the Dwight Old Mission, where the so-called "lapis lazuli" was said to have been found by Mr. Washburn. Your survey in the middle, northern, and eastern part of this county, will be best regulated after you have learnt more of the other localities of interest. When in Conway county, examine the state salt spring. There are also several other localities of interest in this county, on the Cadron, and, perhaps also, on Cedar creek, a branch of that stream, which may require your attention. When in the north-east part of this county, you will pass over a few miles into White county, and examine a locality of coal, of which I have previously given you a note and directions how to find it. The rest of this county has already been explored.

Ascertain where the coal measures of Conway county terminate, and the metamorphic slate formation of Pulaski county commences, in your easterly route into Pulaski. It is, probably, somewhere near Palarm bayou. Some gold ore is said to have been found somewhere near that stream.

One of the most important localities to be examined in Pulaski, is the Kellogg mine of argentiferous galena, some ten miles north of Little Rock, on Kellogg's creek.

As I have been over the road from Little Rock to Oakland Grove, in White county, it will not be necessary for you to pass over that ground again at present, unless you hear of something special that may require your attention.

I know of nothing particular at present to which I can direct your attention, while passing through Prairie county into Monroe, where your geological reconnoissance will terminate for this season; but you will take every opportunity to inquire, before you enter a county, what there may be in it of particular geological interest, and direct your course accordingly.

In each county which you pass through, you will collect sets of characteristic soils, upon the same plan as heretofore followed by the geological corps of Arkansas.

D. D. OWEN, *M. D.*,
Geologist of Arkansas."

REPORT.

———o———

GREENE COUNTY.

As you had examined, personally, the country adjacent to the Chalk bluff, before we separated on our respective routes, it will be unnecessary for me to make any report on that locality.

The northern part of Greene county, included within my instructions, belongs to the quaternary and alluvial period. The quaternary deposits observed, consist of sands, gravel and potter's clay; these occupy the highlands, extending from the Chalk bluff, on the St. Francis river, through the greater part of range seven. They are spread over an area of eight or ten miles in width; and their vertical thickness is from one hundred to one hundred and fifty feet.

The alluvium forms the bottom lands of the St. Francis, Cache, and Black rivers.

A locality in section 36?, township 21 north, range 7 east, one and a half miles from Mr. James W. Payne's, has been rendered notorious on account of a phenomenon, which induced Mr. Payne and others, to believe that gold or other precious metals might be found there. The account given is as follows: When Mr. Payne was out hunting about two years ago, he heard a slight noise at his feet, and on looking down saw the earth open to the width of three or four inches; being reminded of the memorable New Madrid earthquake, which sunk a large district of land in this county, this frightful phenomenon, of course, alarmed him, and he left, supposing the hill was about to be engulfed. After a few days, finding that no serious catastrophe had taken place, he returned to view the condition of things. On examining the ground, he became possessed of the idea that the opening of the earth was a revelation, to notify him of the existence of a vein of gold below. In this belief he was further strengthened by the fact of the tops of the trees, in the vicinity, being dead. Accordingly, with some of his neighbors, he went to work, and sunk three pits, one of which was thirty feet deep. Unfortunately, when I visited the place, these pits had become filled up with the rubbish and washings from the hill above.

After the examination of the material thrown from these pits, and aided by the memory of Mr. Payne, I was enabled to make out the following succession in the deposits:

(*a*) Slope above the shaft, composed of waterworn hornstone and chert gravel, and sand, which are sometimes formed into a ferruginous conglomerate of small extent·········	30 feet.
(*b*) Light colored plastic clay, with small, pure, transparent, lenticular crystals of selenite imbedded ··············10 to	15 "
(*c*) Variegated plastic clay, alternating with beds of clay, in all about?··	15 "
Bottom of the shaft·····································	0 "
	60 "

The deposits passed through in this shaft, are not such as to afford any hope of finding gold, or other precious metals. The labors of Mr. Payne have disclosed, however, in the member marked (*b*), of the above section, a material which will undoubtedly prove to be a valuable fertilizer of land, from the large amount of selenite (a transparent variety of gypsum) which it contains. Judging from its external appearance, the selenite forms about one-third of the whole mass composing this member. An earth, so rich in this ingredient, and so easy of access, must be of great value to the farming community.

The lower bed reached, (*c*), is a good potter's clay, which, by a proper selection, and washing, will be applicable for the manufacture of the coarser kinds of porcelain.

The yellow member of this bed, which is sometimes several feet thick, is a variety of yellow ochre that has commercial value as a cheap paint, used for the coarser kinds of work.

The evidence of the cracking of the earth, at this locality, is still very apparent; and it is probable that such cracks are not uncommon, and may have favored the formation of the selenite, by giving egress to pent-up sulphurous acid or sulphuretted hydrogen gases, which, by oxidation, have been converted into sulphuric acid; this, combining with the lime present in some of the quaternary deposits, has formed the sulphate of lime, (selenite). These cracks may have originated, in part, from the shrinking of the underlying argillaceous strata; and in part, from the slumbering effects of former earthquake action.

The other mystery which aided in drawing attention to this locality, the decay of the tops of the trees, may be explained from the fact, that the soil has been washed away from their base into these cracks, and they are left rooted merely in gravel. Thus deprived of sufficient nourishment, the languid sap fails to reach the top, and the upper branches naturally decay first.

Where the hills are of sufficient height, a bed of waterworn hornstone and chert-gravel is superimposed on the quaternary sand and clay. The pebbles are from one to three inches in diameter; occasionally in some of these are found fragments of carboniferous fossils.

Beneath this gravel bed, a ferruginous conglomerate, or pudding stone, sometimes occurs in sheets of two or more inches in thickness. This is the only instance of finding a hard cemented rock in any portion of Greene county, within the scope of my observation.

In the stratum of potter's clay (*c*) at Mr. Payne's shaft, were found a few specimens of the leaves of oaks (*quercus*), and willow (*salix*), which belong undoubtedly to species now living. No other organic remains were observed; but I have no doubt that if good exposures of this bed were accessible, some associate land or fresh-water shells might be discovered.

Mineral and Agricultural Resources.

Though no metallic ores proper have yet been found in the northern part of Greene county, I consider the selenite bed (*b*) near Mr. Payne's of great importance, in an agricultural point of view; and it may hereafter be the source of no inconsiderable revenue to the county. It occurs in beautiful, small, transparent crystals, abundantly distributed through the clay, which itself contains soda, potash, and perhaps, phosphates and nitrates, forming a combination which will be applicable as a mineral fertilizer to a great variety of soils.

The underlying stratum (*c*) will afford a good, cheap, red, as well as yellow paint; for, by simple burning, the yellow ochre is converted into a red ochre; this latter can be used as a dyestuff for coarse cloth and yarn.

Potter's clay is in great abundance, and of excellent quality for common ware.

In the absence of more durable rocks, the ferruginous conglomerate may be used for the underpining of houses, building chimneys and walling up wells.

The alluvial bottoms, above overflow of the rivers and creeks, are very productive and easily cultivated. The elevated land between St. Francis and Cache rivers, known by the name of Crowley's ridge, is somewhat broken, but highly susceptible of cultivation, producing all kinds of grain; it is particularly noted for its adaptation to the growth of wheat. Mr. A. Muckelroy, who lives on section 19, township 21 north, range 8 east, informed me that he had raised six consecutive crops of wheat on his land without any apparent diminution of fertility; in fact, all the farmers with whom I conversed, spoke in great praise of its wheat growing properties; and when by continued cultivation it may require renovation, there lies close at hand, in the gypsiferous clays, a supply of mineral manure that will keep it in good heart.

The settlers in this part of Greene county, are just beginning to turn their attention to agriculture; heretofore, the great abundance of game seduced them into a thriftless way of living; depending almost exclusively, for a livelihood, on the sale of furs and peltries, which constitute, at all times, a critical and uncertain means of support. As game is now becoming scarce, they are compelled to devote their time to agriculture, or move farther west, where wild animals are more numerous.

The projected railroad, from Fulton, in Texas, to Cairo, at the junction of the Ohio and Mississippi rivers, runs through township 21, range 6, and if completed, will prove of incalculable advantage to a region of country rich in fertile lands; as the want of a ready market for the surplus produce of the country, is one of the greatest drawbacks to its progress.

A plank road from the Chalk bluff, to Point Pleasant, on the Mississippi river, twelve miles below New Madrid, is under construction and will soon be completed.

This road will prove highly beneficial to Greene county, and is the best route for emigrants coming from Kentucky, Tennessee, and the Carolinas, who wish to locate in the northern part of Arkansas. The emigration to and through Greene county, during the fall and winter of 1857, was very great; and as the people of this and the adjoining county of Randolph, receive, from this emigration, no small amount of money, in exchange for produce, it is to their interest to improve the road from the Chalk bluff to Pocahontas, particularly the crossing of Cache river, which is in a wretchedly bad condition, and could be made passable at very little cost. In attempting to cross this river, our mules mired down and came very near being drowned in trying to extricate themselves from the deep mud. We were compelled to obtain assistance, and after disengaging the team had to get the wagon out by hand.

The principal growth of timber on the highland is large white, black, and red oaks, mockernut hickory, (commonly called black hickory,) and a few shell-bark hickories. On the alluvial lands of Cache river, are found, in addition to the above, large poplar, black and sweet gums, and in the sloughs, cypress.

RANDOLPH COUNTY.

The portion of Randolph county, east of Black river, is covered with an alluvial deposit, elevated but a few feet above high water; and, with the exception of a low ridge, which divides the waters of Cache from those of Black river, it is much cut up by sloughs and lakes. Immediately on the west bank of Black river, at Pocahontas, magnesian limestones of the lower silurian period are seen at the water's edge, and extend up into the highest ridges, where they are capped by black and orange-colored sandstone and waterworn gravel of the quaternary period. The country is generally broken, with hills from one to two hundred and fifty feet in height, covered on their slopes with chert, which has weathered out of the limestone.

On the property of Mr. Samuel McLaire, one and a half miles from Pocahontas, is a deposit of black ferruginous sandstone, exposed to the thickness of (23) twenty-three feet, and forming the top of what is considered to be the highest ridge in the county. It is frequently fluted, and resembles in its outward appearance and fracture, a rough variety of pig iron.* At some localities this rock is of a dark orange-color, friable, and readily decomposing into coarse-grained sand. In its lithological character, it resembles very much the indurated and cemented portions of the orange-sand formation of Mississippi and Alabama. Indeed it is so complete a counterpart, that when specimens were exhibited to Dr. E. H. Hilgard, Geologist of Mississippi, he at once recognized the identity with those he had himself collected in the State of Mississippi.

The place of this sandstone is probably in Greene county, below the quaternary clay, which, however, I did not see in Randolph county; it appears to rest immediately on the lower silurian rocks.

The following approximate section exhibits the position of the rocks in this county, extending from the bed of Black river to the waterworn quaternary gravel on the tops of the highest ridges:

*This is probably the locality referred to in my instructions.

(*a*)	Waterworn gravel	1 to 10 feet.
(*b*)	Rough, black, fluted sandstone, equivalent to the "orange sand formation" of Mississippi	23 "
(*c*)	Place of iron ore deposit	1 to 4 "
(*d*)	White cherty limestone; chert in large masses, very brittle and full of cracks	30 to 80 "
(*e*)	Light-gray limestone, mottled with flesh-colored spar, passing down into a light-colored calciferous sand-rock	66 "
(*f*)	Hard compact cherty magnesian limestone, in the bed of Black and Eleven Point rivers, as seen at Imboden's ferry	80 "
		253 feet.

The grayish-buff, hard, and close textured magnesiam limestone (*f.*) forms the bed of Black river, at Pocahontas, and Eleven Point river, at Mr. J. H. Imboden's. Its thickness could not be seen at Pocahontas, but on Eleven Point river it is exposed to the thickness of eighty feet or more. (*e.*) is also best seen on Eleven Point river. At its base, it is a light-gray, calciferous sand-rock, with a sharp grit, and passes upward into a gray limestone, mottled with flesh-colored spar. (*d.*) is a rough weathering magnesian limestone, full of whitish chert segregated in large masses which are filled with cracks, and readily break into small pieces. This member has a variable thickness of from thirty to one hundred feet or more, and may be seen along the road from Pocahontas to the ferry on Eleven Point river. On the top of this rock is the place of the iron ore deposits (*c.*) The iron ore appears to be scattered about in patches, from one to four feet in depth; but it was only found extending over a limited area. Though sometimes mixed with too much sand, it is usually of excellent quality, and belongs to a variety designated by mineralogists as "limonite." It is usually in large cellular blocks, but occasionally presents a globular, and concentric structure.

The rough, ferruginous sandstone, (*b.*) near Pocahontas, possesses a remarkable, fluted structure, and was generally supposed to be manganese ore; but, on examination, it is found to contain only a trace of that metal. In the State of Mississippi, some of the slabs of this rock are so universally, and regularly fluted that they have been used for water spouts.

The bed (*a.*) composed of waterworn gravel, from one to four inches in diameter, belongs above the ferruginous sandstone, but is often seen, where that member is wanting, resting on the older rocks. It usually forms the capping to the highest ridges, and has a thickness of ten feet or more.

Rice's spring, situated on the waters of Mud creek, a branch of Fourche Dumas, on section 14, township 21 north, range 1 west, is a place of much resort for invalids from this and the adjoining counties. The following is the result of the qualitative chemical examination, made at the fountain head:

Temperature of the air 82 deg. F., temperature of the water 62 deg. F.
Carbonic acid (abundant).
Bi-carbonate of lime.
Bi-carbonate of magnesia.
Bi-carbonate of the protoxide of iron.
Sulphates, a trace?

The examination of this spring was made at a very unfavorable time; the unusually heavy rains, which fell in the spring, had completely saturated the surface of the earth, and diluted the spring with fresh water. From the above analysis, it appears to be a weak chalybeate, whereas it is represented by those who frequent it in a dry time to be a strong sulphur water. In its present state, acetate of lead would give no reaction of sulphuretted hydrogen.

Small deposits of hydrated brown oxide of iron (limonite) are seen, at various places in this county. The most extensive are those near J. H. Imboden's on Eleven Point river, and in the vicinity of Old Jackson, close to the boundary line between Randolph and Lawrence counties. It is possible a sufficiency of good ore may be found at the latter locality to supply a small forge.

Agriculture.

East of Black river the soil is principally river deposit; and, where not submerged by ordinary freshets, is easily cultivated and remarkably productive. It is well adapted for corn, wheat, oats, and clover. Samples of soils were collected in this part of the county, from a farm 18 miles from Pocahontas, belonging to Maj. Proudfit. The virgin soil is of a light black color, and the sub-soil a yellow clay. The field, in which the soil No. 2 was collected, had been in cultivation twenty years, nearly all the time in corn, and will now produce with ordinary tillage a crop of 50 or 70 bushels to the acre.

West of Black river, the principal soils for cultivation are the rich alluvial lands adjacent to the river.

The growth of timber on the east side of Black river, with the exception of black walnut, is the same as that noted in Greene county. On the west side of this river the growth is small oak and hickory, on the hills;

whilst on the river bottoms the timber is large, and contains, in addition to the hickory, gum and elm.

LAWRENCE COUNTY.

The geological position of the rocks, along my route, have been mostly determined by their lithological character, owing to the almost total absence of organic remains; in one member alone of the magnesian limestones were any discovered, and they were only a few very imperfect casts of the genus *orthis*, too indistinct for determination; also a simgle specimen of an *orthoceratite*, which is probably new. The want of so essential an aid to the determination of the position of rocks, (especially where there has been a great thinning out of the members, and a condition which indicates a deposition on a very unequal bottom, together with a subsequent cutting away by currents of the deposited members,) renders the identification of equivalent formations difficult and uncertain. The accompanying section may therefore require, upon more minute investigation and comparison, correction in some of the details; and, for the present, I shall only indicate the system to which I think they will hereafter prove to belong, without designating the particular member they may represent.

The strata are lettered in the ascending order.

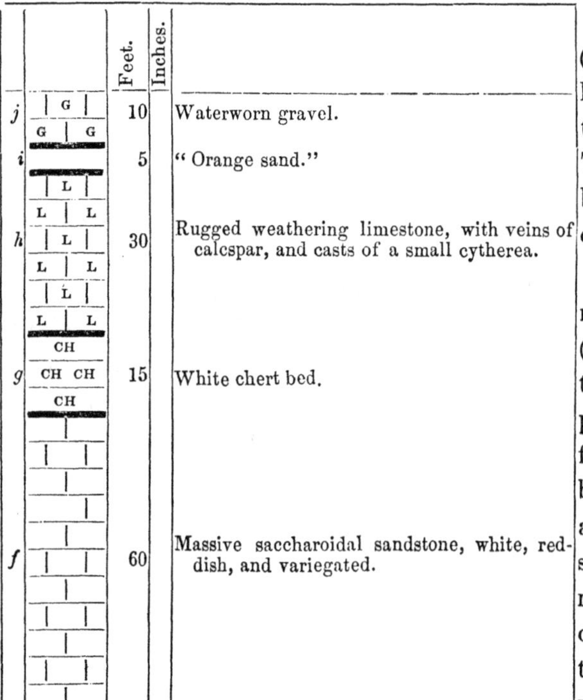

All the members from (*a*) to (*h*) inclusive, belong, most probably, to the lower silurian period. The remaining members (*i*) and (*j*), are of quaternary date.

The thick-bedded magnesian limestone (*a*) and (*b*) are the rocks in which the zinc, lead, and copper ores are usually found. The copper is but sparingly disseminated in some of the calcspar veins ramifying this rock. On the property of Mr. C. T. Stewart, township 17, range 2 west, many small sam-

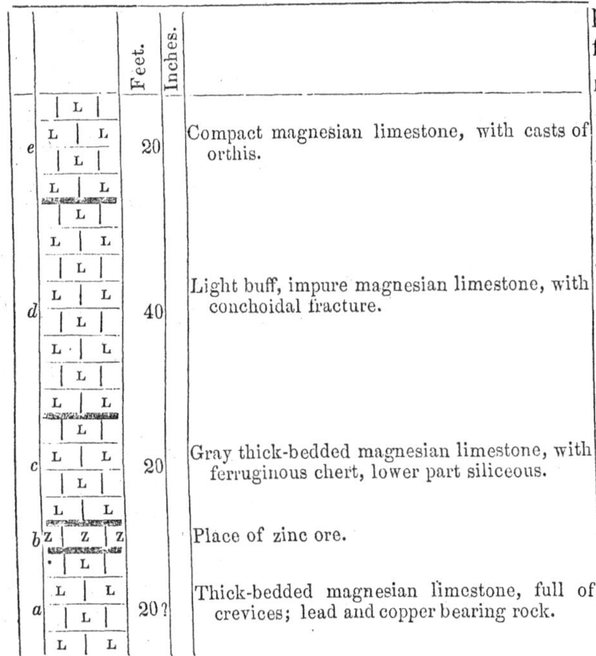

	Feet.	Inches.	
e	20		Compact magnesian limestone, with casts of orthis.
d	40		Light buff, impure magnesian limestone, with conchoidal fracture.
c	20		Gray thick-bedded magnesian limestone, with ferruginous chert, lower part siliceous.
b			Place of zinc ore.
a	20?		Thick-bedded magnesian limestone, full of crevices; lead and copper bearing rock.

ples of copper pyrites found, and a similar variety of ore was also found in the same geological position on the property of Mr. William R. Williams, on section 32, township 17 north, range 6 west.

The veins of calcspar in which the copper occurs, have no constant direction, where seen; but it is probable that, when the country comes to be examined more in detail, they may be found connected with some system of true veins.

The principal working for lead, in these rocks, in Lawrence county, has been made on the property of Mr. E. W. Houghton, six miles from Powhatan, on section 10, township 17 north, range 2 west, where as many as twenty pits have been sunk, from which between one and three thousand pounds of galena have been taken out. No profitable lode was reached, therefore the diggings were discontinued. Surface lead ore ("float mineral") has been occasionally picked up, over a district about one-fourth of a mile in breadth, and extending several miles in a north-west direction; but no continuous vein has so far been discovered.

In the openings which have been made in this county, the cap rock is first reached; after penetrating it, at a depth of thirty or forty feet, members (*a*) and (*b*) of the preceding section are reached; in these, small crevices occur, in which the lead ore is found, accompanied with clay, charged with oxide of iron ("*gossan*"). These crevices have a bearing north-east and south-west, but do not extend continuously any great distance. The abandoned shafts, at this locality, had become mostly filled with rubbish, so that I had no opportunity of seeing the position of the ore at the bottom. When more time can be devoted to the examination of this county, a more satisfactory conclusion may be arrived at, in regard to this lead region, than could be gained in the time allowed for a simple reconnoissance of the country. All that can be at present stated, from the best information, is that the ore was rather more abundant at the greatest depth reached, than near the surface, as if it might concentrate into a true vein. For want of sufficient capital to sink deeper, these mines have never been thoroughly proved.

Associated with the lead at Houghton's diggings, is a yellow, earthy-looking rock, resembling indurated mud; hence, labeled mudstone, which proves on examination to be remarkably rich in carbonate of zinc; for the chemical constituents of this ore, see the Chemical Report.

Many other localities in this county have afforded some lead. On the headwaters of Reed's creek, on the property of Mr. Robert G. Shaver, township 15, range 4 west, lead ore is found, associated with carbonate of zinc and zinc-blende (sulphuret of zinc). At this place, digging has only been made to the depth of two or three feet, entirely insufficient to prove the richness of the deposit. The crevices in which the lead is found, traverse the strata in a north-east and south-west course. This locality has the appearance of being a very favorable place in which to find a good vein of galena; at least, it is worthy of a more systematic search than has yet been made. The rocks in which this lead occurs, belong also to *a* and *b* of the section.

Carbonate of zinc, belonging to the variety known as "smithsonite," is very abundant in this county, and, for the purpose of converting this ore into the metallic zinc of commerce, works have been erected by a company of gentlemen from St. Louis, known as the Independence Mining Company. Their works are located on section 22, township 16 north, range 4 west, and are called " Calamine," after the zinc ore of that name.

So far as can be ascertained by the present openings, the zinc ore does not run in veins or crevices, but occurs in beds, associated with a red ferruginous clay, resting on a dolomitic limestone. Both the matrix of red clay and specimens of the associate limestone, which were analyzed by Wm. Elderhorst, M. D., the Chemist to the Survey, have been found to contain a small per centage of zinc. The ore, imbedded in the clay, is usually of a porous or cellular character; but sometimes compact, and covered with crystals stained with oxide of iron. That which is found in contact with the dolomitic bedrock, is mostly in mammillary or botryoidal masses, having an opalescent appearance on the fresh fractured surface. The corroded and irregular surface of the dolomite seems to indicate that large portions of it must have been removed, perhaps by some material interchange of the elements of the rocks and the metallic solutions pervading it. The small fractures, which traverse this bed rock in every direction, are, at some of the localities, filled with beautiful rose-colored crystals of carbonate of zinc, resembling pearlspar.

The follwing section will show the succession of the rocks at "Calamine," and the relative position of the zinc ore:

Slope to the top of the hill covered with chert and scattered masses of brown oxide of iron, resting on limestone with cherty segregations	35 feet.
Zinc ore, resting on cherty magnesian limestone (*b*) of the previous section	35 "
Calciferous sandstone	10 "
Magnesian limestone	16 "
Spring at "Calamine" furnace	0 "
	86 "

The ore bed in the above section is only a few yards from the smelting furnace, and is called the "Koch mine," after Dr. Koch, one of the members of the smelting company.

The most extensive deposits of calamine seen, were at the "Hoppe mine," section 19, township 16 north, range 2 west; "Bath mine," section 29, township 17 north, range 3 west; and the "Raney mine," three miles south-east of Smithville.

At all of these localities of calamine, the ore occurs under precisely the same conditions; consequently a description of one, will answer for all.

The "Hoppe mine" is opened on the north-west side of a low and very gradually sloping hill, some fifty feet above the valley. A great many tons of calamine have already been taken out from the present opening, which is about six feet deep; and the ore has been proved to continue to a depth exceeding fifteen feet, by trial shafts, sunk for this purpose. The greater portion of the ore, lies in irregularly curved and hollow masses, sometimes covered with rusty-looking crystals of carbonate of zinc, having its interstices, as well as the intervening spaces between the blocks, filled with a tenacious, red, ferruginous clay. This clay is found resting upon a magnesian limestone, about four feet thick, presenting the appearance of a segregated mass, and is traversed by small veins of the carbonate and sulphuret of zinc; the former, sometimes, in beautiful rose-colored crystals. The calamine resting on, or in close proximity to, the dolomitic bed rock, usually presents a brecciated appearance, caused by the mammillary opalescent carbonate of zinc, enclosing fragments of an amorphous zinc ore, which has the appearance of dolomite, and which had very probably that composition, but has become carbonate of zinc by a process of displacement.

Some specimens of the ore found at these mines, convey the idea of a simultaneous deposition of the zinc and dolomite; while others rather indicate an infiltration of the zinc through interstices of the previously formed rock. Perhaps the most plausible explanation of these phenomena, is that the ore was first in the state of sulphuret, and was subsequently changed into carbonate by some reciprocal play of chemical affinities acting from the interior upwards. The increase of the sulphuret, as you descend in the rocks, and the general structure of the deposits, which resemble inverted cones, showing a divergence at the surface from a central point of action; together with the existence of carbonate of zinc, in the associate rocks and clay, rather favor this view of its formation.

It is a remarkable fact, to which attention was first called by Dr. Koch, that, where deposits of calamine are found at the surface, the only vegetation to be seen is a small, black *lichen*, closely adhering to the ore or accompanying rocks; and the soil, to the depth of a few inches, is of an intense black color.

There are, in addition to those already mentioned, four other mines, opened and belonging to the Independence Mining Company, on the following sections, viz: Section 28, township 17 north, range 3 west; sections 12, 28, and 29, township 18 north, range 4 west.

At the town of Powhatan, in the street leading to Smithville, I discovered a deposit of carbonate of zinc, the extent of which cannot be known without digging; but it is no doubt considerable, and there is every reason to believe, that good calamine will be found abundant in the immediate vicinity of this town.

Powhatan is situated on Black river, a stream navigable for small boats, at all seasons of the year; it has under construction, and partly graded, a plank road leading to Gainsville, in Greene county, which will intersect the Cairo and Fulton railroad twelve miles distant. This, together with the fact, that it is surrounded by, and close to, the main deposits of zinc ore, renders it the most desirable point for the location of a zinc smelting furnace. In addition to the advantages to be gained at this place for shipping the metallic products of the furnace, abundance of charcoal may at all times be had, from the extensive forest bordering on Black river.

These suggestions, for the location of a zinc furnace at Powhatan, are made from the fact that the "Calamine" furnace, from mismanagement, did not go into successful operation; and experience has shown that its location is not a favorable one. At all events, before the members of the zinc company remodel their establishment and engage experienced smelters, they should take into consideration the advantages of a change in the location of their works to Powhatan, or some equally accessible point on Black river; because the success of the enterprise certainly depends, in a great measure, on the proper location of the smelting establishment.

Considerable beds of excellent brown oxide of iron have been found in this county, strewed about over the ground in loose blocks. The original place of this ore is between *c* and *d* of the previous section.

This ore not only occurs in the usual stalactitic botryoidal and mammillary forms; but, also, crystallized; the form of the crystals being modified octohedrons (pyramido-octohedrons), which seem to be pseudomorphs from magnetic iron ore.

By far the most usual form of this ore is a stalactitic or mammillary structure on one side, whilst the other side is flat, as if it might have been attached to rocks, over and from which the ferruginous waters flowed and dripped, gradually depositing their iron.

The most abundant localities seen, for iron ore, were on the property of Alfred Bevens & Co., on the waters of Williams creek, sections 23, 25 and 30, township 16 north, range 4 west. On section 25 this mineral has assumed the form familiarly known amongst miners as "pot-ore," imbedded in a red ferruginous clay, resting on dolomite. This bed is from two to five feet thick. The upper part is sandy, the middle nearly free from sand, and the lower part usually of excellent quality for smelting. The surface of the ground, above this bed, is covered with a mixture of siliceous, and good-working blocks of stalactitic ore.

Alfred Bevens & Co. have erected a forge on Williams creek, one and a half miles north-east of the zinc furnace at "Calamine," for working this ore; it has two fires, and is driven by a good water-power. When visited, this forge was undergoing thorough repairs, and preparations were being made to introduce the hot blast in place of the cold blast, formerly in use, by which alteration it was expected to increase the amount of swaged bar iron manufactured from (500) five hundred to (1600) sixteen hundred pounds per day. Though the quantity of iron produced at these works is not great, owing to the mode of manufacture, which is wasteful of ore, and especially so of fuel; yet it is of excellent quality and meets with a ready sale on the spot, without seeking a market.

Another very promising supply of iron ore, for a small forge, was seen near Dr. John Bevens, township 15? range 3 west.

On Big creek, a branch of Strawberry, there is a white cellular quartzose rock found in abundance, intercalated amongst the sandstones of the section of this county, which may afford good millstones; indeed, millstones have been made out of it for some of the mills in the vicinity. A pair of stones made from this rock, may be seen running in Jone's mill on Big creek, six miles from the mouth, and have proved of excellent quality for corn.

The coarse-grained saccharoidal sandstone (*f*) in the vertical section of the rocks in Lawrence county is mostly of a dark red color, but locally very white, and occasionally ornamented with buff-colored bands. This sandstone makes its appearance in the south-eastern part of the county, near Mr. Campbell's, caps the hills on Big creek (Williams creek), four miles south of the zinc furnace at Calamine, and extends in a north-west course through "Evening Shade," or Hookram, as it is usually called, and continues on through Fulton and Marion counties; universally covered with a luxuriant growth of yellow pine.

The orange sand (*i*) and the water-worn gravel bed (*j*) were seen in the vicinity of Powhatan, the former corresponds to the ferruginous sand belonging to the quarternary in Greene and Randolph counties. The western limits of these two deposits is somewhere near range 4 west, since I was not able to discover either it or the gravel bed west of that line; in fact, I was not able to detect the ferruginous sand west of the line between ranges three and four.

At Powhatan the citizens were extremely anxious to know if stone coal did not exist close by, as fragments had been found on the river sand-bars, which, it was supposed, had been broken from the main deposit and transported by the water. For their information, I may here state, that the true coal-bearing rocks do not exist in the counties through which Black river flows; nor yet in Greene county, where some of its tributaries take their rise; hence there is no probability of discovering beds of bituminous coal; but there are beds of lignite amongst the quarternary deposits of this latter county, some of which has very much the appearance of coal. I am disposed, however, to think that the lumps of coal found on the sand-bars, were most likely dropped from the steamboats navigating the river.

Agriculture.

The upland soils of Lawrence county, west of Black river, are derived chiefly from the cherty and earthy magnesian limestones of the lower silurian period, and its overlying sandstones. Soils derived from the quarternary are limited to some of the ridges bordering on Black river, east of range four. The soils selected in this county, for analysis, were collected on section 15, township 17 north, range 2 west, overlying and derived from the buff, earthy, magnesian limestones of the lower silurian system.

East of Black river the soils are essentially alluvial, like those of the eastern part of Randolph. The "Buncomb ridge" may be especially cited for its productiveness; and, being more elevated than the adjacent land, is not subject to overflow.

The timber on the highlands, with the exception of the pine ridges, where the sandstone prevails, is a thin growth of stunted oak. On the bottom land, the growth of timber is large, and comprises white, black, red and postoaks, gum, hickory and black walnut.

JACKSON COUNTY.

The northern part of this county, examined by me as far south as the town of Jacksonport, on White river, is entirely destitute of solid rock. The geological formations are those earthy deposits, such as usually constitute alluvial lands. The low ridge, dividing the waters of Black river and village creek, is composed as follows:

Siliceous soil and subsoil......	7 feet.
Tough yellow clay	18 "
	25 feet.

These are underlaid by a light-colored sand, the thickness of which could not be seen; this sand forms the substratum, which affords unfailing supplies of good water, and is reached by sinking wells, at a depth of from 15 to 30 feet. From the qualitative chemical examination, made of this water, taken from Mr. John Robinson's well, two miles north of Jacksonport, it was found to contain

Carbonic acid,
Bi-carbonate of lime, (small quantity),
" " magnesia, " "
Sulphates, a trace?

The examination of this water is important to clear up the prejudice of those persons, who have looked upon the well water of this portion of Jackson county, as deleterious to health. It contains the usual mineral ingredients of hard spring water; these, when not in quantities so large as to produce medicinal effects, cannot be looked upon as injurious to health, since they contain elements essential for the growth of the body, in a form, easy of assimilation.

The northern part of Jackson county contains a large amount of highly productive land, easily cultivated, and especially adapted to the growth of cotton, wheat, oats and corn. A set of the alluvial soils of Jackson county were collected for analysis from Mr. H. J. Dowel's land, section 32, township 14 north, range 2 west, fourteen miles north of Jacksonport;

also, a set from Mr. M. L. Robinson's land, two miles north of Jacksonport. At the latter place, No. 2, the cultivated soil, was selected from an old field fifty years or more in cultivation, and has produced for the last twenty years successive crops of cotton, with an average yield of about eight hundred pounds of seed cotton per acre, rating in the New Orleans market in quality equal to the Mississippi cotton, and having a rather better staple than the cotton from Tennessee.

The principal growth of timber on this land is black, white and post-oak, sweetgum, blackwalnut, and some hickory.

The Cairo and Fulton railroad crosses White river near Jacksonport, and runs along Village creek, through the northern part of the county. I was informed that as many as one hundred and fifty hands were employed this season in its construction in Jackson county, and it is hoped that the completion of so important a work to the State, is placed beyond a doubt. The large grant of lands bordering on the road, it is estimated will be sufficient to pay for its construction.

INDEPENDENCE COUNTY.

The geological formations in the part of this county explored by me, are exhibited in the following section:

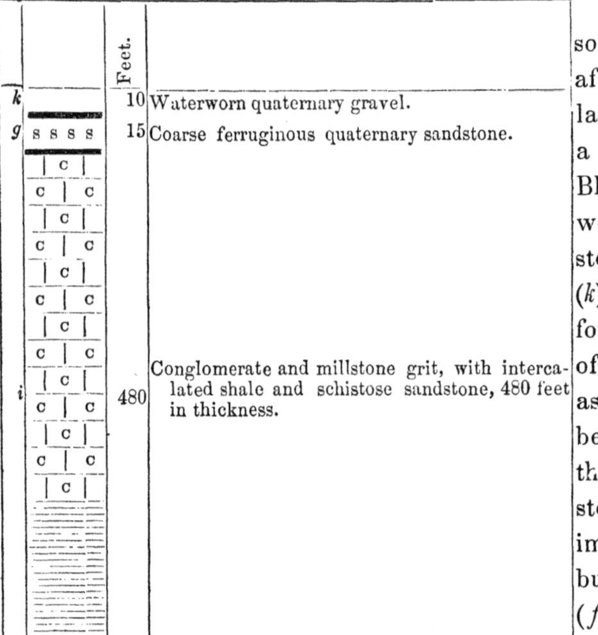

On the road from Jacksonport to Batesville, after reaching the highland some five miles in a westerly course from Black river, the waterworn quaternary hornstone and chert gravel (*k*) of this section is found capping the tops of the hills as far west as range 4. This gravel bed sometimes rests upon the ferruginous sandston (*j*), and sometimes immediately upon the buff-colored sandstone (*f*); but was nowhere recognized in connection

	Feet.	
i	480	Conglomerate and millstone grit, with intercalated shale and schistose sandstone, 480 feet in thickness—Continued.
h	20	Black entrochital limestones.
g	20?	Place of dark shales, usually under the black limestone.
f	180	Buff-colored fossiliferous sandstone, with intercalated, dark shale; lower part thin-bedded and schistose.

with the intermediate members.

The coarse ferruginous sandstone (*j*) is seen, in many places in the eastern part of Independence county, resting, usually, on the buff sandstone (*f*). At some localities, it is very rich in iron ore; but too much mixed with sand to admit of its being used, profitably, as an ore for the manufacture of iron.

The conglomerate or millstone grit (*i*) was not seen on the north side of White river, but makes its appearance in the southern part of the county, near Rocky Point post-office, where it contains embedded pebbles. This rock has been quarried, and is held in good repute for millstones. Though not more than fifty or sixty feet in thickness at the above locality, on the south side of Salido creek it increases, with its associate shales, to four hundred and eighty feet. I have not observed any coal associated with these rocks in this county.

The black limestone (*h*) belongs to the subcarboniferous limestone

	Feet.	
e	35	Black bituminous shale.
d	400	Subcarboniferous or cavernous limestone, with intercalations of sandstone and shale; contains large deposits of manganese, some iron, and copper pyrites.
c	75	Massive saccharoidal sandstone.

period; where it crops out, north of Rocky Point post-office, it has a thickness of about twenty feet. It is quite fossiliferous: the most abundant fossils are, *Productus cora*, and *P. elegans.* One layer, full of entrochites, is hard enough to take a polish, and the fossils generally showing white on a black ground, it will make a handsome marble for ornamental purposes. This limestone is usually underlaid by the dark shales (*g*) of the section.

Sandstone (*f*) is buff-colored, and rather soft; usually in prismatic blocks near the base, and contains casts of subcarboniferous fossils belonging to the genera *spirifer*, *orthis*, *lingula*, *productus*, *nucula*, and *bellerophon*, also fragments of *trilobites.* At Mr. McDonald's, on the head waters of Mud creek, 13 miles from Batesville, this member is but a few feet in thickness, and rests upon dark, sheety shales; the sandstone is bedded in blocks from three to four inches thick, having an earthy look, and low specific

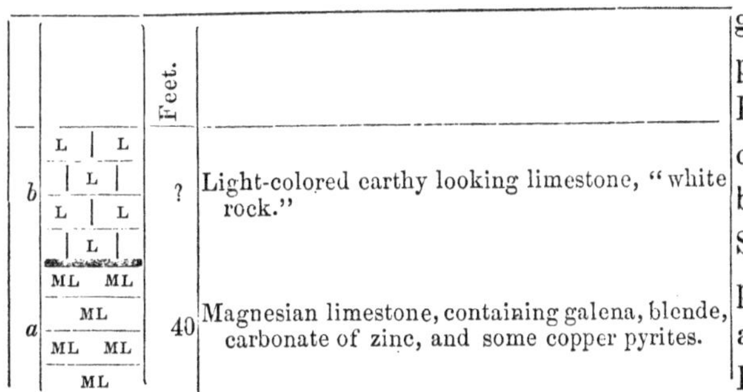

gravity. Between Sulpher rock and Parson Rogers' dwelling, it is only eighty feet thick; between Batesville and Spring creek, it has expanded to one hundred and eighty feet or more. It forms the substratum upon which the town of Batesville is built, and crops out about one mile to the north. Seven or eight miles south of Batesville, this member dips beneath the drainage of the country. East and west, along its strike, it can be traced as the surface rock from the highland, on Black river, passing through Sulphur rock and Batesville, to the western boundary of the State. Though very persistent, in its lithological character, this member is, at some places, almost entirely replaced by limestone, with, locally, one or more beds of intercalated dark argillaceous shale.

Member (*e*) was first observed, along my line of survey, at Mr. McDonald's, in a little branch called Shakeray, a tributary of Mud creek, where it is not more than three or four feet thick, the upper part of a dark-gray color, and splitting into large thin sheets. The lower part is ferruginous, more compact, and quarries into blocks six or eight inches thick; it will probably be found, when analyzed, to contain a considerable amount of iron; in fact, I was impressed with the belief, while at some of the localities of this shale, near Sulphur Rock and Batesville, that it would prove to contain enough iron to justify smelting.*

Going west from McDonald's, this black shale increases in thickness, and is found in the bottom of wells, and in the deep cuts of ravines, as far west as Spring creek, three miles north-west of Batesville, where it attains a thickness of thirty-five feet or more; and though undoubtedly belonging to the subcarboniferous period, has the lithological character of the devonian black shales of Indiana and Kentucky. It is charged with bitumen, possesses a strong, fetid odor, splits into thin sheets, and decomposes too easily to permit of its being used for roofing buildings. At Spring creek, this member contains the same black, compact, and ferruginous stratum found in the vicinity of Sulphur Rock, which is here

*Owing to some unknown cause, the packages shipped by me, early last spring, to the office of the Arkansas Survey, have not yet been received. One of these packages contained the principal specimens of this shale, collected in Independence county, the manganese ores from near Batesville, and many other important samples of the rocks in that region: consequently no analysis can, at present, be given. Enquiries have been instituted, and it is hoped these missing boxes may yet be found at some of the shipping points along their route.

increased to a thickness of ten or twelve feet, and has been quarried to build, in part, the race at Ruddle's mill, on this creek.

The organic remains seen in this shale, comprise imperfect casts of the genera, *cardium*, *lingula*, *avicula*, and *orthoceras*, bi-furcated teeth of fishes and stems of plants.

The cherty subcarboniferous or cavernous limestone (*d*) which commences at Black river hills, in township 14, often encroaches upon and replaces the greater portion of the overlying sandstone (*f*). This cherty limestone has its southern limits one mile north of Batesville, caps the mountains in the northern part of the county with its detached chert, and continues in the direction of its strike, a little north of west to the Cherokee territory. In the western part of the State, north of township 15, it is in great force, and extends northward into Missouri, beyond the lead mines of Granby.

In the western part of Independence county this limestone forms a perpendicular cliff on White river, above the mouth of Lafferty creek, from four hundred to five hundred feet in height, making a conspicuous landmark for navigators of this river, and bears the name of "Pinter's Bluff." Between this point and Batesville it forms the substratum of extensive table-lands, well adapted for agriculture. Characteristic samples of this soil have been collected from the farm of Mr. R. A. Childress, section 36, township 14 north, range 8 west, ten miles from Batesville.

One and a half miles north of Batesville, on the property of Mr. Mull, there is an oolitic member of this limestone, having a thickness of thirty or forty feet, which takes a good polish and can be quarried in blocks of any required size for building purposes, and has the reputation of being a durable stone. Mr. Mull is now engaged quarrying this rock, for the manufacture of lime, for which use it is well adapted, on account of its purity and whiteness. Lime made from the oolitic limestone, on the Ohio river, below Louisville, always brings a higher price and meets with a more ready sale than that which is made from the associated dark limestones.

The ores found in this member (*d*.) are oxides of iron and manganese, galena and some little copper pyrites. The two former of these promise to be abundant. This is the same geological formation in which the fine deposits of iron ore occur on the Cumberland river, in Kentucky and Tennessee, that supply the western furnaces located in its vicinity.

North of Batesville, near Mr. Cason's, there is a strong axis of disturbance in the strata, bearing south-east and north-west. Small quantities of copper pyrites are found disseminated amongst these titled strata, chiefly in a close textured limestone rock, which has a slight greenish color. Its occurrence, in proximity to this line of disturbance, may be regarded as a favorable symptom and indicative of its origin from beneath.

In this formation, in the vicinity of Lafferty creek, rich beds of manganese ore have been found at several places.* The most remarkable occurrence of this ore, within my range of observation, is on the property of Mr. Martin Cason's in section 34, township 14 north, range 6 west, three miles north of Batesville. Here it does not occur in veins, but in regularly stratified beds, splitting up into rusty slabs two or three inches thick, and containing imbedded sub-spheroidal concretions of a harder and more metallic appearance than the matrix ore; in size they vary from a half to one inch in diameter. This segregated ore is not inappropriately called, "Button ore."† It is well exposed at Mr. Cason's, on the slope of a hill in his field, where, in fact, he actually turns it up in great sheets while cultivating his land with the plow. After it has been exposed to the atmosphere for a short time, decomposition takes place, producing a black soil more fertile than any other portion of his farm. Shafts have been sunk into the ore at this place, fifteen feet in depth, without reaching the bottom. The ore-bed is overlaid by a coarse-grained entrochital limestone, which has four feet of its base colored red and filled with the aforementioned button-shaped concretions of manganese ore.

The position and appearance of the ore, at this locality, render it highly probable that beds of limestone, previously existing, have been replaced by infiltrated oxide of manganese.

The saccharoidal sandstone (*c*) was best seen in the eastern and northern part of the county on Bayou Doty and Bayou Cury, where it has a thickness of fifty or seventy-five feet. It is a coarse-grained, slightly cemented rock, possessing a variety of shades of color, from pure white to deep red. This variegated sandstone underlies the subcarboniferous limestones (*d*.) and rests on magnesian limestones of lower silurian date, but being destitute of fossils we are, at present, not prepared to say positively to what geological period it belongs.

The earthy looking limestone (*b*.) is found associated with and over the lead bearing magnesian limestone of the lower silurian period, and is usually known in the vicinity where it occurs, by the name of "white rock," or "cotton rock." This is a very constant member in the slopes of the hills, in the northern counties, where lead ores have been discovered.

The massive magnesian limestone (*a*.) is a continuation downwards of

* See Report of Dr. D. D. Owen, State Geologist.

† The specimens collected at this locality, and shipped, have not yet arrived. The economical value cannot therefore be reported on.

the above formation, and is frequently intersected by small imperfect veins of galena, associated with calcareous spar, copper pyrites and zinc.

Some five years ago a company was organized in Batesville, to search for lead in this rock, on Bayou Cury. Several pits or shallow shafts were sunk under the direction of Judge T. C. Bricky, one of the company, and a considerable amount of lead taken out; the means at the disposal of this company were inadequate to make the necessary investigation for proving the ground. In consequence of the shafts having caved in, no opportunity was afforded to see the character of the veins. In the rubbish, thrown out of the shaft, I saw a considerable amount of the sulphuret and carbonate of zinc, and collected specimens for analysis; * these specimens of sulphuret of lead are of the steel-gray variety, but disseminated amongst spar and rock, rendering it difficult to obtain large specimens of the clear ore. The geological formation is certainly perfectly analogous to that in the lead region of Marion, Carroll, and Lawrence; which circumstance renders it probable that the ore will be found under the same circumstances as in the above mentioned counties.

Agriculture.

A considerable diversity of soil is to be found in Independence county, corresponding to changes in the underlying geological formations. Though the surface is considerably broken, still there are extensive areas of table-land underlaid by the cherty subcarboniferous limestones. These soils are rich, and being based on red clay, are retentive and durable; they are similar in composition to the land in the barrens of Kentucky. There are, also, extensive tracts of bottom land, bordering on the numerous small streams which water this county, that are well adapted for cultivation.

The principal growth of timber is white, black, red, and postoaks, hickory, gum and elm; on the cherty limestone land, the most abundant trees are blackjack, sassafras and persimmon.

FULTON COUNTY.

In the southeastern corner of this county, near Judge Billingsley's, the substratum is a hard impure limestone, rough weathering, and full of cross cracks; superimposed on this, are thirty or forty feet of thin-bedded siliceous limestone, disposed in layers like pavement stones, on the surface of which remarkable fucoidal impressions are apparent. Above this flaggy

* For result of the analysis, see appendix to Chemical Report.

limestone is an impure, cherty member, about twenty-five feet thick. This succession continues nearly to Salem, and the country is strewed with the reddish and variegated chert, derived from these formations.

Half a mile north of Salem, is an isolated, comical hill, called the "Pilot Knob." A measurment made with the aneroid barometer, gave its height four hundred and forty-five (445) feet above the town of Salem. The summit is capped with a reddish, quartzose sandstone, and disintegrated fragments of the same are strewed on the sides of the "Knob;" thus entirely concealing from view any other rocks which may exist at the base. This is a conspicuous knob that may be seen from a distance of many miles; hence it served, in early times, to direct the course of the pioneers.

Four miles west of Salem, there is a considerable bed of hydrated brown oxide of iron, in connection with an impure siliceous ore, laying exposed on a ridge, about one hundred feet above the general drainage of the country.

The geological position of this ore is probably the same as that which has been before noted in Lawrence county.

Both copper pyrites and galena, have been found in small quantities in the magnesian limestones, in the southern and western part of the county.

Between Salem and Bennett's bayou, the substratum is a white earthy limestone, resembling the "white rock" (*b*) of the Independence county section, alternating with a greenish, marly shale, which weathers easily and forms broad grassy valleys between the hills destitute of timber. Bennett's bayou, along which is a rich agricultural district, cuts its way principally through this stratum.

In the western part of this county, on the North fork of White river, there are seen, in the base of the hills, ninety feet of irregularly bedded, impure, cherty limestone; the chert is very brittle, and has a tendency to break into cubes. This is overlaid by one hundred and eighteen feet of cherty limestone, alternating with a grayish-buff, siliceous rock.

In the southern part of the county, on Piney creek, the saccharoidal sandstone (*c*) of the Independence county section, forms the tops of the ridges, and is covered with a heavy growth of yellow pine.

Agriculture.

The valleys of the numerous streams, watering this county, afford a rich fertile soil, well adapted for cultivation; and that forming the small grassy valleys, derived from the decomposition of the "white rock" and its marly shales, is generally black and quite productive for all kinds of small grain. Characteristic soils of the latter land were collected from a farm belonging to Judge Billingsly.

The principal growth of timber on the limestone and chert ridges is blackjack, blackoak, postoak and hickory, and where the sandstone prevails, yellow pine. In the prairie-like valleys, besides the tall barren-grass, there is an abundant growth of "Rosin weed," *Camphorosma resinosa* (*Gray*).

MARION COUNTY.

In the eastern part of Marion county, there is an alternation of the magnesian or lead-bearing rocks of the lower silurian period, with sandstones, and the tops of the highest hills are covered with chert belonging to the subcarboniferous rocks, as proved by the characteristic fossils which it contains; these are, however, in most instances only casts. A number of fine specimens of fossils, found in this chert, were presented to the survey by Mr. William Flipping, among which are several crinoides, belonging to the genera *platycrinus* and *actinocrinus,* also *Spirifer striatus*, and a large undescribed *nautilus*. The light impure limestone "white rock," with its associate greenish marly shale, is seen over a great portion of this county, and forms the substratum to the gently undulating tracts of land, known by the name of "Barrens." The principal of these are the Flipping, Rapp, and Talbot barrens. Characteristic soils have been collected from the latter, which will give a fair average of this kind of land. It is very black, and in addition to barren grass, supports a luxuriant growth of "Rosin weed," *Camphorosma resinosa* (*Gray*).

On the immediate bank of White river, in section 28, township 20 north, range 15 west, in what is called the Horseshoe bend of the river, a magnesian limestone, alternating with sandstone, forms a conspicuous bluff; in all, some two hundred and fifty feet thick. A number of rock-house caves have been formed by the disintegration of the magnesian member of this series, in which large quantities of nitre earth have been formed.

The principal of these caves is known generally as the Bean cave, and seems to have been worked in early times, as an old decayed leaching-hopper has been found in it. A story is related by some of the first settlers in the country, that a man of the name of Bean once made nitre at this place in partnership with another man, who he is said to have killed in a quarrel. This circumstance, it is believed, caused the enterprise to be abandoned; and to this day, the cave is known under the name of the

"Bean cave." It is about thirty feet wide at the entrance, and runs back some one hundred feet or more, when it becomes much wider. Its height will average about eight feet. The walls or sides of this cave are composed of a laminated, tough, ferruginous clay, the laminæ having a varied color, from pale yellow to dark red. The upper and lower portions of this laminated clay, forming the walls of the cave, are partially dry, whilst the center, for about two feet, is quite damp. Though this clay, as it is dug from the bed, contains a considerable quantity of nitre, and most in the upper and lower part, yet it is only after it has been broken down and left on the bottom of the cave for some time, that it acquires sufficient nitre to be worked with profit. After it has been broken down in the cave, it rapidly loses its moisture, and crumbles into a fine powder. A considerable quantity of this dry earth, equal perhaps to one-third of the dimensions of the cave, is found on the sloping sides and floor.

These nitre earths yield from 3 to 6 per cent. of salt-petre, as will be seen by consulting the Reports of Dr. D. D. Owen and Dr. Elderhorst; the red, dry, crumbled earth on the floor being the richest in these nitre salts.

After lixiviation with water, this earth can also be used as a coarse paint, being nearly free from grit; it contains so much oxide of iron as to give it the color of Spanish brown, the depth of which is increased by ignition.

I was informed by Mr. Flipping that a drift had been made into the laminated clay of this cave in search of lead, and that some little was found, but not sufficient to encourage further investigation.

About one hundred yards from Bean's cave, in the same bluff, and occupying the same level, is another cave, one hundred and sixty feet wide at the mouth, and nearly as many feet in depth. The thickness of the deposit of laminated nitre earth, though not as great as in Bean's cave, is nevertheless, from four to seven feet, and there is good reason to believe that the earth will be found continuous from one cave to the other.

There are several other nitre caves, of less extent, and filled with this same description of earth, reported to exist in this bluff, which I had not time to visit.

Messrs. Smith & Co., of Elgin, Jackson county, Arkansas, have recently purchased land on White river, including these caves, and made arrangements for the manufacture of salt-petre from the nitre earth which they contain. I was informed by one of the partners, when at Elgin, last spring, that the yield of nitre was fully equal to their expectations, and they were quite sanguine that it would prove a profitable investment. He stated also that they used the lye for evaporation in the kettles, without increasing its strength by passing it through hoppers, containing fresh earth; if so, the expense for fuel is unnecessarily increased. To evaporate the lye in the most economical manner, it should be brought to the strength of 12 or 14 deg., by passing it repeatedly through fresh earth, in order to extract the soluble salts. A very useful instrument for ascertaining the strength of the lye, is the saltpetre hydrometer.

The best method of arranging the lixiviating troughs, or casks, is to place them at such heights, one above the other, that the lye passing through the first shall run into the second, and so continue, until the requisite per centage of saltpetre is obtained, before proceeding to the boiling and graining process. In lixiviating, no more water should be used than is actually necessary to extract the nitre; and lye, under 12 or 14 deg. of the hydrometer, should be returned through fresh earth, before boiling, until that strength is obtained.

There can be no doubt that works properly constructed, and judiciously and systematically managed, will produce salt-petre sufficient to make it a remunerative business. The location is immediately on White river, which is navigable at all times, as high up as Jacksonport, and, for a small class of steamboats, during the greater portion of the year, up to the caves. The mouth of the cave is so close to the river bank, that, by means of a chute, the earth can be very conveniently projected to the river, where the water for lixiviation can be easily obtained. Fuel is close at hand, and will cost but the chopping and transportation.

For further information, in regard to the geology of this county, as well as for the particulars of the analysis of the nitre earth, see the Report of Dr. D. D. Owen, State Geologist, and also that of the Chemical Assistant, Dr. William Elderhorst.

CRAWFORD COUNTY.

After separating from you at Van Buren, I proceeded to examine the coal, on Frog bayou, owned by Mr. Phillips. The principal opening is on the west half of south-west quarter of section 18, township 19 north, range 30 west, being one mile south of the stage road leading from Van Buren to Little Rock. The same seam is also opened, on this bayou, about one mile north of the stage road. This coal, known as the " Phillips bank," is one foot thick, it has a semi-metallic lustre, and though easily mined in large blocks, its cohesion is so slight that it soon breaks into small lumps by handling. It is the principal coal used by the blacksmiths in the southern part of Crawford, and the greater part of Franklin county, and is in good repute with the workmen. By analysis, it is found to contain, in 100 parts:

Volatile matter	16.2	Moisture	1.0
		Volatile combustible matter	15.2
Coke	83.8	Fixed carbon	80.8
		Ashes, (yellowish-red)	3.0
	100.0		100.0

It belongs to the class of semi-bituminous coals, and is free from earthy impurities, as shown by the small amount of ashes in the analysis.

As a fuel, the semi-bituminous coals are in high estimation, being rich in carbon; and, without any superflous volatile matter, they have a sufficiency of gas to render them easy of ignition.

On Frog bayou this coal lies under a bed of twelve feet of blue shale, which has to be removed in order to get out the coal. So long as this coal can be reached by this amount of stripping, it can be obtained, but not without considerable expense, which will be greatly increased when it shall become necessary to follow it by a drift, as much waste material will have to be removed to make head room in the mine.

The black shale forming the roof of this coal contains fossil plants, belonging to the genera *lipidodendron*, *sphenopteris*, *calamites*, and *pinularia*, and also a shell belonging to the genus *avicula*, of which only a fragment was found, too imperfect for determining the species.

At the Phillips bank, the argillaceous shale is all that can be seen over the coal; but the following section, taken in the hills near by, shows the overlying beds:

Top of the hill, soil and subsoil	?
Thin bedded sandstone, alternating with red marly clay, (base of millstone grit)	25 feet.
Blue argillaceous shale with segregations of carbonate of iron	60 "
Black bituminous shale with fossil plants	1.
Semi-bituminous coal	1.
Fire clay	0.6
	87.6

Thirteen miles from Van Buren, and about one mile north of the stage road, on the property of the Messrs. Herds, a mineral spring breaks out at the base of a hill, from beneath an exposure of bluish-colored, rough, sheety sandstone, with concretionary markings. The water comes, most likely, from a blue shale, which is concealed below the surface; as strata of this character were reached in Mr. Herd's well, twenty feet below the surface, and a similar water obtained.

A qualitative chemical examination of this mineral water, at the fountain head, showed its principal constituents to be:

A small quantity of free sulphuretted hydrogen.

Bi-carbonate of lime.

Bi-carbonate of magnesia.

Sulphate of soda (glauber salts).

Sulphate of magnesia, (epsom salts).

Chloride of sodium, (common salt).

Chloride of magnesium.

The chemical reactions indicate only small quantities of saline matter. It is, therefore, a weak saline sulphuretted water, and its medicinal properties will be that of a mild laxative, it will also be found beneficial in all cutaneous diseases.

On section 30, township 10 north, range 30 west, at Mr. Etherly's blacksmith shop, a thin coal was struck in digging his well, overlaid by twenty feet of hard blue sandstone and blue argillaceous shale. From the shale thrown out, specimens of lipidodendron and stigmaria were obtained. This coal is most likely the equivalent of the Frog bayou coal, or another thin seam in close proximity.

For further remarks, on the geology of Crawford county, see Report of Dr. D. D. Owen, State Geologist.

FRANKLIN COUNTY.

The millstone grit series prevails in the northern part of Franklin county, composed of conglomerates and thick-bedded coarse sandstones, flagstones, and red and blue shales. Only thin beds of coals can be expected to be discovered in such materials as lie below the true productive coal measures.

A slight wave in the strata, carries the coal of Crawford county beneath the surface in the northern part of this county, and it is not until you reach the waters of Horsehead creek, in Johnson county, that this coal again makes its appearance at the surface, on the north side of the Arkansas river.

One and a half miles north-east of Benner's mill, near William Parker's house, there is an excellent chalybeate spring, which was found on examination to contain:

A trace of free sulphuretted hydrogen.

Bi-carbonate of lime.
Bi-carbonate of magnesia.
Bi-carbonate of the protoxide of iron.

This water appears to contain a considerable amount of oxide of iron, and it is therefore somewhat remarkable that it should also indicate, with acetate of lead, the presence of sulphuretted hydrogen, a combination that can only exist when the oxide of iron is held in solution by a free acid.

This water will have a tonic effect, combined with an action on the skin and kidneys.

At and near Mr. Parker's spring, is seen the following succession of rocks: coarse-grained sandstone, alternating with flagstones, reddish-yellow and gray shales; in all about two hundred feet. In the gray shales, ten feet above the spring, there is a thin coal-dirt.

On Mulberry river, the thick-bedded sandstone of the millstone-grit series attains a thickness of more than three hundred feet. From the base of one of the cliffs of this sandstone, on Mulberry river, section 30? township 11 north, range 28 west, there issues a saline water, from a fissure in the rock, that is known as the State salt spring. This spring has lately been given up by the State and is now the property of Messrs. Basham & Ward. It contains:

Chloride of sodium, (common salt).
Bi-carbonate of lime.
Bi-carbonate of magnesia.
Bi-carbonate of the protoxide of iron.
Sulphates, a trace.

This is a weak brine, which might become much stronger by deep boring, as it occupies the same geological position in which the strongest brines are found in the western states.

There is another saline spring, reported to be of about the same strength, situated higher up on Mulberry river, which I did not have an opportunity to visit.

The qualitative chemical examination of a mineral water, on Spirit creek, a branch of Mulberry, township 11 north, range 28? west, resulted as follows:

Carbonate of the protoxide of iron (strong).
Bi-carbonate of lime.
Bi-carbonate of magnesia.

This is a good chalybeate water, and its effects will be that of an active tonic.

A chalybeate spring was also examined at Mr. William Ham's, on Mulberry river. This water contains the same ingredients as the preceding though the oxide of iron is not in such large quantities.

Between Mr. Ham's, on Mulberry river, and Ozark, the following section was obtained:

Siliceous flagstones	130	feet.
Siliceous iron ore, 5 to	6.	"
Yellow, red, and gray shales	60.	"
Coal-dirt, or thin decomposed black shale	1.	"
Space concealed, to bed of creek	60.	"
	257	feet.

Agriculture.

The northern part of Franklin county, though much broken, contains a large amount of good tillable land on the creek and river bottoms, which is very productive, when properly cultivated. The principal growth of timber is white, black, and redoak, blackjack, postoak, and hickory, sweet and black gum.

JOHNSON COUNTY.

A number of openings have been made into a seam of semi-bituminous coal, on the waters of Horsehead creek, in Johnson county. The principal of these are the Wilmoth coal, section 18, township 10 north, range 25 west; Butts' coal, section 8, township 10 north, range 25 west; Lee's coal, section 15, township 10 north, range 25 west; Flemming's coal, section 1, township 9 north, range 25 west. These coals are all opened in an extensive plateau formed by the easily-weathering mass of shales underlying the massive sandstones of the millstone grit series, which are seen prominently capping the mountains, a short distance to the north.

The Wilmoth coal bed, from 20 to 22 inches thick, is worked by drifting; it has a dip of 6 or 8 degs. to the south-east, and rests on a dark fireclay bottom, filled with stems of stigmaria. In mining the coal, some eight inches of the roof falls down and has to be carried out, which gives a head room equal to about thirty inches. In this dark earthy looking shale, is found a small, undescribed species of fossil shell, belonging to the genus *modiola*, and fragments of plants belonging to the genus *pecopteris*.

A section of 650 feet of the rocks overlying the coal, was obtained and is here given in the following section:

Millstone grit or conglomerate, a massive sandstone in three members, with shale between, and forming three distinct benches on the mountains, in all	350	feet.
Vermicular sandstone, in thin beds, with remarkable impressions	80	"
Schistose sandstone with intercalated hard bands	100	"
Yellow and reddish shales	50	"
Dark argillaceous shales	60	"
Brown earthy shale forming roof of coal	0.8	"
Whitish-gray shale, mottled with dark spots	9	"
Semi-bituminous coal	1.10	"
Fire clay	0.00	"
	650.9	feet.

Mr. Thomas Butts has opened this coal on his property, where it is 18 inches thick, and dips 10 deg. to the south-east. It is here overlaid by the same character of shale as seen at the Wilmoth coal, and there are found in the roof the same fossils.

An opening has also been made into this vein of coal at Mr. Russel Lee's. The spring rains had filled up the opening so that the coal could not be seen, and Mr. Lee being absent, I did not ascertain its thickness. I believe it to be identical with Butts' coal, as fossils of the same character occur in the roof shales thrown out of the opening. If this inference be correct, the thickness of the two coals will probably correspond.

Mr. Fleming's coal is opened on a little branch, which runs into Horsehead creek; it is 18 or 20 inches thick, and is mined by stripping off the roof. The overlying shales and organic remains are identical with the above. It is undoubtedly an extension of the Wilmoth coal.

Mr. Hodges has opened, and works by stripping this same vein of coal, two miles north of Clarksville. It is here 18 inches in thickness, and the same characteristic fossils were found in the shale. At this locality the coal is not quite so free from sulphur as at the other openings, nor will it stand exposure to the atmosphere as well as the coal at Mr. Wilmoth's.

The coal taken from the different mines in this county, meets with a ready sale. On account of the difficulty experienced in working so thin a vein of coal, the miners receive 10 cents per bushel for raising; and it is sold at the bank to the consumers at 20 cents per bushel.

At Mr. Hodge's, the coal has but very little, if any dip, and it is only carried above and below the drainage of the country by local undulations in the strata. Though the coals, at these various openings, differ somewhat in quality and appearance, yet I believe they will be found to be all an extension of one and the same bed. Experience has shown that local changes in the composition of the same vein of coal are not unusual, and cannot alone be relied upon as a means of identification. The organic remains of the roof shales and observations on the superposition of the strata, are much surer guides in the determination of the position of beds of coal.

For further remarks on the coals of Johnson county, see the Report of Dr. D. D. Owen, State Geologist.

East of Clarksville, and north of the Arkansas river bottoms, the heavy mass of dark shales, associated with the coal, disappear beneath the surface, and the overlying sandstone becomes the surface rock, with some intercalations of shale towards the base. The siliceous soil, derived from this sandstone, supports a growth of large yellow pines, on the high ridges between Clarksville and Dwight mission.

Agriculture.

The tillable up-lands of this county are derived principally from the shales lying below the main mass of millstone grit rocks. Sample of soils were collected for chemical examination, from Mr. Arthur Davis' farm, one and a half miles east of Clarksville, where the growth was principally postoak.

The bottom lands, bordering on the Arkansas river, are highly esteemed and very productive.

POPE COUNTY.

The geology of Pope county is almost a counterpart of that of Johnson. The northern part is broken and mountainous. The mountains are composed of massive sandstones, belonging to the millstone grit formation at the summit, and thin-bedded and shaly sandstones at the base. Near the head waters of Illinois bayou, the upper bed of sandstone is a true conglomerate charged with pebbles, huge blocks of which have rolled from above into the valley beneath.

On Indian creek, the subcarboniferous limestone appears beneath these rocks, interstratified with reddish shales. This is the only limestone observed in the county.

South of Dover, between Illinois bayou and Galley creek, and south of the Carrion Crow mountains, the country is comparatively level, where the siliceous, red and dark argillaceous shales, having no capping of hard sandstone to protect them, have been worn away and filled up the inequalities of the surface.

Throughout all this southern part of the county, thin beds of semi-bituminous coal are found. One of the principal openings for coal, is in the bed of the Illinois bayou, near Dwight mission; but, at the time of my examination of this county, the river was too high to admit of its being seen. Mr. Edwards informed me that it was 15 or 20 inches thick. The geology of the adjacent country leads me to believe that it will be found to occupy the same geological position as the coal described on Horsehead creek, in Johnson county.

The following section exhibits the succession of the rocks at Mr. Edward's dwelling, Dwight mission, Illinois bayou:

Thin-bedded sandstone, top of the hill	10	feet.
Reddish, ferruginous, argillaceous shale, with nodules of iron ore	60	"
Shaly argillaceous carbonate of iron	3 to 5	"
Dark shale with fossil plants, lepidodendron and stigmaria	2	"
Band of sandstone in two layers (local)	2	"
Alluvial bottom	20	"
Bed of Illinois bayou	0	"
	99	feet.

The shaly argillaceous carbonate of iron in this section, is of excellent quality and sufficiently abundant for the supply of smelting furnaces. It contains 32.2 per cent. of metallic iron, and is similar in its composition to the best quality of the ore from the Cross Basket mines, in Scotland, used at the Clyde iron works. Iron made from this class of ores is of the finest quality, combining strength and ductility.

This description of ore, will no doubt be found at many other localities in the vicinity of Dwight mission, and must eventually attract the enterprise of the iron manufacturer, from its vicinity to the Arkansas river and proximity to large forests of pine timber, and to the workable coals of Johnson county; especially the Spadra mines described in Dr. Owen's Report. The coal which is exposed in the bed of Illinois bayou, at low water, may be reached by a shallow shaft at the base of the section at Dwight mission, and may be worked by the removal of 8 or 10 inches of the shale roof.

Considerable quantities of argillaceous iron ore were observed in the vicinity of Dover, but not in the same abundance as further south.

Six hundred feet of the rocks, exposed in section in the Carrion Crow mountain, near Mr. Potts', on Galley creek, are here given:

Millstone grit in three benches of thick-bedded rock, having shale between—in all about	400	feet.
Space concealed by debris, mostly flagstone and shale	140	"
Argillaceous shale	60	"
Semi-bituminous coal	1.3?	"
Galley Creek	0	"
	601.3	feet.

The above thickness of the individual members will be subject to a correction for a slight north-west dip.

Some iron ore was observed in the Carrion Crow mountain, under the upper bench of sandstone; but the greater portion of it contains too much silica to be considered valuable for the manufacture of iron. The coal at the base of the mountain has the same appearance as the semi-bituminous coal of Frog and Illinois bayous. It was not sufficiently opened to be seen well.

Agriculture.

The cultivated lands lie chiefly in the southern part of this county, east of the Illinois bayou. There are extensive districts of level tracts, chiefly in townships 6, 7, 8 and 9, ranges 19 and 20 west, that are very productive, especially adapted for wheat. The soil of this region overlies, and has mostly been derived from, the disintegration of the reddish and dark shales at the base of the millstone grit, sufficiently intermixed with siliceous washings from the overlying flagstones to correct their otherwise tenacious and refractory character. Samples of soil were collected from John P. Langford's land, on the Illinois bayou, five miles north-east of Dover. The timber was very large and mostly oaks with some hickory.

CONWAY COUNTY.

The northern part of Conway county is skirted by a continuation of the same chain of mountains that traverse the preceding counties of Pope and Johnson, and has a corresponding geological structure. Sandstones of the millstone grit form its summit, overlying flagstones and shale. The hills diminish very much in the southern part of the county, seldom exceeding three hundred feet, and are composed mostly of thin-bedded sandstones, underlaid by reddish siliceous, and dark argillaceous shales. In the level portions of the eastern part of the county, the latter shaly members underlie the fine tracts of grass land, which affords excellent pasturage for cattle.

Thin beds of coal have been opened, in many places, on the waters of the Cadron, in the eastern part of the county, and range in thickness from 4 inches up to 20 inches. In section 7, township 5 north, range 12 west, on the Black fork of the Cadron, a 4 inch seam of coal is intercalated amongst the shales. It is a more solid coal than those beds previously described, in Pope and Johnson counties, highly bituminous and very black; it has but little tendency to crumble, and breaks with a smooth angular fracture. A few fossil plants were found in its roof shales, belonging to the genus *pecopteris* and *neuropteris*. This is probably a different seam of coal from that, before mentioned, on Illinois bayou and the waters of Horsehead creek. It is, however, too thin a seam to be of much commercial value.

Three layers of subcarboniferous limestone crop out on Turkey creek, a branch of the Cadron, in all four or five feet thick, dipping about 3 deg. south-east. It is a dark, earthy-looking rock, containing encrinite stems and indistinct carboniferous fossils. This is the only limestone that has been observed, south of Little Red river and north of the Arkansas river, in this part of the State; as this rock will make a good strong lime, it is important to a country where limestones are seldom accessible.

In the north-east part of Conway county, close to the Bull mountain, the dark shales under the millstone grit are fractured, dislocated, and traversed by veins of quartz, associated with talc and other allied magnesian minerals; the shales, for some distance on either side of these veins, are indurated, altered, and more or less metamorphosed. I observed, at one locality, an almost vertical bank of dark, siliceous rock, one foot wide, charged with iron, and possessing a cubical structure, the blocks averaging about three inches by two. This siliceous vein traverses the disturbed shales, in a north-east and south-west course, for several miles.

Where these quartz veins pass through the property of Dr. David Lewis, in section 24, township 6 north, range 11 west, several shallow pits have been sunk to investigate their character. All that were discovered, proved to be talcose slates and fine transparent crystals of quartz, three or four of which had enclosed a drop of water. These pits I consider too shallow to prove the metalliferous character of the veins. The apparent connection of these veins with those in Pulaski county, which contain argentiferous galena, leads me to suspect that similar ore might be found at a greater depth; especially, as the Bull mountain veins reach the surface through a hard, siliceous slate, which overlies the metalliferous shales in Pulaski. The following is a section of the rocks at the Bull mountain, near Dr. Lewis' house:

Conglomerate, thin-bedded and shaly sandstones, in all········	310 feet.
Dark, siliceous shales, with bands of prismatic shale, much disturbed, and traversed by veins of quartz, in all·············	75 "
	385 "

Near the mouth of the Cadron, veins of milky quartz are found, traversing the millstone grit; this appears to be the western limit, on the north side of the Arkansas river, of that subterranean action which has filled or injected the slates, south of the Cadron, in Pulaski county.

At Springfield, the county seat of Conway county, a qualitative chemical examination was made of the town spring, which issues, in a bold clear stream, from the reddish and dark-colored shales under the millstone grit. It proved to be a good chalybeate water, possessing decided tonic properties. The principal ingredients are:

Carbonic acid;
Bi-carbonate of lime;
Bi-carbonate of magnesia;
Bi-carbonate of the protoxide of iron (strong).

Another chalybeate spring, of the same character, occurs at the Peach-orchard-gap, in section 20, township 6 north, range 10 west, in the edge of White county, and belongs to Mr. Elliott.

Agriculture.

The most important tracts of arable land, occupy she southern part of the county, in townships 6 and 7, ranges 11, 12, 13, 14, 15, 16, and 17, on the waters of the Cadron and Point Remove creeks. They are the same description of lands, already spoken of, in the south-east part of Pope county, and have been derived from the same geological formations.

PULASKI COUNTY.

North of the Arkansas river, the stratigraphical character of the rocks, in Pulaski county, is very much the same as that previously noted, in the counties laying to the west. The millstone grit still forms the capping to the highest hills, while the cuts in the valleys have laid bare the reddish and dark underlying shales, which seem to augment in thickness to the south and east; while the sandstones of the millstone grit appear to become more schistose in structure.

Imperfect crystals and veins of amorphous milk-white quartz have ramified the strata, close to the junction of the sandstones and shales, near Mr. Irvin's, and not far from the stage road leading to Little Rock, where the adjacent walls of sandstone and shale are metamorphosed for 18 inches on each side of the veins, but especially on the south side, where the wall is slaty and micaceous. The whole strata, through which the vein runs, are so much disturbed that, for a width of fifty feet, they dip 35 deg. to the north east, with a north-west and south-east strike. Beyond this, the strata gradually assume a more horizontal position. No mining explorations have been made along the line of this vein, in search of metallic ores; though I believe the conditions under which the vein appears, favorable for discoveries.

The hill at the toll-bridge, on Palarm creek, is 220 feet high, measured from the bridge floor, which is about 30 feet above the bed of the creek. The rocks of which this hill is composed, are thin-bedded, soft, brownish-colored sandstones, dipping about 40 deg. north-east, and intersected with veins of milky quartz. On the surface of some of the sandstones, quarried out to improve the road over the hill, clusters of transparent crystals were found attached. The upper part of this quartz-bearing sandstone, which caps the hill, is a coarse-grained, reddish rock, which crumbles easily to sand.

About two miles west of Winfrey's old stand, a remarkably hard, black metamorphic rock, in semi-crystalline blocks, traversed by numerous fine veins of white quartz, crosses the road. It is one foot wide, and dips about 35 deg. north-east. The strata, on each side of this tilted band, appear to be nearly horizontal.

The most important mineral locality which has yet come under my observation, in Pulaski county, north of the Arkansas river, is situated on Kellogg's creek, and known as the "Kellogg lead mines." The principal mines are in township 3 north, range 11 west, and about ten miles north of Little Rock. When first discovered, these mines created considerable excitement, and the right of mining was leased by the proprietor of the land, Mr. Kellogg, to a company, who were to hold this right so long as they paid him regularly a stipulated amount of the ore. Some forty or fifty tons of this ore were mined and shipped to Europe, for the purpose of ascertaining its value. No account was ever received, at the mines, regarding the sale or disposition of this shipment of ore; and the company, whose means were limited, becoming involved in debt and discouraged, finally abandoned the enterprise.

From long disuse, the shafts from which this ore was raised, have become filled with water, rubbish, earth and rocks, washed in or detached from the mouth of the pits, so that there is no opportunity, now, of inspecting the condition of the ore in place. In giving an opinion, therefore, in regard to these mines, we have to judge from the material thrown out, from the general geological structure of the country, and from information derived from Mr. John W. Purdom, who lived close by the mines at the time the ore was mined. It appears that the ore was found, not in a single vein only, but occupying a number of veins, which traverse the argillaceous shales under the millstone grit at this place; these seem to have very much the same distribution and relation, as those previously mentioned as occurring on the property of Dr. Lewis, at the Bull mountain, in the north-east part of Conway county, as well as those observed near Mr. Irvin's in this county.

To convey a clearer idea of their geological relations, I subjoin the annexed vertical diagram; which illustrates not only the succession in Pulaski county, but also in Conway county:

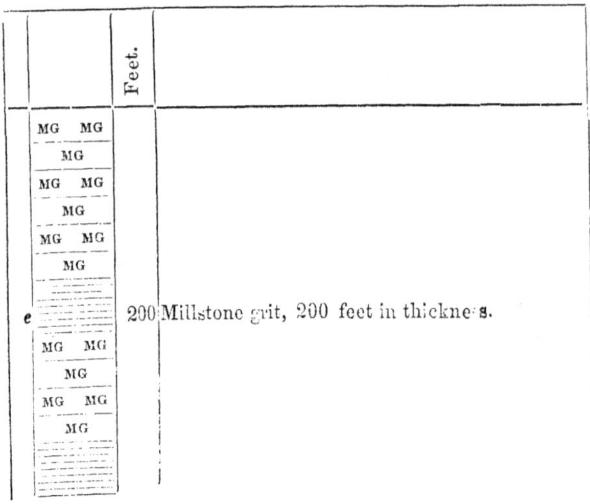

		Feet.	
e	MG MG / MG / MG MG / MG / MG MG / MG / MG MG / MG / MG MG / MG	200	Millstone grit, 200 feet in thickness.

The millstone grit, marked (*e*), at the top of the section, occupies the highest position, not only in the hills adjacent to the mouth of Palarm bayou, and in the ridge dividing the waters of that stream from Kellogg's creek, in Pulaski county, but also in the Bull mountain, in the north-east corner of Conway county.

		Feet.	
	MG MG MG MG MG MG MG MG		Millstone grit, 200 feet in thickness—Continued.
d		15	Siliceous and argillaceous shales, with thin bands of hard rock.
c	S S S S S S	40	Thin-bedded soft sandstone.
b		30	Hard shale.
a		200	Argillaceous shale, traversed by metallic veins.

The underlying siliceous and argillaceous shales (*d*) are exposed, in section, on the Arkansas river, near Mr. Irvin's, at Palarm bayou; as well as on Bull bayou, in the north-east part of Conway county. It is through them that the veins of quartz reach the surface, on the property of Dr. Lewis, in Conway county, and near Mr. Irvin's in Pulaski county. Locally, a bed of soft sandstone (*c*) is intercalated amongst these shales, succeeded by thirty feet of hard shale or slate, (*b*), intersected with lines of cross fracture, probably caused by shrinkage.

The lowest stratum (*a*) of this section comprises the shales forming the valley of Kellogg creek, which are traversed by a system of metalliferous veins, containing a rich silver-lead, associated with quartz, talc, (tallow rock of the miners), copper pyrites, spathic iron, and blende. The principal veins have a course nearly east and west. At the Kellogg mines, metalliferous veins are found, occupying a belt of country from north to south, of more than half a mile, and the whole system of quartz veins and tilted strata, of which the Kellogg veins form a part, must have a width, in the same direction, exceeding twelve miles.

From 40 to 50 tons of silver-lead ore have been taken out of one of the shafts sunk at the Kellogg mines, according to information derived from Mr. Purdom, and one lump carried to Little Rock, as a sample, weighed 108 pounds. In following the vein, this shaft was carried 108 feet through shales (*a*) of the section, after which the work was abandoned. The vein was found to contain more or less lead throughout the whole depth. Another shaft, known as the "Well or Moreland diggings," passed through 200 feet of the same shale, which still continued beneath. This vein also afforded a considerable amount of argentiferous lead, associated with the minerals before mentioned as belonging to this locality; but the amount of ore taken out of this shaft could not be accurately ascertained. Mr. Purdom was of opinion that it had not produced as much as the 108 feet, or "Johnson shaft." A large quantity of copper pyrites was found amongst the rubbish thrown out of these shafts, and it is believed that good veins of this ore might be reached by following the veins.

The lead and copper bearing shales of Kellogg creek are underlaid by the subcarboniferous limestone, which, we have every reason to believe, would be more favorable to mine in than the overlying shales; besides, the surface indications of this system of veins give evidence, that the deeper they are followed, the richer they become; for the quartz veins of the Palarm, which I conceive to be an extension upwards of the veins of Kellogg creek, have not as yet yielded any ore, either of lead or copper. I believe it, therefore, to be a fair inference, that the deeper the veins are followed, the richer they will become; more especially when they reach rocks more favorable for the reception of ores.

The analysis of two samples of lead, from the Kellogg mines, gave the following result: No. 1, a bright crystalline looking ore, gave, by reduction, 81.7 per cent. of metallic lead. By cupellation, this lead gave a silver bead weighing 1.06 per cent. of the lead employed, which is equal to 339.2 ounces of silver in a ton of 2,000 pounds.

No. 2, a porous fine-grained ore, with particles of talc disseminated, gave 73.45 per cent. of metallic lead; this, by cupellation, gave 0.7 per cent. of silver, equal to 224 ounces in a ton of 2,000 pounds.

The silver-lead ores of Great Britain and Ireland, worked in 1852, according to Mr. Hunt, (as quoted in Whitney's "Metallic wealth of the United States)," ranges as low as 6 ounces of silver in a ton of lead; the highest, being that of Devon, contains 40 ounces of silver in a ton of lead. The Cardiganshire and Montgomeryshire lead ores sometimes contain as much as 75 or 80 ounces of silver to the ton. At Wildberg, in Prussia, the lead contains 80 ounces of silver to the ton. The silver-lead of the Upper Hartz, belonging to Hanover, contains from 13 to 123 ounces of silver to the ton. From 70 to 80 ounces of silver is obtained from a ton of the argentiferous lead of Obernhof, in Saxony.

From this it will be seen, that the silver-lead from the Kellogg mines greatly exceeds in richness the silver-lead ores of Europe, and in the comparison, leaves a margin for profits so broad, that no doubt can be entertained of the practicability of working these ores, not only for the lead, but the silver.

Why these mines have been so long abandoned, after having been once partially worked, I was unable to learn. The situation is highly favorable for rich lodes of metal, not only silver-lead, but also copper.

If the property, belonging to these mines, can be obtained on reasonable terms, and a judicious and economical system of mining instituted, there can be but little doubt of a profitable result. The stratum of argillaceous shale is easily mined, and there is no difficulty in sinking a shaft through it. From the increasing thickness of the shale to the south-east, it is difficult, at present, to state exactly, what the total thickness of the shales on Kellogg creek may be, before reaching the limestone; it may, probably, be 300 feet or upwards.

The qualitative chemical examination of the Newton spring, on the property of John W. Purdom, in section 26, township 3 north, range 12 west, 8 miles north of Little Rock, gave, as its principal constituents,

Bi-carbonate of lime.
Bi-carbonate of magnesia.
Bi-carbonate of the protoxide of iron.

This is a strong chalybeate water, and will be found an excellent tonic for patients suffering from debility.

Two and a half miles east of Mr. Purdom's, between the old Batesville and Memphis roads, there is a large body of bog-iron ore, which will, no doubt, be found to contain sufficient iron to pay for working, judging from its appearance. A strong chalybeate spring breaks out from this bed of ore. Several persons have been induced to sink prospect holes, for lead, in this vicinity; all of which reached bog-iron ore, proving this ferruginous deposit to be extensive. Its thickness, where it was only partially exposed, is two feet. This is, therefore, a locality worthy of the attention of the iron manufacturer.

Agriculture.

Large tracts of level land exist over the area of the above mentioned shales, from which the soil has been chiefly derived in this county. Where the reddish-colored ferruginous shales of this group prevail, the land is productive and easily cultivated; but where the purely argillaceous shales exist, the soil is stiff, refractory, and inclined to be sprouty, and difficult to bring into a good condition for cultivation; however, when subdued, it becomes fertile. These flat clay lands, in their wild state, support a luxuriant growth of "barren grass," excellent for stock. The timber is mostly postoak and gum. The soil of the hill land is mostly derived from the sandstone of the millstone grit series, and is easily cultivated, though not so productive as the bottom lands. The principal growth of timber, on the highlands, consists of white, red, and blackoaks, black hickory, and black-jack oak. A set of soils was collected, characteristic of the latter lands, from Mr. John W. Purdom's farm, in section 36, township 3 north, range 12 west.

PRAIRIE COUNTY.

At the time I reached this county, the flies were found to be so numerous that it was impossible for the horses to travel during the day; consequently my observations in this county have been limited.

It is a level prairie country, as its name implies, and its substratum is composed of the orange-colored sand belonging to the quaternary period. The only solid rocks observed, are in the north-western part of the county, and belong to the millstone grit formation. The greater portion of this county is well adapted for cultivation, and though mostly open prairie, there are considerable bodies of good timber bordering along the numerous small streams that water this county. There is, at all times, an inexhaustible supply of wild grass, for stock, and large droves of Mexican mustangs, and Texas horses, passing through the country, are, annually, brought to this county to recruit upon its rich, wild pastures. Samples of soils were collected from the John Percifield old place, in the Grand prairie, seven miles from Brownsville, section 10, township 2 north, range 7 west. This soil is said to be excellent for small grain, and will produce twenty-five bushels of wheat to the acre. It is not so good for corn, the average being from twenty-five to thirty bushels to the acre.

MONROE COUNTY.

West of White river, this county is formed of high level prairie lands, similar in character to the lands of Prairie county, just described, except a short and narrow strip bordering on White river, in the vicinity of Aberdeen, which is broken by hills, about one hundred feet in height, composed of yellow clay and orange sand. East of White river, in this county, the land is generally low, and much cut up by lakes and sloughs, which, in time of high freshets, overflow large tracts of country. The remaining portion of this part of the county is composed of ridges that never overflow, and is amongst the finest cotton land in the state, producing 1200 or 1500 pounds to the acre. Soils characteristic of this land were collected from Alfred Mullen's farm, in section 25, township 1 north, range 3 west. No. 2, soil fourteen years in cultivation, and now in cotton. The principal growth of timber, in this section of the county, is large sweet-gum, elm, hickory, and dogwood.

I did not see any solid rock formation in this county.

CONCLUSION.

---o---

It will be seen, on review of this Report, that the northern part of the counties lying north of the Arkansas river, are bounded by a chain of mountains, which are crowned, on their summits, with massive conglomerate or thick-bedded sandstones, locally pebbly, belonging to the millstone grit series. These massive sandstones are underlaid by reddish and dark-colored shales of great thickness, especially towards the south-east, as three hundred feet have actually been measured where they still extend beneath the drainage of the country. Thin seams of coal are found in the upper part of the dark shales, in all the counties from Crawford to Pulaski,* one of these veins appears to be persistent, and has been identified, by its organic remains, over a great extent of country. Though often interrupted by extensive waves, which must have taken place in a great degree before the deposition of the superimposed sandstones, the general horizontality of the strata is well preserved. The axis of these waves appears to be parallel to the strike of the strata, and the elevated ranges produced from this cause are always capped with the millstone grit, with sometimes one or two hundred feet of shale overlying it. After reaching the eastern boundary of Pulaski county, the dark underlying shales, with the incumbent sandstones, disappear either by dipping to the south-east, or what is most likely the case, they have been removed by denudation, and buried beneath heavy deposits belonging to the quaternary period.

Permit me to take the present occasion, to acknowledge the many acts of kindness experienced at the hands of the citizens of the various counties through which I passed, which have promoted and facilitated the objects of the Survey. Where these are numerous and universal, it would be invidious to particularize individual cases.

EDWARD T. COX,

Assistant Geologist.

---

* Though I did not see any coal in Pulaski, I was credibly informed by Mr. Elliott, that he had found a thin seam not far from the Kellogg mines; and he promised, if possible, to meet me at the mines and show it.

INDEX.

---o---

ERRATA.

p. 84, line 3 from bottom, [illegible] for [illegible].
p. 43, " 14 " top, " [illegible] " standstone.
p. 148, " 17 " " " *ferruginous* " feruginous.
p. 219, " 2 " " " *Sulphur Rock* for Sulpher rock.
p. 227, " 30 " " }
p. 253, " 19 " " } " *lepidodendron* " lipidodendron.

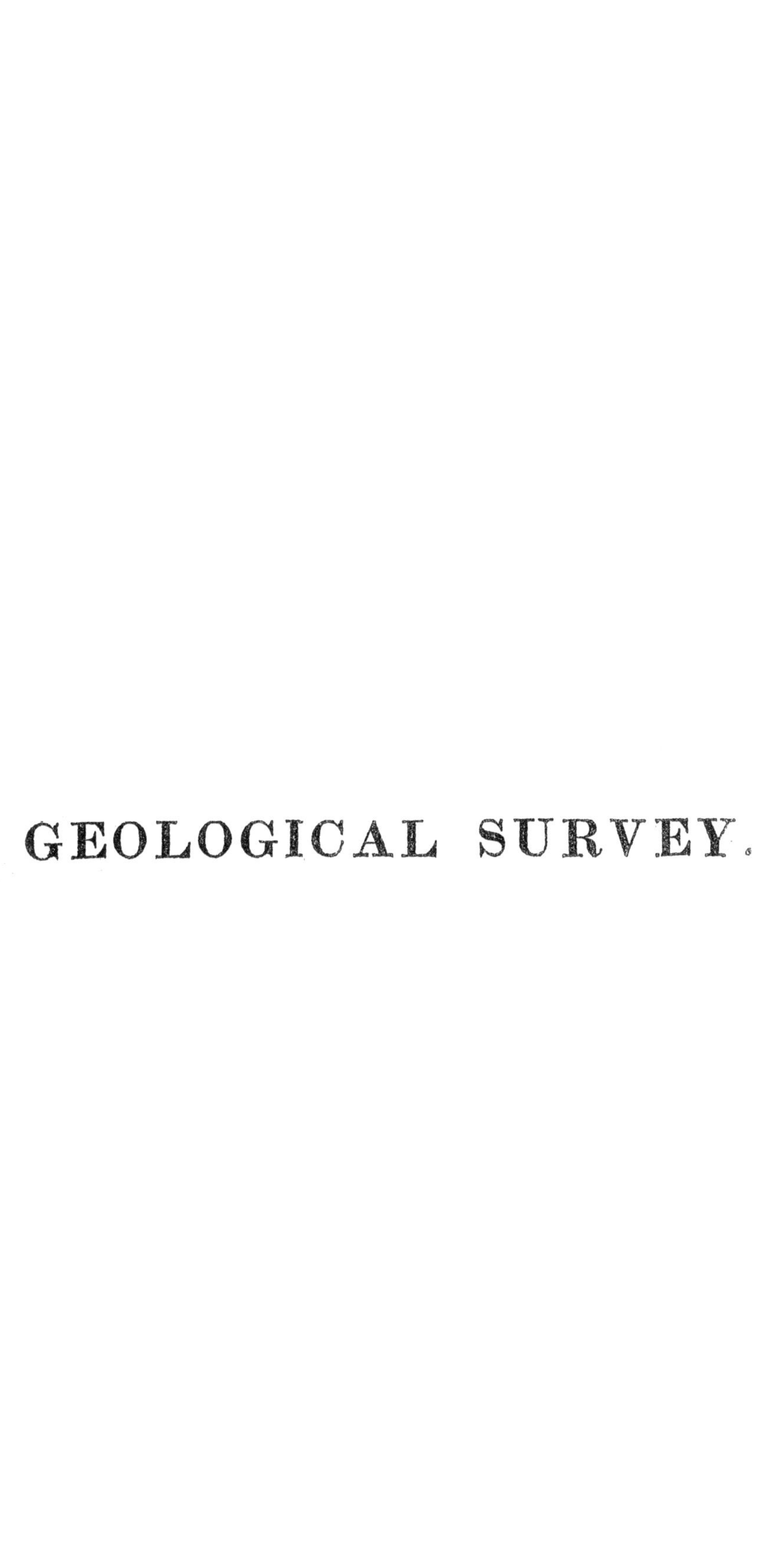

GEOLOGICAL SURVEY.